Imagining the Jewish Future

Imagining the Jewish Future

Essays and Responses

Edited by David A. Teutsch

91-36445
CIP

Y OF NEW YORK PRESS

Published by
State University of New York Press, Albany

© 1992 State University of New York

All rights reserved

Printed in the United States of America

Production by Cathleen Collins
Marketing by Bernadette LaManna

For information, address State University of New York
Press, State University Plaza, Albany, N.Y., 12246

Library of Congress Cataloging in Publication Data
Imagining the Jewish future : essays and responses / edited by David
    A. Teutsch.
        p. cm.
    ISBN 0-7914-1167-2 — ISBN 0-7914-1168-0 (pbk).
    1. Judaism—United States—Forecasting—Congresses. 2. Jews—
United States—Intellectual life—Forecasting—Congresses.
3. Jews—United States—Attitudes toward Israel—Forecasting—
Congresses. 4. Israel and the Diaspora—Forecasting—Congresses.
5. Jews—United States—Social conditions—Forecasting—Congresses.
I. Teutsch, David A., 1950-   .
BM225.I42 1992
296'.0973'01—dc20

10 9 8 7 6 5 4 3 2 1

Contents

Acknowledgments

This book arose out of discussions sponsored by the Reconstructionist Rabbinical College, at a conference coordinated by the most able Barbara Nussbaum. She was assisted by Susan Kitty, Gail Gibbs, Cindy Krassenstein, Geri Marcus, and Joan Marie Somers.

The conference was made possible by generous support from the Samuel S. Fels Fund, Mandel Family Philanthropic Fund, Myer and Rosalie Feinstein Foundation, and Canadian Friends of the Reconstructionist Rabbinical College. It also received support from Charlene and Howard Gelber, Paul Hitlin, Herman Levin, and Harry Stern. Robert Kritz, then RRC's vice president for development, worked with the funders.

The planning committee chaired by the editor helped to give shape to the conference and this volume. The ongoing support of Arthur Green, the president of RRC, and of Jacob Staub, the dean of RRC, have been invaluable in completing this book. Muriel Weiss, Gail Gibbs, and Evelyn Gechman were thorough and uncomplaining in their typing of the manuscript. Reena Spicehandler helped with copy editing. Lillian Kaplan and Joseph Blair did proofreading.

Rosalie Robertson of SUNY Press was unfailingly helpful and cheerful in seeing the book through to publication.

My wife Betsy and children Zachary and Nomi have uncomplainingly cleared space for me to finish this book. Their constancy and caring are the staff on which I lean; their presence is my greatest joy.

The views expressed are those of each essay's author. While I am grateful for the helpful advice of many people in shaping this volume, the final responsibility for it is mine alone.

Introduction

David A. Teutsch

Dreaming and planning strike most of us as inimical to each other. Planning—the focused action of applying what we know and what we can do to what we want to achieve—seems so concrete. Dreaming, by contrast, seems soft. Imagination—images that are the product of fantasy—seems far removed from the calculated measures that can affect the future. Yet I believe that dreaming and planning go hand in hand.

This book is about imagining the Jewish future because only imagination can inspire the images, ideas, and feelings from which can emerge the motivating vision needed to shape our future. Every student of political science knows the power of "creating facts." Things that are unthinkable before they are done become the basis for reorienting everything else thereafter. This is true of the effects of wars and inventions no more than of new ideas. When the U.S. Supreme Court struck down the "separate but equal" doctrine in Brown v. Board of Education, the once unthinkable process of integration began in America's schools.

Visions and dreams can also change history. When in reaction to the Holocaust and a variety of post–World War II events the United Nations voted for partition and allowed the creation of the State of Israel, the prime cause was a 2,000-year-old dream. Thus imagination, ideas and hopes can do much more than shape plans; they can motivate the planners to fulfill them. The goal of this book is not to plan based on what we know. It is to take the time for imagining the Jewish future as we wish it would be.

We cannot know what the future will bring. Yet most efforts at preparing for the future assume a certain knowledge, as if to place odds on what will be. That assumption is the basis for strategic planning, which attempts to anticipate problems and devise ways to overcome those new difficulties and challenges. Though the goal is to help us keep up in a world changing with increasing speed, planning often fails to predict many key changes with which we have to cope.

Forty years ago who would have predicted the impact of television, computers, and jet travel on the average American's life-style? And who would have predicted the enormous economic influence of Japan, the emergence of Islamic fundamentalism in Iran, or the move away from communism in the Soviet Union and Eastern Europe? Efforts to predict the technological and political future rarely meet with much success. The way that cultures regenerate themselves is just as difficult to anticipate. At the time of the destruction of the Second Temple, who would have predicted that 1,000 years later rabbinic Judaism would be flourishing? And who 100 years ago would have thought plausible the existence of a Jewish state where Hebrew is the daily language and Jerusalem is the capital? Nor did most Jewish leaders realize 40 years ago the full extent to which the Holocaust had seared the European and American Jewish psyche. Or how the existence of Israel would shape the identity of every American Jew. Equally unpredicted is the renewed desire for Jewish belonging and spiritual sustenance, which is steadily becoming more common today. These examples should lead us to distrust the perennial cry of each generation that its successor is more degenerate, dissolute, and destructive of society than any before in history. The future seems obvious only when it has become the past.

This book is not about prediction. Instead, the writers are together attempting to imagine the Jewish future. Imagining here means conjuring up images of what we wish the Jewish world were like right now. This kind of dreaming is critical to a different kind of planning—normative planning, or idealized design, an approach discussed by Russell Ackoff in *Creating the Corporate Future*. Normative planning requires us to agree on a picture of what we would like to become and to acknowledge the seriousness of the problems we face. The gap between the current situation and the one we wish we were in is the planning gap. Filling it requires us to describe the impediments to living our vision. Such impediments may be political, economic, sociotechnical, or scientific. Once the impediments have been identified, we can determine what it will take to overcome them and construct a plan with the means to do so. At that point the vision may need to be adjusted slightly to fit what we are capable of accomplishing. The resulting plan gives us a way of approaching the future that contains the elements of transformation.

We can consciously shape our tomorrows only if we know what we want them to be. That is why it is so important to imagine the Jewish future as we wish it would be, face the impediments to our visions, and energize the leaders of the Jewish community so that they plan to live in the light of our shared visions. Intended to aid in that process, the essays in this volume were prepared for a conference sponsored by the Reconstructionist Rabbinical College in December 1988, which laid the groundwork for the planned launching of RRC's Institute for the Jewish Future. Through policy studies, conferences, and consulting for Jewish organizations, the institute hopes to suggest new approaches to the moral, cultural, political, and religious issues confronting the American Jewish community.

Each of the essays included here addresses issues relevant to the institute and to anyone interested in the future of American Jewry. Together they portray a critical reality about the Jewish experience—the interrelatedness of all of the aspects of Jewish experience and culture. It is obvious that American Jewry has been profoundly shaped by life in the United States. Patterns of education, employment, homes and neighborhoods, leisure-time activities, family structure, and commitment to autonomy are just a few of the characteristics that American Jews have increasingly come to share with their fellow citizens.

But it is no less true that American Jews remain somewhat different from other Americans. Despite their high level of integration and assimilation, American Jews continue to have unique patterns that depend upon complex and interlocking elements of Jewish ethnicity, religion, and culture. It is true that changes in American culture mean changes for Jews. It is also true that changes in any part of Jewish culture contain the seeds of change in all other parts. Thus, for example, the rise of ethnicity in America has increased the impact of the emergence of the State of Israel, which has increased commitment to the use of Hebrew in synagogues. Thus the dreams, impediments, and concerns that appear to be particular to one aspect of culture need to be fit together to build a unified vision.

Autonomy and Personal Fulfillment

The values of autonomy and personal fulfillment in American culture have had a huge impact on American Jews. Those values play powerful roles in moving us away from the strong model of community that still existed a hundred years ago in Europe. They move us toward the very weak notion of community characteristic of American Jewry, something that Arnold Eisen talks about at some length in his essay. Those same values are attached to the fragility of Jewish neighborhoods and the breakdown of the family, which in turn has had, and will continue to have, a major impact on Jewish identity formation, as Egon Mayer points out. To some extent, the breakdown in community has negatively affected the availability of sophisticated audiences for Jewish poets, dramatists, and others in artistic endeavors—a situation that Marcia Falk, Richard Siegel, and Omus Hirshbein discuss. But the fact that so many Jews live between cultures and experience alienation in such specific ways may help to encourage creativity by bringing a wide range of artistic techniques and experiences together with a fresh look at Jewish living.

One important response to the problems associated with the breakdown in Jewish neighborhoods and families lies in family education. Family education can focus effectively on inculcating values and practices in entire family units, an approach that Jonathan Woocher, Kathy Green, and Joseph Reimer explore in their essays. We clearly have reached a watershed in Jewish identity to which this shift in tactics responds. No longer can we assume that the generation of the parents has a way of Jewish living with which they themselves are comfortable. The knowledge and observance levels of Jewish parents are, in fact, often a sore spot. More parents than ever want something for themselves, often something to which they have had little or no previous exposure. That desire is both a hope and a challenge. If we dream of a vibrant Jewish community, we are dreaming of active and Jewishly educated adults. Given what is possible in religious schools, for the most part that means adults educated *as* adults. We must rethink the role of Jewish schools, their relationship to parents and to educational opportunities within the Jewish community as a whole. Education is the key not only to richer Jewish lives for adults and families; it is also a key to strengthening Jewish community.

The popularization of *havurot* suggests that the desire for community is widespread. That so many synagogue *havurot* are casual in their educational commitments, meeting only monthly, may reflect the lack of groundwork that could support greater commitment. Or it may reflect a relatively low interest on the part of most Jews for greater commitment to community. Opportunities for community such as *havurot* deserve full development, for greater commitment to community is a critical factor in Jewish revival. Such commitment will have to be based on a voluntary curbing of autonomy. The development of theological and moral arguments that provide a basis for community is critical to such a revival. But these arguments will be of little use unless the educational vehicles exist to popularize them, unless the organizational structures exist to support that reinvigorated community. The benefits that such belonging brings must justify the sacrifices. Are such hopes phantoms? That depends partly upon whether Jews choose to believe in them and support the efforts to make them a reality. Unless the effort is made, no one will be certain of the nature or strength of the impediments. And if more intensive community existed, would it not provide more support for the embattled family's many current forms? That is certainly what has happened in my neighborhood—but we won't know more without diverse efforts in this area.

There are those who argue that broad structural issues such as employment opportunities and the system of secular education are the chief culprits in the weakening of Jewish community involvement. While it is certainly the case that these uncontrollable factors have wielded considerable influence, it should not be lost on us that most American Jews were willing partners in this shift. As Charles Silberman noted in *A Certain People,* recently the first signs have appeared that some Jews are seeking a greater sense of belonging and believing. I believe that the personal satisfactions that flow from living in strong family and community far outweigh the costs. It would be a delightful irony if the value of personal fulfillment—a key in the dissolution of Jewish community—were now the source of its renewal.

Reshaping the way we think about the American Jewish family along the lines discussed by Martha Ackelsberg, Esther Ticktin, and Elliot Dorff, and providing more support for it through increased family education are critical to the family and to our blueprint for Jewish education. Such imagining and implementing of fresh visions typifies normative planning.

The Relationship of American Jewry to Israel

The relationship of Israel and American Jewry suggests, again, the interconnectedness of issues and the need for fresh vision and planning. The role of Israel in the lives of American Jews is so strong that it is hard to imagine growing up as an American Jew today without it, a point made by Steven M. Cohen and Martin Raffel. The American Jew's relationship to Israel is the one part of the Jewish psyche that is regularly reinforced by the daily papers. Far more American Jews read about Israel every day than learn Talmud. The ethnic component of Jewish identity is intricately tied to what is happening in Israel. Pride in the Zionists' redeeming swamp and desert, in the achievements of the Israeli citizen-soldier, in the military victories of 1967 and 1973, and in the building of a sophisticated, contemporary Israeli culture has helped to shape the life of every American Jew. Similarly, American Jews have been profoundly influenced by their worry about the threat of further war in the Middle East, Israel's treatment of its Arab inhabitants, the problems between Orthodox and non-Orthodox and between Sephardim and Ashkenazim, and the host of other problems Israel faces.

While it is possible to describe the relationship of American Jewry to Israel as Judaism by proxy, I believe it is fairer to say that American Jews take with great seriousness the traditional idea that *kol Yisrael areivim zeh bazeh*, that every Jew is connected to all others and responsible for them. With the American Jew's sense of ethnic identity rooted deeply in the success and problems of Israel, the successes and failures of Israel have a substantial impact on American Jews.

Yet the cultural gap between Israelis and American Jewry is continuously growing. Israeli society does not have as strong a commitment to the civil liberties, religious freedom, and democratic processes that are so much a part of American Jewish life. Because Israelis constantly live with overwhelming problems of war and peace, they have been willing to compromise in areas that American Jews consider essential. And Israeli culture has taken on a life of its own, a life from which American Jews are separated not only by thousands of miles, but by a language barrier and radically different life experiences. The gap in experience is reflected in the issues of women's rights, Jewish pluralism, and separation between church and state. American Jews have discovered the gap in political cultures; the response to the intifada and problems associated with negotiating with the Palestinians have further strained the effort to maintain close ties.

The resulting alienation of American Jews from aspects of Israeli life has political, social, religious, and cultural dimensions. That in itself is worrisome, but when we think of Israel's role in American public life, the dimensions of that alienation could become considerably more complex and dangerous. The powerful involvement in Israel of the American Jewish federations is one example.

The tie to Israel is a critical factor in recruiting volunteers and raising money for domestic projects. Involvement with Israel is deeply embedded in the operations of such national organizations as the American Jewish Committee, American Jewish Congress, Anti-Defamation League, AIPAC, and dozens of others; for many, Israel is the central focus of operations. Any shift in the relationship between American Jewry and Israel poses a major threat to the stability of many of the most important institutions in American Jewish life. At the least, some would have to undergo major policy revisions; at worst, some would find their very survival endangered and their service to the Jewish community severely constricted. Philip M. Klutznick explores some of these institutional issues in his essay.

Because Israel has taken on a major sacral dimension of its own, what happens in Israel also has a major impact on life in the synagogue. Israel symbolizes the post-Holocaust rebirth of Jewry; Yom Ha'atzmaut, Israel Independence Day, is now a major synagogue event and communal event. Observance of the holiday illustrates the powerful interaction of the religious and ethnic, personal and communal, synagogal and federation aspects of the American Jewish connection to Israel.

A deepened commitment to forging more and stronger relationships between individual Israelis and individual American Jews—the dialogue and empathy that come from personal relations—may hold a key place in reducing future difficulties. But the necessary relationships will be costly to build. Massive funding would be needed for American Jews—particularly younger ones—to spend enough time in Israel to build such relationships. And no less important is bringing Israelis who will return to Israel to America to spend a year or more living among Jews here.

These direct linkages can break down the global drift between Israelis and American Jews and can make political and ideological problems into personal ones. They can perhaps help to normalize the relationship. Such normalization will show us how the sacral, the ethnic, the moral, and the political form a seamless whole encompassing every Jew. Given the political and moral tensions in the current relationship between Israeli and American Jews, normalizing the relationship may well have a profound effect on the ability of American Jews to build strong and healthy communities here. And if the steps toward normalization represent the kind of watershed some of us imagine, the effects will be cultural, social, religious, ethnic, and even familial. Making this effort requires an enormous reorganization of Jewish communal funds. But if the present situation is as fraught with danger as it appears, and if the dream of a deep interpersonal connection between Israel and the Diaspora is as powerful as it seems to be, then planning the steps to get to this fresh vision should not be delayed. The strategic planning that dominates the Jewish community today would have to shift to a normative planning model. Making that transition poses an enormous challenge.

Reconnecting Jews and Judaism

A third problem nexus is the need to win and maintain Jewish loyalty. The institutions that have proved most successful at helping Jews find their way to Judaism these days take many forms—Jewish camping and youth groups, missions to Israel, adult bat mitzvah, *ba'al teshuvah* yeshivahs, and young leadership groups, to name but a few. Private activities such as reading the torrent of new academic and popular Jewish books exist alongside large-scale cultural activities and more intimate *havurah* settings. Some of the challenges posed by forms of Jewish involvement are explored by Deborah Lipstadt, Everett Gendler, Hillel Levine, Rela Geffen Monson, and Deborah Dash Moore. No single method works so well that it can supersede the others. The necessity of many forms of involvement reflects the diversity of interests and commitments within contemporary American Jewry.

What does seem clear is that reaching out to the largest possible number of American Jews requires multiple tactics and seeing the Jewish community in its diversity. It must be considered in segments, with attention to the special needs, requirements, and interests of each. In this volume Lawrence Kushner, Burt Jacobson, and Lee Friedlander address one example of this approach—life-cycle needs in the synagogue setting. They show the complicated psychological situation of the family, the sensitive counseling the family requires, and the importance of ritual to fragile families. Life-cycle moments provide opportunities to reconnect families to the life of the Jewish community. Despite their obvious importance, endeavors to meet the needs of the family do not generally seem to receive the careful consideration they deserve.

As the emphasis in many families has shifted over three generations from daily to weekly to yearly to life-cycle Jewish observance, the opportunities for reconnecting the family to the community have become rarer. The religious, psychological, and communal significance of life-cycle events has deepened in the face of this reality. Significant life-cycle moments beg to be embodied in pivotal spiritual and communal events, around which much of the other Jewish activity in families' lives could be planned. The religious school is seen by many families as the place to go for preparing for bar or bat mitzvah. For the school to surmount the pressure for privatization, links must be built between the religious school population and other members of the synagogue. This broadening of the notion of education not only redefines the forces of Jewish acculturation, it reaffirms the commitment to community.

Young leadership groups that create opportunities for men and women to meet each other by involving themselves in Jewish organizational life are doing two important things. Sometimes they provide substantive opportunities for Jewish learning and for discovering other Jewish communal institutions to which their members can develop longer-term commitments. When that happens, young leadership groups, too, become major forces for Jewish connection. And often they provide exposure to a broad variety of Jewish arts and culture, helping to acculturate their members and to provide an audience for the writers and performers who are helping to shape Jewish culture.

Groups focused primarily on social-justice activities can similarly provide an entry point for Jewish return. This is most likely when the group does not limit itself to involvement in a single narrow cause and when Jewish study within the group makes a connection between the group's activities and values and sources within the Jewish tradition. Such possibilities are suggested in the essays by Arthur Waskow and David Wortman. A shared social setting, moral action, and Jewish learning can combine to provide a transcendent sense of meaning and belonging.

What do these three settings—a young leadership group, a synagogue, and a social action group—have in common? They all illustrate that unless we act upon a vision of maximalist involvement, we are missing key opportunities for Judaization. Of course there are many Jews who would not be reached even if such a shared vision were widely implemented. And of course as pluralists we should not be judgmental toward those Jews who do not share our vision. But that maximalist vision turns each Jewish contact into an opportunity further to excite and involve in learning, action, spiritual deepening, and community. We squander the resources for building the Jewish future when we fail to formulate and act upon such a vision. One key to that vision is finding the words to express it. Arthur Green and Judith Plaskow in their essays describe the effort to create language that can link the theological to the moral and political.

Everyone who attended the conference sponsored by the Reconstructionist Rabbinical College, at which the papers in this volume were delivered, was excited. Why? I know of several reasons. Some of the most exciting minds in the American Jewish community came together to talk about matters of deep concern. They were unconstrained by organizational agendas or demands for exacting scholarship. On the contrary, they were urged to dream, imagine, and paint vivid pictures. They were urged to state fully their disagreements with each other. The result was a conference filled with passion and freshness yet free from the acrimony that so often marks the need to defend institutional interests.

That conference and this volume represent one way to reach out to some of the best-trained scholars whose primary concerns revolve around the future of Jewry. Part of the challenge facing the RRC's planned Institute for the Jewish Future is to harness the ideas and energies of such people for the sake of the community and to bring their ideas and approaches to organizations that can apply them. It is still the case in the American Jewish community that the approaches of most of the large organizations are cautious and slow. The Institute for the Jewish Future posits that this is a time requiring dreaming, bold innovation, and experimentation. Stimulating such developments and supporting those organizations willing to undertake more innovation is part of the institute's mission. It can fulfill that mission only within the context of encouraging a pluralistic, experimental, and open-ended approach to the contemporary Jewish situation. Since that approach stands in contrast to a change-resistant, unity-seeking mode that operates by cautious consultation, it will not have universal appeal. But the risk-taking and change that are needed will show their value over time.

We need to encourage those capable of recommending fresh directions. History suggests that they will probably not be those closest to the problems, probably not practitioners invested in current conventions. We need to make more room for the academics who have greater latitude and perspective to express their views and try out new ideas. Aside from a handful of stars on the scholar-in-residence circuit, most of the scholars who have those insights do not attract the audience or support needed to justify their attention to practical solutions. And those deeply involved in speaking to Jewish organizations tend to tailor their message to what those organizations expect to hear. I believe that the Institute for the Jewish Future can provide the needed bridge between the Jewish community and the scholars less deeply involved with Jewish organizations, without demanding from either scholars or community the concessions that both have shown themselves unready to make. This is a critical part of creating the open marketplace of ideas and developing the tactical skills necessary to implement fresh visions.

Imagining the Jewish future is not just an armchair exercise. And it is not just a chance to voice optimism about the Jewish future. This imagining should lead to concrete action, strategic planning, and the redesign of programs along the gamut of Jewish organizations. This vision should inspire Jewish leaders—and through them Jews of all kinds—about what the future can bring if we start fulfilling our visions this very day. The essays that follow can shape our visions and move us toward action if we listen for their message. They illustrate an approach to Jewish life that is visionary and vigorous, rooted in pluralism, dialogue, and openness—an approach American Jews need in much greater abundance.

The fundamental issues raised in this volume are not significantly altered by such recent momentous events as the Gulf war, the coming of democracy to Eastern Europe, the massive immigration of Soviet Jews to Israel, and the disintegration of communism in the Soviet Union. The gap between Israeli and American Jews continues to grow; the National Jewish Population Study of 1990 shows increasing American Jewish assimilation; and the threat of nuclear proliferation in the Third World continues. The need to take a unified normative approach remains. The challenge for American Jews, as for any group involved in trying to bridge the gap between a dream and its realization, is to unite around fresh visions—to see the dream through to the light of day.

Section I

Religion and Theology

1

God, Prayer, and Religious Language

Arthur Green

I begin this discussion of prayer and its future with an article of faith, the faith of a religious humanist. The human need to pray is universal and constant. Even in our seemingly secular age, worship exists in one form or another throughout the world—in all of the traditional cultures and in many garbs within contemporary culture, even by those who would deny engaging in it. The prophet's statement that "in every place incense and sacrifice are offered in My name" (Mal. 1:11) indeed describes the human situation. The need to pray exists prior to any particular theology or definition of God. In fact, theology is a response of intellect to the reality of the need to pray and an attempt to rationalize it. It is the mind's articulation of truth the heart already knows.

The need to worship covers a wide range of human moods and life experiences. It includes the fullness of heart experienced by Jews in the songs of Kabbalat Shabbat as well as the moments of dread and awe conveyed to us in the liturgy of Yom Kippur. Exultation and awe, joy and terror dwell together in prayer, the tune to which we dance on this knife point called human existence. The "valley of death's shadow" ever remains an important part of the human experience; it too plays a role in our need for prayer. The individual confrontation with mortality is heightened in our day by a collective sense of potential danger, making this an age in which the role of prayer is increased rather than diminished.

As we are the first generations to grow up aware of the imminent possibility of universal destruction by the human hand, the consciousness of mortality that colors our prayer-life has taken on a universal hue. For all the continued growth of human knowledge in biomedical and other scientific areas, the sense that the keys to both life and death lie in hands that reach beyond human understanding or control has not been lost. Now as the greatest of human fears shifts from that of nuclear holocaust to that of ecological devastation (a shift that has taken place before our eyes), the sense of divine involvement in the fate of the world will grow. The longing to assert some ultimate meaning to our commitment to the preservation of life on our planet will become the most essential task of religion, even among those who are not "believers" in the traditional Western sense of that term. It is not only those who believe in a simplistic version of a God who "hears" or "answers" who need to pray in an age like ours.

It seems appropriate, as we discuss the future of Judaism in the early to mid-21st century, first to offer some thoughts on what the world as a whole will look like at that quickly approaching time in human history. Of course this imaginative construction can only be derived from the present situation and leaves aside the distinct possibility of some new calamity or transforming historic event that cannot be predicted. The world I describe here is as I think it is most likely to appear based on current evidence and trends. It is not entirely the world as I wish to see it, but rather the world as I expect it will be, including the good, the bad, and the terrifying.

The great international conflict between East and West that so dominated later 20th-century history is already a receding memory. By the mid-21st century, the great powers of the day (United Europe, a now vanished Soviet Union, China, Japan, and the United States) will be close to a state of full détente—in effect, world government. This will have come about not because of the advent of Messiah or any dramatic change in the nature of the human heart, but rather because of an overwhelming realization that the planet as a whole so imminently faces destruction and the end of human habitability that only the combined efforts of all nations will allow for the earth's survival. The terror wrought by the rise in global temperature, the frightening rate at which the earth's ozone shield will have been depleted, the imminent destruction of forest reserves, and the near-irreversible pollution of air and seas will force upon humanity an unprecedented degree of unity. It will be clear that the great patchwork of private, corporate, and national practice in relation to the environment has led to a disregard and flouting of warnings that the human community simply is not able to tolerate. This realization will bring about tremendous changes in human history and the world's political structure, the United Nations giving way to a stronger body, but one dominated by an entente of major powers. Membership in this community of nations will be essential for the survival of any individual nation-state. The vital nature of such membership will be enforced both by economic and military threat. At least for a time, the greater weapon that will stand as the club behind a new principle of organization will be the economic one. There will be cases of near expulsions from the community of nations: perhaps Brazil for not controlling the burning of Amazon forests; Burma for not bringing an end to the growing of poppies in the Golden Triangle; the United States for not levying sufficiently severe punishments on industrial giants that conspire to circumvent environmental regulations. Such expulsion from the international community would mean a degree of total economic isolation that no nation would be able to withstand.

The first half of the 21st century will be the time when humanity is forced to take seriously the paucity of earth's natural resources and the need to transform human society so that it begins to live within the bounds of those resources. This will involve strict international controls of resource use, as I have said, within the context of a single world economic order. It will also have to involve a universal and tightly enforced commitment to population control. It will be widely accepted, in all circles other than those of certain religious fundamentalists, that unless world population growth is severely limited, all attempts to maintain standards of quality for human life within the bounds of preservation of resources will be doomed. Earth can remain livable for future generations, it will be realized, only if the numbers of those generations do not get out of hand.

We now turn to the place of religion in this emerging society of the mid-21st century. The most important development on the religious front will involve the growth of a series of semiscientific new religious groups based on meditation and other disciplines of consciousness control, exhibiting both the best and worst uses of such powers. These will be officially encouraged by various regimes as offering the benefit of leading their adherents toward life at a slower pace, a major goal of an environment-conscious world that wants to slow growth in every area. In these groups and in some of the ongoing traditional religious communities, borders between East and West will continue to diminish. As travel becomes increasingly easy and the world grows smaller, Christian–Zen retreat centers in both Eastern and Western settings will be common. Yoga classes taught in churches and synagogues will surprise no one. Christianity itself may be somewhat diminished as a force in world affairs. The evangelicals, after the great sweep of millennial revivalism at the turn of the new century, will come up looking and feeling somewhat empty on its other side. Liberal churches will be fully absorbed in decrying resource abuse and in supporting world federalism, identifying both with the promised desolations and glories of biblical tradition. The Catholic church is likely to be significantly divided and battered. Some quarters within the church will continue to be among the most progressive in support of ecological concerns, just distribution of resources, and the governmental structures needed to maintain them. Catholic traditionalism, however, will be significantly discredited as the Vatican is forced by international pressures to renounce its opposition to birth control, a position the world community will not be able to tolerate from such a major force in world affairs. A significant minority of the church will refuse to submit to this ban, and Catholicism will suffer the consequences.

I fear that Judaism in the generation of which I speak will be represented in the world by two rival claimants, whose polemical and adversarial relationship will already have a history. These two groups, the Orthodox and the combined liberals, will continue to be bound together by certain common concerns, especially those involving a prejudice by bigots who continue to make no distinction between them. Ties of family and personal friendship will also help to prevent a total break. But traditionalists will live under rather sharp public scrutiny, as will those other traditionalist religious groups associated with attitudes harmful to the societal order, including both protracted antagonism toward others and violation of birth control legislation. This traditionalist Jewish group will itself remain very much divided, and a great deal of its strength will be spent on internal conflict. It will, however, live with a sense of strength and price, augmented by its self-perceived position as a persecuted minority.

The nontraditionalists, or liberal group of Jews, will continue to be viewed as a religious community in North America and mostly as a cultural/ethnic entity in Israel and Europe. The links between American, European, and Israeli nontraditionalist Jews will be strengthened. All of these groups will have been deeply shaken by the internationally imposed settlement of the Israeli/Arab conflict. Questions regarding the meaning of Jewish existence, the legitimacy of Jewish nationalism, and the validity of religious and national separatism in an age of such great international striving for unity will also be very much alive in their midst. At the same time, these communities will continue to enjoy a modest revival, mostly affecting small circles of the most committed, with regard to religious observance, historical study of Judaism, and cultural creativity.

Our interest here is in the religious life of that community, and especially in the religious language and liturgical forms that will be current in it. By their very nature, religious language and liturgy are highly conservative vehicles of a group's collective self-expression. They serve as ways for a community to verbalize the link both between its present-day adherents and their historical past, and between the ordinary human being and eternity itself. As such, the liturgical text needs to give the worshipper the feeling that it is deeply rooted, ancient, and unchanging. It is for this reason that liturgy tends to take on a quasi-scriptural status in religious communities. Though liturgy is not quite canonical in the formal sense, change in it takes place with great hesitation and amid tremendous controversy. The reaction to the liturgical changes of Vatican II, the great conflicts around 19th-century Jewish Reform liturgy in Germany, and the public burning of the first Reconstructionist prayerbook are all cases in point. There is little that distresses religious traditionalists as much as a threatened change in their beloved forms of liturgical expression.

But now we have to turn to the heart of the matter. What will the act of prayer and the use of religious language mean to this group of Jews in the century to come? Let me begin with two comments on prayer in the contemporary American Jewish setting. Jewish life in this century has given a disproportional prominence to public worship while undercutting its private and personal core. The notion of "synagogue-centered Judaism" was once loudly touted by the Conservative and Reform movements, along with "synagogue attendance," as the pollsters' measure of Jewish loyalty, and there were attempts to fit Judaism into standards of behavior and measurement appropriate to the American Protestant world. By the end of the 20th century, more sophisticated religious leaders and social scientists have come to understand that other measures of Jewish loyalty are at least as appropriate as attendance at worship services.

But at the same time that public worship was so elevated in importance, it may be said that true prayer (from the devotional point of view)—the art of opening the heart to God, the pouring out of both joy and anguish before the One who created the world—has suffered a tremendous decline. Part of this has to do with the general secularization of culture and lack of clarity about religious matters. Before whom does one pray? Is there a God who hears? Does prayer change anything? If not, does it make any sense? This authentic theological doubt and confusion combines with a typically modern impatience and unwillingness to give time to the cultivation of inward skills. The pace at which moderns have been trained to live makes such prayer seem nearly impossible, even for the would-be faithful. The fact that traditional Jewish worship involves the mumbling of a great many words at a rapid speed does little to enhance its status as a valid way of prayer in an age that needs to slow down radically its pace of living. No wonder that Eastern—or Quaker—modes of silent prayer or meditation seem more attractive and "meaningful" than those of Judaism. How can the novice ever learn *kavvanah* when there is so much to be said, and at so rapid a pace?

I feel that Jews in the generations of which we speak will know little of the real act of prayer, and their mostly negative associations, either with traditionalist rapid mumbling or with the formalism of the large liberal synagogue, will continue to serve as roadblocks. Only rabbis in smaller congregations and groups of Jews in informal *havurot* will be able to make accessible to Jews outside Orthodoxy a sense that prayer, including liturgy, needs to be the most spontaneous and least routinized of human activities. The popularity of such leaders and groups will be great, and not only among the young. One of the great challenges of Jewish religious leadership, and therefore of theological education in our own time, is the ability to convey the importance of prayer as an essential human and humanizing act. If religious language is going to survive among our descendants, we will have to give it new meaning. As Jews stand farther than we can imagine from the great well of emotional power that prayer had for our premodern and mostly East European ancestors, we will have to find new and creative ways to reinfuse it with energy.

While experimentation is certainly called for, a sense of authenticity and deep-rootedness in tradition will remain the greatest bearer of that power and should not be sacrificed. For all the changes in prayer and religious language that will take place as we enter a new age in Jewish history, we must never lose sight of the fact that the deeper task of religion is common to all ages and indeed to all humans. In the life of prayer we seek to create a constant awareness of the divinity that surrounds us at all times. We live in the divine presence as did our ancestors and as will our descendants. Prayer offers to the individual and the community something of an echo of eternity, and that single echo is borne by the multiple echoes of history and antiquity. This is why I believe the Hebrew language will remain a vital vehicle in the prayer life of the Jewish community. No translation bears for the Jewish soul even a faint reverberation of the tremendous power contained in the Hebrew liturgical text. We cannot allow the power contained in that ancient and much loved text to be lost. The way that text is understood, however, is already changing and will continue to change radically. It is a new understanding of the *act* of prayer—more than a new prayer text—that is needed by contemporary Jews.

If there is to be a link between authentic Jewish prayer of the past and the new understanding of prayer in the era of which I speak, such a link will be best provided by the sources of Hasidism. I have been under the spell of these texts for many years now; they have "saved" the value of prayer for me as I have come to terms with my own disbelief on a literal level. I have tried to collect some of the most important of these sources, with brief comment, in *Your Word Is Fire* (together with Barry W. Holtz). Perhaps the most important single line for me is the statement attributed to Rabbi Pinhas of Koretz, a contemporary of the Ba'al Shem Tov: "People think that you pray to God," he said, "but that is not the case. Rather prayer itself is of the essence of Divinity." Much of what I have to say on prayer can be viewed as a commentary on this line.

For us post-Freudians and post-Jungians, the human being is not a simple conscious self, for whom the act of prayer would be a calling out to a "wholly Other," who then might or might not be said to exist, listen, and respond. Our notion of prayer is more complex, as our notion of person is more complex. We see consciousness as having multiple levels. The great labyrinth of the mind, including the emotions, is perhaps the most magnificent of those creations for which we express thanks in prayer. In thanking God each morning for "establishing the land over the sea," we symbolically recognize that waking consciousness is a thin and sometimes precarious veneer over a deep and churning unconscious life. We see in prayer an important avenue in which the deeper preconscious self calls out to the conscious mind for verbal expression. Our most ancient and primitive joys and fears, including thankfulness for being alive and terror of night, are permitted expression in the language of prayer. We need look only at our daily evening service, ranging in emotion from *ha-ma'ariv 'aravim* to *hashkivenu* to see how much of the human emotional range is captured by our liturgical language. In prayer the hidden child within us breaks through the repressing bonds of adult conscious control, which does not allow for the spontaneity and wide variety of emotion that the child in us yet needs to express.

As we reach ever deeper into the human mind to call forth the most profound—and vulnerable—parts of ourselves, we occasionally find ourselves standing before moments of great mystery or transcendence. The inner depths called forth in our prayer seem to be without end or limit. Sometimes the voice that speaks—or the silence that resounds—within us seems clearly to be not of our own making.

It is the source of such inner moments that we identify as God. But this God is hardly the wholly Other or the radically transcendent Being of conventional Western theism. On the contrary, this reality is so tied to our deepest inner self that we feel false in seeking to disengage this intimate connection. We seem to know God best at the place where self and Self can no longer be distinguished: the eternal One as manifest in the individual human soul. Prayer is a reaching forth of the individual conscious self toward the universal Self that lies within us, and at the same time the striving of that innermost One for expression at the surface of consciousness, which can be provided only by individual humans and human community. I believe this sort of religious humanism (I use the term as did Martin Buber) is not too great a distortion of Rabbi Pinhas's message.

For us, as for the Hasidic author, that dual process of our seeking the divine and the divine speaking through us is the sacred process. The faith that sustains our commitment to this process is in no way separable from our belief in the nobility of the human spirit. The human and the divine meet in an inward encounter in which the I/Thou may even be transcended, though the spiritual modesty dictated by Jewish language stops short of describing that ultimate mystical union of self and Self. Such a faith describes a God who is not radically other than either soul or world. We believe in a continuum of consciousness and in a divinity that stands as the inner essence of all existence, present throughout being insofar as we are open to discovering and responding to that presence. Divinity is accessible to us through a contemplative inner ascent or an exercise in the development of human consciousness. Human consciousness serves as a unique channel for that which lies within to achieve expression. Prayer is both our seeking out of this divinity and the "attempt" of that divinity to "respond" by speaking through us. It is the reality of God that we come to know in the heights and depths of prayer and contemplation that will become the basis of our future theological conversation.

Prayer is the most private of all human acts, needing to traverse intimate and emotionally vulnerable territory within the human self. At the same time, it is a universally shared human activity, one that surpasses all boundaries of language, culture, and even theology. To say it again in language influenced by Hasidism, prayer is the process by which the spark of divine light within each of us seeks out other sparks, the lights within all creation, and joins with them in the return to the one great source of light. In the course of this journey, the seeking out of those sparks that reside in other human souls, especially members of that soul family who speak the same religious language, becomes appropriate. For us Jews, prayer at its most personally profound and the activity of communal prayer should not be seen as conflicting with one another. Prayer in community should involve a reaching out to the soul of the other and a joining together as a community of human souls together reaches toward God.

In order to perform the "horizontal" aspect of such reaching, I must come to know the other. Shared prayer without shared caring makes no sense. The prayer community, therefore, should ideally be small and rather intimate, and must exist in the context of a supportive and caring community. This is why I have long been involved in the *havurah* movement and have been an advocate of the small synagogue or *minyan* as an alternative to the formal and depersonalized prayer act as performed in most American liberal synagogues. I continue to be a firm believer in this position and in its growing acceptance among Jews in the coming century.

It is at this place also that prayer is joined to that which too often in our world is confined to the separate realm of social action. How can I pray with another human being if I do not know the needs of that other? What does it mean to pray together if I do not have the consent of the others with whom I pray? But the other may say to me in the course of this process, "Care about me first as a person! Cease oppressing me or merely 'using' me as a member of your religious community. Help me be free enough to join in this search in my own way." Ultimately, we realize that we are joined in such a prayer community to all of Israel and then to all of humanity. Since the light of each and every soul is needed for the ultimate restoration of the One great light, there is no escaping the real life demands that being a person of prayer makes upon us. There is no authentic praying without a life of doing. Prayer and action are completely united with one another, and for many, action itself will speak as the loudest and most authentic testimony of prayer.

I will not attempt to describe any further the nature of the single light that is formed in this great collective act of inner reaching. The One that is both source and product of human unity remains beyond description. It is the transcendence pointed to by our collective human experiences of divine immanence, but its nature remains mysterious. It is the question that remains after all our answers. It is Y-H-W-H: the One whose only name is nothing other than "breath" or "Being." Ultimately Buber is right in saying that this One can be spoken *to* more readily than it can be spoken *of*. But I have also tried to say here that this "speaking to" is not that which it at first appears to be.

Since this view of prayer is clearly tied to a God concept that reaches far beyond the god-as-person images of our traditional liturgy, some words must be said about the reason for maintaining such language, and even a verbal (as distinct from silent meditational) form of prayer altogether. If what we seek is contact with the deepest Self within, why not turn in our verbal prayer for a series of contemplative exercises? Clearly, the God of which I speak here is not the super-person of biblical and rabbinic tradition. The old rabbinic God concept, still so familiar to us in our ancient prayer book, was already refined and transformed many centuries ago by the legacies of both Jewish philosophy and mysticism. It is clear, even to the relatively casual student of Jewish intellectual history, that neither great Moses of medieval Jewry—neither Maimonides nor De Leon, the author of the Zohar—was a literal believer in the old rabbinic concept of God. True, they allowed the liturgy to remain mostly intact, and it seems that they were content enough that the masses continued to believe in a rather anthropomorphic deity. The intellectual elitists of both camps believed that enlightenment as they taught it was simply not appropriate to the mental capacities of most people. They lived in an age of faith, and their departures from conventional piety, as important as they were, left most of the society intact.

The situation in modernity is entirely different. In a secular age, in which only a minority struggle for faith altogether, religion has to be presented in the most sophisticated manner possible. Ours is an age marked not only by secularism, but by a Jewish community of unparalleled general educational sophistication, coupled with abysmal Jewish ignorance. Only a Judaism that is presented in the most sophisticated terms will appeal to a community such as our own. Jewish leaders, and particularly rabbis in recent decades, have frequently been guilty of underestimating the spiritual sophistication of seeking Jews, leaving would-be devotees out in the cold insofar as positive affiliation with Judaism is concerned. In an age such as this, it is important to say openly that the God of which we speak is not in essence a person or a willful, personified being. The turn to God is for us a turn inward to the core of ourselves and the core of all being, a recognition by the individual human consciousness that it is but a surface expression of a deeper underlying reality that is expressed through every other human mind and voice as well.

Why then do we continue to use personal metaphors in prayer? If we recognize that the personhood of God is a human projection onto a faceless core of being, why do we continue to pray as though we were addressing that projection? Is this, in fact, not praying before the mirror? Are we not worshipping the human rather than the true divine in such prayer?

The answers to these questions are manifold and not simple. In this matter too I turn to Hasidism for guidance, and here I am an advocate of the Bratslav Hasidic school as opposed to the very different teachings of the Habad (Lubavitch) school, which is indeed more contemplative in focus. I believe that prayer is about intimacy. The way into the core of being is only through our most pained and personal selves. In the search for the great inner One there is no detour around individual inwardness. Self-confrontation is crucial to the act of prayer. Indeed, the root of the word used for prayer in Hebrew, *tefillah,* probably is derived from a source that means "self-judgment." To whom do we open our most intimate selves if not to another person? With whom do we think we can talk about what pains us? With whom can we share our joys, our loves, our doubts, and our fears, if not another person? While Buber may have considered it possible to have an I/Thou relationship with a tree, for most of us intimacy and the interpersonal go hand-in-hand.

The understanding that projection plays a key role in our theological imagination, so central to the modern understanding of religion since Feuerbach, Nietzsche, and Freud, is not original to these moderns. Maimonides's claim that prophecy contained a perfect mixture of intellect and imagination already points in this direction. The Kabbalists refer to this insight in their distinction between *ein sof,* the boundless, undefined, and essentially impersonal divine reality, and the *sefirot,* which may be called the masks of God. But even before the new intellectual refinements of the Middle Ages, the rabbis knew that our images of God were projections brought about by human need. The midrash claims that there are two great moments when Israel actually saw the divine form. At the crossing of the Red Sea, they saw God as a young lover and hero. At Sinai they saw God as an elderly law giver and judge. Each revelation was in accord with the need of the hour. In the day of battle, a frail, elderly God could hardly be the right vision for the moment. On the Day of Judgment, no one could be satisfied with a God who looked any less distinguished than the jurists of the day, "the elders who sit at the gate." What is this midrash if not a primitive understanding of projection? A particularly startling Hasidic interpretation of the Prophet Ezekiel's vision says that "the figure with the appearance of a man" who sits on the divine throne that Ezekiel saw is there only because we place him there.

None of this is to say, of course, that divinity is not real or that religion is "just made up." Quite the contrary. It is because religion is so real and addresses the human spirit at such great depth that we are forced to turn into ourselves and bring forth the most profound creations of the human spirit as reflecting mirrors with which to catch the divine light. All the prophets but Moses, say our sages, prophesied "through a darkened glass," which really means through a mirror. One interpretation of prophecy, quoted in the name of an ancient midrash, says that the seeker is like an animal wandering through the forest who suddenly comes upon a pond. He looks down into the pond and thinks he sees another. That other is his reflection, of course, but in seeing himself projected outward in the form of another, he is allowed to see himself for the first time.

Religion, and particularly the act of prayer, requires personification. We who want both to sing to the universe of our love of life and to cry out to it in anger, protest, and pain, need to paint that universe as having a human face. It is that human face or that human ear, which we experience as the other, that sees us, listens to us, and receives our prayer.

The divinity that we believe lies within and throughout the natural world seeks through us to be discovered and raised to consciousness. Thus it becomes the inspiration for the lives we lead in its presence. This is the very essence of our religious faith, based on longings and intimations of truth that well up from deep within us. In this process, consciousness plays a crucial role. For us to say that God is less than conscious, to say that only we have consciousness and there is no mind higher than our own, would betray both faith and experience. Those who have been granted some glimpse of the infinite rungs of consciousness know how narrow the perspective of the ordinary human mind can be. We thus may speak of God as the mind of the universe, or as cosmic consciousness. But our verbal description of God as conscious should not lead us to forget that even this is an inadequate expression of what we really seek to say. God as consciousness is not the same as God as person.

There is no religious language other than that of metaphor and symbol. The danger of our tradition is that we are too much wedded to a single form of metaphoric expression. That picture of God, the loving, yet judging, male elder seated on the throne, leaves us too little variety of metaphoric play and too easily veers into idolatry. One of the most important lessons we learn from the Kabbalah is its insistence upon a multiplicity of spiritual metaphors. In one moment God may be that elder, but in the next, the divine is young woman, flowing spring, great sea, Temple, moon, lover, other and even destroyer. The mixing of personal and nonpersonal metaphors is helpful here, as is the significant mixing of feminine with masculine religious metaphors, especially in a literature until now created almost entirely by men. It would be helpful for us today not to seek to do away with traditional religious language, but to add to it within this great multiplicity of metaphors. Particularly as women are enfranchised in Jewish life, it is clear that new prayers using female metaphors will become a more accepted part of Judaism. Some of these may well be based upon imagery used in the Kabbalah (to me, a welcome change). The mixing of personal and impersonal metaphors, as well as symbols taken from nature with those taken from Torah and tradition, will serve to enrich Judaism, as did the Kabbalah of the Middle Ages. To be sure, there are dangers in such an approach, and there may be points at which boundaries have to be set, particularly insofar as the preservation of Judaism's distinctiveness is concerned. But we would do well to encourage more rather than less spiritual and liturgical creativity as we face a new age in Jewish history.

As we move toward the growth of new religious language, I would like to say something in particular for the traditional "father figure" God of Jewish liturgy, one that I think must be preserved (along with other images) for important psychological reasons. I believe that the mostly loving and compassionate Father/King of this liturgy represents a tempering of the wild and warlike deities who preceded the God of Israel and are still reflected in some parts of the Hebrew Bible. This taming of the ancient warring gods, and then the "conversion" of the desert God into the deity of rabbinic religion, is a totemic representation of the taming of human (and particularly male) anger and violence, a representation of the need for sublimation of our inner violence and hostile feelings. As psychologist David Bakan has noted, the rabbinic father, projected as "our Father, compassionate Father, compassionate One, have mercy upon us" is really father turned into mother. "He" has taken on some of the classic archetypal characteristics of "she." This process of reducing the radical difference between "male" and "female" in the God figure should be treated with some seriousness and care. We should be cautious of a situation in which proposed feminine god language or god figures alongside the masculine lead to a polarization wherein the "male" figure is pushed back into those negative "masculine" characteristics that Judaism has so long labored to transform.

Our archetypes need to remain complex and richly textured. Just as "mother" should not be all love and compassion, but should have elements of judgment and power as well, so should "father," the projected male totem of our Jewish society, combine elements of rule and compassion. I do not suggest that there is an easy or automatic solution to this problem, nor can living symbols be entirely molded to suit any generation's idea of correctness or propriety.

I also think it is important to speak openly about the essential character of the second-person usage in Jewish worship. In order for prayer to be real, it has to call forth, according to the greatest Jewish masters in this art, both love and awe. For prayer to be effective, these two at their greatest heights must join together; the words in fact serve primarily to evoke these emotions. (Prayer without love and awe "has no wings," say the Hasidic masters, "and cannot fly upward.") I believe that the need for love and awe in worship requires the use of the second person. I do not tremble when I say "I love nature" or "there is a beautiful tree." I do tremble when I say to another "I love you." Here, too, Martin Buber is crucial to our discussion. The saying of "you," he claims, makes a claim on my whole being that no third person or cohortative first person can make. In saying "you" in prayer, I open myself and make myself vulnerable. Without that vulnerability—that laying oneself open before the other present in the saying of "you" (even though we understand that the "you" is not ultimately other)—we cannot enter the emotional state needed to pray.

I thus believe that insofar as liberal Judaism maintains a liturgy into the next century, it will and should remain an essentially traditional, Hebrew-centered liturgy. But there will be some important changes and additions to that liturgy. The past two centuries have already provided precedent for ongoing, relatively moderate changes in the liturgical text. Though some Orthodox leaders fulminated with rage on each occasion, such changes continued. Even a return to greater tradition in liturgy, notable in the recent efforts of all three liberal movements, has not and will not eliminate the desire for certain carefully thought out departures from tradition. There are two areas where I believe current circumstances will affect the religious language of Judaism in the mid-21st century: the issues of ecological survival and of nationalism/universalism.

The importance of ecological concern will lead Judaism back to a largely creation-centered theology. Jewish theology foundered through the 20th century on the twin rocks of revelation and providence. Accepting Franz Rosenzweig's formulation of Judaism as the religion of revelation par excellence, Jewish thinkers struggled endlessly with the question of what remains of the Word of God after the ravages of critical Bible scholarship, comparative ancient Near Eastern religion, and literary form studies as applied to scripture. Thinly veiled behind the great concern with revelation was the issue of authority, particularly the authority of religious law. Though these two did not necessarily have to go hand-in-hand with one another, it was generally claimed that only a rather literal belief in scripture as the revealed will of God would suffice to justify the institutions of Jewish law.

The question of providence was forced upon Jewish theology by the terrible events of mid-century. As naive a formulation as it may be, the question "where was God?" has continued to haunt the would-be Jewish faithful for several generations. As the 20th century draws to a close, however, the balance seems to be shifting toward a theology of creation, in recent years an issue mostly neglected by nonfundamentalist Jews. The essence of religion is now seen to lie in a profound openness to a divine presence within the natural order, an appreciation of God as the One who "renews each day the act of creation." Awareness of divine presence and willingness to act upon that awareness and construct a life and society appreciative of the universe as God's handiwork seem to comprise the sort of religious attitude appropriate to the turn of the new century, given the picture of that century's chief concerns as outlined above.

Here the insights of the 20th century's greatest Jewish thinkers begin to combine in surprising new ways. Martin Buber's idealized reconstruction of Hasidism, focused on awareness of the divine presence in each "here and now," and Abraham Joshua Heschel's emphasis on a profound sense of mystery and wonder about existence as the starting point of religion, will be joined with Mordecai M. Kaplan's insistence on a this-worldly and intellectually honest Jewish faith. These together will produce a Judaism at once driven by the excitement of spiritual quest and focused on the natural order, its existence and sustenance, as the great testimony of God's presence.

This new creation-centered Judaism does not take the biblical creation story literally, but rather uses it as symbolic expression either of a highly immanentist theology, in which talk of creation stands for the holiness of all existence, or a somewhat vague theism/religious humanism, which emphasizes the notions of human stewardship over and responsibility for the created world. It is, for the sake of clarification, completely alien both in origin and spirit to so-called Creationism, a rear guard attempt to support biblical literalism current in Christian fundamentalist circles. This new Jewish emphasis on creation is, in a certain sense, a return to Maimonides, who well understood that Jewish theology had to address itself to universal questions of human existence, and that foremost among these is the act of creation. While we are far from the medieval need to "prove" creation from the laws of physics, we share with this mentor an awareness that life's meaning and life's origins are tied to one another.

The universal quest for human meaning usually begins with the most personal and this-worldly of questions: "Who am I?" "What is the purpose of my life?" The most essential Jewish answers to these questions are rooted in our shared account of creation: "You are the image and likeness of God, put into this world to continue the ongoing sublime act of divine creation. In your use of speech, you may imitate the speech-acts of God in creating the world. In reflection and sanctification of time, you repeat the primal Sabbath. In making life holy and in the moral improvement of the universe, you are ever completing the unfinished act of creation. As a creature of intelligence, freedom, and moral choice, the way is open before you—for life or death, destruction or creativity.'' This message will be one of tremendously increased religious power as the world faces a time of crucial decisions and potential disaster.

A second area in which external history is likely to impinge on Jewish religious language is the age-old conflict in Jewry between universalism and particularism. Liberal Jews toward the mid-21st century will be driven by a great conflict: internationalist in sympathies, most will support a strong world government and recognize how deeply life in the new threatened ''global village'' needs to be transformed to assure a future for human society. They will be cultural cosmopolitans, enjoying the full benefits of the blending of cultures that will have resulted from the breakdown of international borders and speedy and accessible global travel. In their musical and artistic tastes, they will remain largely linked with the internationalist avant-garde. These Jews will have suffered more than a generation of embarrassment over the nationalism and the Israelocentrism of their own tradition and of their compatriots, the Jewish traditionalists. Though most will remain supportive of Israel throughout its protracted and morally difficult struggle to retain independence and political/ military hegemony in the Middle East, they will be deeply torn and embarrassed about this as well. At the same time, the drive to maintain a unique Jewish identity and preserve the Jewish heritage will not be abated. North American Jews, the great-great- or great-great-great grandchildren of immigrants, most of whom live highly assimilated and comfortable lives, will continue to pay more than monetary dues and lip service to the idea of preserving Judaism.

This inward conflict will be reflected in extended experimentation with Jewish liturgy. Some texts within the prayer book, rooted in Reform tradition and eschewing national aspirations, will again become popular, having largely disappeared with the Reform move to the right in the late 20th century. Such formulae as ''make peace for us and for all Israel'' will have given way in such liturgies to universalist formulations. References to Israel as ''the chosen people'' will be absent from such prayer books, which will consider the Reconstructionist liturgy of 1945 as a progressive vanguard statement.

On the other hand, prayer books will also be sought that affirm the national identity of the Jewish people and its ties with the State of Israel. Inclusion or noninclusion of a prayer for the State of Israel may be something of a touchstone on this question. It will be important for some Jews that the prayer book affirm liberal Jews' unity with nonsynagogue Jews and communities. In these prayer books an important place will be given to modern Hebrew poetry in translation, along with other creative contributions of modern Jews. Evidence of the continuing historical struggle of the Jewish people for survival and recognition will make such a liturgy imperative. Unlike the more classically Reform prayer books, here references to the land, to Jerusalem, and even historic references to the priesthood and the Davidic dynasty will be restored under the influence of the need for greater connection to Jewish history. Some Jews will come to appreciate their liturgy as a testament to the evolving character of Jewish civilization, bearing within it traces of each period through which the people have lived. Liturgical affirmations of the messianic future in particular will grow in importance as Jews take their place as an active part of a society that works to avoid a new apocalyptic doomsday. Within the liberal Jewish community, controversy will continue over liturgical change and several versions of the prayer book will remain current, even as the old denominational labels shift in meaning.

In the face of these two great issues, I believe that the liturgical crisis of the 1980s—the questions of gender—will be seen with a good deal of historical perspective. The hysteria on all sides generated by the empowerment of women in the Jewish community will be a thing of the past, and the playing out of that hysteria on the board of liturgy will be the subject of interesting historical and sociological research. Jewish worshippers (men and women) will be able to say *barukh atah* again without having to feel embarrassed before real or imagined feminist critics. Inclusion of references to the matriarchs in the prayer book, *kavvanot* addressed to the *shekhinah,* and new prayers invoking the spirit of Rachel, Miriam, or Hannah will be commonplace and widely accepted by both men and women. Nonsexist translations will be *de rigueur,* but the hypersensitivity of our own decade to the gender question will have gone by the wayside.

In all of these matters, I believe a wide variety of prayer styles should be legitimized in the Jewish community. As we collectively grope toward the religious language appropriate for a new age in our people's history, a century in which "a thousand flowers bloom" is not at all a terrifying prospect to me. Jewish law, insofar as it remains a significant guide in this area, is rather open with regard to what is truly required in prayer. Maimonides concludes that the recital of the *Shema* and the spontaneous prayer of the heart are biblically ordained obligations and that all other liturgy has the lesser status of rabbinic ordinance. I could readily conceive of a Jewish community in our age in which twice-daily prayer, at sunrise and sunset, consisted of a period of meditation to be concluded with a communal calling out of the one line *Shema.* That is a synagogue I would like to attend sometimes, though I would also like to go to one where there is still *davnen,* for another kind of spiritual nourishment. The synagogue that offers thoughtful new prayers, including some that reflect the cosmological and scientific language of our time, converted into worshipful appreciation, is also one I would like to visit sometimes. A congregation that experiments with some of the new forms of meditation and spiritual growth techniques that will abound in the 21st century, seeking to bind them to the earlier sources of Jewish spirituality, will also have a real contribution to make. I continue to believe and hope that all of these, along with a good many others, will survive in our liberal Jewish community as we face the challenge of an unknown, sometimes frightening, but ever exciting new age in our people's history.

A Response

Judith Plaskow

When I look into the 21st century, I see set before us possibilities for life or death: the greater international cooperation and ecological awareness that Arthur Green envisions; or greater fragmentation and international struggle, not between East and West, but between North and South, rich and poor, and with this struggle a potential postponement of ecological responsibility until it is too late, as the North seeks to defend its hegemony and the South tries to cope with explosive social and economic needs. I do not know which future, if either, will come to be, but I do know which we are obligated to choose. And I have some ideas as to how we as liberal Jews can consciously shape our liturgical future to reflect and strengthen our commitment to life—shape this future not just so that it coheres with our political choices but so that it expresses our real connection to the power of being that sustains life in our perilous times.

As I study it for guidance in this project which I know we share, I find in Arthur Green's essay two rather different Arthur Greens. One is the writer who insists that "religious language and liturgy are highly conservative," who stresses the links between present-day Jews and our historical past, and who says that liberal Jewish liturgy "will and should remain an essentially traditional liturgy." This is the writer who chooses to italicize the following sentence: "While experimentation is certainly called for, a sense of authenticity and deep-rootedness in tradition will remain the greatest bearer of [emotional] power and should not be sacrificed." I experience that sentence as a warning and a threat. And while I cannot say I exactly disagree with its author—I am very much aware of the importance of communal and personal memory as central elements in the effectiveness of liturgy—I see traditional authenticity as one ingredient in the creation of prayable and satisfying prayer.

The other writer is the one who says that "the danger of our tradition is that we are too much wedded to a single form of metaphoric expression," who acknowledges the verbal idolatry that this narrowness of expression can entail, who learns from Kabbalah "insistence upon a multiplicity of spiritual metaphors," and who suggests that we speak of God using a variety of personal and impersonal, natural and traditional images. With this vision of "a thousand flowers"—which certainly does not abandon authenticity and yet leaves ample room for experimentation within and beyond it—I wholly agree.

For me, however, the quest for new imagery, for forms of liturgical experimentation, and for the religious experience out of which all effective liturgy
comes, is inseparably bound up with feminism and will be bound up with it well
into the 21st century. The feminist critique of liturgy has never been limited to
a critique of God's gender: gender simply provides an obvious starting point
from which to name a much deeper dissatisfaction with the God of conventional
piety, and to begin a quest for that sophisticated understanding of God that contemporary Jews can believe in. Whatever "hysteria" there has been on this
question of gender comes almost entirely either from those who do not understand the symbolic character of religious language, or from those who do, yet
suddenly revert to another level of discourse when women's claims to religious
authority threaten male privilege. Certainly, feminists did not spend much time
praying to "God-She" or the "Queen of the Universe" or "She whose womb
covers the earth" before we realized that, while such images are important in
signaling the symbolic nature of religious language and challenging past verbal
idolatry, they do not convey our seriousness as feminists and as Jews. Feminists
are seeking a new, or old/new, conception of God—a search that, though partly
shaped by feminist sources and experiences, is certainly not ours alone, for it
merges with a larger Jewish quest and struggle.

Once I look past Green's too-easy dismissal of feminist concerns to the
substance of his theology, I find a concept of God similar to that emerging in
feminist theology and liturgical experimentation. This is a God "not radically
other than either soul or world," a God who is the "inner essence of all existence, present throughout being insofar as we are open to discovering and responding to that presence," and a God whose "independent or 'transcendent'
existence" is "a secondary and largely moot" question, yet is somehow also
implicit in "our collective human experience of divine immanence." Catherine
Keller has described Nellie Morton's theism in very similar terms. "Self-
relation," she says, " . . . is not separable from relation to the whole, and the
whole not separable from its own transcending center." Like Green, Keller uses
the language of self to speak of God, and also like him, she is not willing to
collapse theism into pure immanence. The deeper wisdom in which we participate, Keller says,

> is never just my own immanent depth, or inner self, nor is it ever . . .
> identical with what already is. It creates the space in which something
> new can occur. So it is "transcending" in the sense that it is also im-
> manent in the experience of everyone and everything else; and that it
> always pushes "up from down under," beyond what is given and es-
> tablished. It moves through the body . . . but is not . . . reducible to
> physical mechanics. It moves with the voice of the prophets . . . up
> through the suffering of the downtrodden.[1]

Given the similarity between Green's understanding of God and these quite
mainstream feminist words of Keller's, what leads him to view feminism as a

quarrel about gender? On the other hand, what does feminism have to offer to the issue of liturgy and religious language that is not also being discussed in non-feminist terms? The first question I do not attempt to answer; the second is the subject of my response.

I believe that in raising fundamental religious questions from the perspective of our own lives and experiences, feminists are both bringing particular issues and emphases to bear on a wider Jewish theological conversation, and testifying to the deep connection between our contribution to this conversation and our empowerment as Jewish women. Aware that there will be no fully Jewish conception of God and no fully Jewish liturgy until women participate in creating them, we seek to confront the full range of issues with which modern Jews must deal—but on the basis of our experiences as Jewish women. Because the project of creating a Judaism that reflects the perspectives of women and men intersects with all Jewish issues, it is not surprising that there is a broad consonance of direction and purpose between the feminist agenda and that of other progressive Jews. Yet feminism also offers a particular angle of vision on the world that can make a distinctive contribution to the issues of God and liturgy, as well as other issues in contemporary Jewish life.

Let me illustrate this point by looking at several of the specific questions Green raises. He discusses, for example, the importance of ecological concerns and the recent surge of interest in a creation-centered spirituality. The human relation to the natural world has been a central issue for feminist spirituality in general and Jewish feminism in particular, partly because of the historical and social connection of women with nature and physicality. The ideological links between women, goddesses, nature, and sexuality, and the actual historical experience of women in tending and nurturing physical life have led feminists to take a hard and critical look at theologies and liturgies that connect God and nature only through the disembodied word. Looking for and finding God in that most despised Other—the bodies and sexuality of women—feminists have learned to find God in all that is. The discovery and celebration of a God immanent in the natural world is clearly expressed in the liturgy of Marcia Falk, who has begun to create the impersonal and natural metaphors Green calls for as part of a full naming of God, and who has blessed God as source, fountain, and wellspring of life. In keeping with the feminist insight that there is a deep connection between neglect of and disregard for nature and disparagement of our own bodies, we need also to find metaphors that reveal the presence of God in human sexuality and embodiment.

Arthur Green discusses the conflict between universalism and particularism. This too has been an important issue for Jewish feminists as we have confronted issues of distinctiveness, hierarchy, and difference both in dealing with our subordinate role within traditional Judaism and thinking about images of God. Struggling for equality in a Jewish community that has not yet learned to respect internal difference and mine it as a source of enrichment and power, feminists are acutely aware of the analogies between our own situation and the situation of the Jewish community in relation to the wider world. Maintaining Jewish uniqueness while acknowledging our connections to a larger national and global order is part of the same project as affirming our identity as Jewish women within the context of a Jewish community that genuinely values diversity. Moreover, issues of universalism and particularism affect liturgy not simply in terms of its depictions of the social order, but also in terms of its understanding of God. Any particular image of God is just one aspect of the divine totality that embraces the diversity of a universal community. Only when our metaphors for God are sufficiently inclusive that they reflect the multiplicity of a pluralistic Israel *and* of a cosmic community will God truly be one—which is to say all in all.

A third issue Green discusses that clearly overlaps with feminist concerns is the issue of community. Indeed, it may be in the affirmation of community as the locus of personal development and the divine/human relation that Judaism and feminism most fully come together. Certainly, it is no accident that *havurot* have provided a first prayer home for many feminist Jews, at the same time that they have created an intimate space for the experience of God's immanence.

Feminists have also stressed, however, the significance of the empowerment that can come through community and the relation of that empowerment to God and to worship. Women discovering in community the power of our individual and collective voices have realized that this power is connected to a greater one that grounds and sustains it. If, for both Judaism and feminism, community is not in conflict with selfhood but allows and nurtures it, so community itself is rooted in and succored by a more embracing reality that is also the ultimate horizon of the self. The feminist experience of personal empowerment in community can lead to a sense of participation in an energy and process that finally enfolds the cosmos and that is responded to and enacted by the individual and community. Richard R. Niebuhr, in his description of rejoicing, captures perfectly the experience of many feminists that discovering our own autonomy also means discovering our relation to a larger project that embraces and transcends humanity.

> [Rejoicing] entails consciousness of liberation into the stream of life,
> a sense of collectedness, a feeling of the union of one's own power
> with power and energy itself, and finally a sense of effectiveness and
> of recognition as an agent in a human commonwealth that transcends
> the present.[2]

For me, this experience of empowerment in community provides the experiential baseline for Jewish feminist God-language. I see it not only as a central feminist experience but as resonating with the experience of a certain group of slaves who miraculously and frighteningly found themselves agents of their own destiny, and in so doing named the God who guided and covenanted with them. I would like to see this experience of empowerment find expression in a host of personal and nonpersonal metaphors imagining God as source and sustainer of the world, friend and goad of humanity, and cocreator with us in the task of redemption.

I believe that it is also in this experience of empowerment and the metaphors we use to capture it that the social action or political dimension of feminist prayer becomes most clear. I agree that ultimately we form a prayer community with all humanity—I would add with the whole cosmos—and that therefore we cannot escape the demands that prayer imposes upon us. I also believe that prayer can help us to sustain the sources of motivation and power that lead and allow us to enter fully into the task of *tikkun*. One of the most serious problems with the traditional liturgy is its one-sided emphasis on human frailty, impotence, and nothingness. While these are aspects of human experience I certainly would not deny or exclude from prayer, I am nonetheless convinced that it is not the apprehension of our nothingness that leads us to effective action. Indeed, it seems to me that the language of domination that permeates the liturgy is in fundamental tension with the language of covenantal responsibility because it denies the reality of human power and responsibility that the covenant presupposes. When we know God in our selves and in community as the one who creates, sustains, and empowers the great web of existence, we are most able to join with others to make a home for the divine presence in the world.

If prayer can help us touch the sources of power in ourselves that lead to effective action, then the metaphors we use in prayer point in the direction of that action. This is where the gender of God does become a feminist issue and, in fact, where all the issues under discussion here come together. When we expand our metaphors for God to include femaleness as well as maleness, we remind ourselves that the community of prayer to which we are responsible is truly a community of women and men. When we speak of God as ground or fountain of life, when we use other images from nature, when we do not neglect our sexuality in prayer, we remind ourselves that the community of prayer is a cosmic community that begins in the experience of our own bodies. When we speak of God using the vast store of images of a universal community, we remember what we already know, that the prayer community is universal. When we do not use such images, when we continue to depend on the narrow store of metaphors the traditional liturgy provides, prayer cannot be a vehicle for the memory that we need. On the contrary, our prayer life contradicts and can potentially undermine our impulses toward creative change.

I would like to conclude by returning to the issue of authenticity. Are these feminist reflections on God and prayer Jewishly authentic? They seem so to me. At least they are no less authentic than any other form of liberal experimentation! Yet feminists must also question the criteria of authenticity that determine whether a particular liturgy adequately expresses the link between contemporary Jews and our historical past. I have implied it already, but it cannot be said often enough that the sources that validate authenticity are male sources. We do not yet have the sources and stories of past Jewish women that we can remember and celebrate. Thus, although I have followed Arthur Green in focusing on issues of contemporary images for God, for feminists, creating Jewish liturgy always also means recreating the past as the basis for a present-day Jewish community that will truly be a community of women and men. The ongoing task of reshaping Jewish memory so that it remains in continuity with changing Jewish values is itself a perennial and authentic Jewish project, and one most effectively carried out through the vehicle of liturgy. It is only as we open up our understanding of who constitutes the Jewish community and what our collective past has been that authenticity becomes an inclusive and empowering criterion challenging us to claim our history, rather than a weapon against those who have hitherto been voiceless.

2

Tradition and Religious Practice

Deborah E. Lipstadt

For a number of years observers of the Jewish scene, both within the academy and outside of it, have debated the nature, quality, and future of Jewish life in America. The debate has focused on issues of Jewish identity, literacy, culture, and religion, and assessments have varied markedly. Some believe the present and the future are full of promise; others predict doom and gloom.

The publication in 1985 of Charles Silberman's book *A Certain People* intensified the nature of that debate.[3] Silberman, enthusiastic about the developments he had witnessed, argued that the community was in the midst of a creative renaissance. Convinced that it was undergoing a transformation from a traditional to a modern society, he argued that the traditional barometer of evaluating Jewish life had become outmoded, and a new standard of measurement must be found. Silberman dismissed concerns about intermarriage, assimilation, shrinking populations, and Jewish illiteracy as unwarranted, contending that any negative trends are overshadowed, if not nullified, by an array of positive developments.

Now that the heat of the debate has passed, it is valuable to return to some of the issues it raised and to ascertain whether a deeper understanding of them offers any guidance for planning for the Jewish future. Several questions seem to be central to this debate: What does it mean to build an authentic Jewish community and Jewish identity in the United States? Do the patterns of behavior in the contemporary Jewish community offer the promise of a flourishing and creative future? What relationship, if any, might that future have to traditional Jewish patterns of behavior, standards, and values? What are those standards and values, and what role do they play in Jewish communal life? Given the pluralistic nature of American Jewish life, is it possible to delineate authentic Jewish teachings that would be universally accepted by all groups?

Prognosticating about the religious or spiritual outlook of the community 30 years hence does not come easy to a historian familiar with the talmudic dictum that, since the completion of the Tanakh (the Hebrew Bible), prophecy has been reserved for "children and fools." Consequently, I assess the nature of contemporary Jewish life in America and critically analyze the path it might take in future years. Even those who believe a revival has taken place must ask some serious questions about its longevity and quality. Perhaps this essay will prompt such questions.

Though Silberman's book made the so-called Jewish revival a topic for sermons, popular lectures, and newspaper columns, in truth he was joining a discussion that had begun long before. Beginning in the 1970s, a number of observers of the American Jewish scene were taken aback by the rapid changes in the community. Intense reaction to the Six-Day War, the evolution of the *havurah* movement, the emerging *ba'alei teshuvah* (return to religious observance) phenomenon, Jewish studies programs on campus, and the proliferation of traditional and nontraditional day schools had led scholars to call for a reassessment of the American Jewish community. In the aftermath of the community's unprecedented response to Israel's need during the 1967 war and thereafter and the renewed interest in Jewish life, Nathan Glazer added a chapter to his classic work *American Judaism* that acknowledged this new turn of events.

In the early 1980s Jonathan Woocher called attention to the development of "civil Judaism" in the ranks of those who had chosen "secularized" kinds of activities within Jewish communal life.[4] Woocher argued that those involved in these arenas were really expressing a strong spiritual connection, a religious link to the community, and were not simply or solely engaged in social welfare activities. Studies show that communal lay leaders are evidencing an enhanced connection to Jewish tradition and conceive of their activities as having a transcendental and personally redemptive quality. Activities that in previous periods were seen by those who performed them as an expression of "noblesse oblige" are now seen as a personal and spiritual expression. None of these developments had been predicted.[5]

Steven M. Cohen's studies of different Jewish communities also prompted a reassessment of the quality of Jewish communal life. His work called special attention to positive and unexpected trends in the American Jewish community. Cohen focused on issues of Jewish identity as well as demography. For example, he noted that the tendency of Jewish women in their twenties not to have children did not indicate a decision to remain childless, as had originally been interpreted. Women had simply postponed having children to an age that had once been considered beyond the childbearing years. So, too, young Jewish adults postponed—but certainly did not reject—joining synagogues and other Jewish organizations.[6] Despair was therefore inappropriate.

In their book *The Transformation of the Jews,* Calvin Goldscheider and Alan Zuckerman argued that there had not been an erosion of Jewish identity but a "transformation." Kinship, friendship, and a broad array of other connections between Jews emerged as "important sources of Jewish communal strength."

Because they saw the Jewish community as being rooted in its interaction, as opposed to its shared values, they argued that "the greater the interaction in the largest numbers of spheres of activity the greater cohesiveness of the group."[7] They found that in social, occupational, residential, and political spheres there was evidence of enhanced Jewish interaction.

Not only did developments seem to point to increased arenas for group cohesiveness in the American Jewish community, but Jews compared quite favorably with other American groups in terms of different forms of association and cohesion, including friendship, residential patterns, social networks, and educational arenas.[8] Even the developments in the professional and occupational life of the Jewish community were interpreted by Goldscheider, in *Jewish Continuity and Change: Emerging Patterns in America,* as having had positive results. Occupational mobility had not "resulted in the occupational assimilation of Jews, but it has become a powerful base of ethnicity and ethnic continuity."[9]

These developments excited the optimists. They saw a group emerging that was "more Jewishly educated, more identified, more involved in Jewish matters,"[10] than had previously been the case. They saw a community that was "neither diminishing demographically nor weakening Jewishly but one that was more Jewish, stronger, more articulate, more cohesive as a community." Having been transformed, it was "entering a period of flourishing and creative development" rather than "entering the final gasps of a declining, weakening, struggling to survive remnant."[11]

The optimists could be said to have been reacting in part to a decisive change in the nature of modern Jewish identity. Until recently, the modern Jewish experience has been marked by an overwhelming desire to fit into and be accepted by the surrounding non-Jewish culture. As the operative slogan of 19th-century Jewish emancipation put it: Be a person in the street and a Jew in your home. The Enlightenment offered Jews the opportunity to move freely in the non-Jewish world and yet to adhere privately to Jewish tradition. No longer was the choice, as it had been for many centuries, between the social, religious, and cultural isolation of the ghetto or the "liberation" of the baptismal font. In contrast to the traditional Jewish relationship to non-Jewish society, separation was rejected by Jews as a philosophy of a life.[12]

In the latter decades of the 20th century, the motto of "man in the street, Jew at home" was reversed. Jews were more comfortable proclaiming their Jewish identity in the public sphere than they were adhering to Jewish traditions in the private sphere.

Initial evidence pointed to a real change, which was most evident in those arenas where Jews had been particularly reluctant to call attention to their minority identity, among them the college campus, the political world, and the corporate sector. In the 1950s and early 1960s the college campus was considered a veritable Jewish wasteland and even a threat to Jewish identity. Jewish parents and communal leaders feared that Jewish students would encounter

professors openly contemptuous of Judaism who would lure them to follow all
sorts of intellectual "false gods."

In contrast, on Rosh Hashanah and Yom Kippur during the 1980s it was
common to find campus services heavily populated by the most prominent professors. On prestigious campuses, Jewish faculty groups thrive. Jewish studies
programs are common fixtures at many universities. [13]

Goldscheider has observed that "educational attainment is not the source
of Jewish secularization nor does it lead to alienation and disaffection from the
community." [14] Whereas education once drove a wedge between immigrant parents and their children or between first- and second-generation Americans, it
now is a tie that binds generations. More important, rather than being threatened
by advanced education, ethnic identity and communal continuity are strengthened by it, according to Goldscheider's findings.

In the political arena Jews had traditionally been uncomfortable about publicly articulating a Jewish agenda. Few Jews ran for public office even in dis-
tricts with a predominantly Jewish electorate. [15] Jews who participated in
political activities generally devoted their energies to helping other groups and
causes. In contrast, by the 1980s the Jewish caucus on Capitol Hill had over 30
members. Jewish political action committees of every variety had been established. Irrespective of one's feelings about the wisdom of PACs or the correctness of the viewpoint they expound, the willingness of Jews to participate
publicly *as* Jews in the political arena is in marked contrast to the tradition of
shtadlanut, or backdoor diplomacy. [16]

Successful young professionals and entrepreneurs of the kind who would
have shunned most forms of public Jewish identification but a few decades ago
now find Jewish organizational young leadership groups not only attractive but
populated by their successful counterparts. Law firms that once refused to hire
Jews now are the site of weekly Talmud classes. Groups of Jewish business and
professional women meet regularly throughout the United States to discuss areas
of common concern to them as Jews.

In view of these developments, many observers are tremendously upbeat
about the great success Jews have had not only in entering the American scene
but in adapting Jewish life to America. But a number of other disturbing phenomena have caused many observers to step back and reassess what at first
glance seems so positive. In so doing they have joined the ranks of those who
have long expressed concern about the future direction of Jews and Judaism
in America.

It can be argued that some of the optimists, such as Silberman, were doing
more than simply objectively analyzing the current state of the American Jewish
community. Their work may be seen, at least to some extent, as a response to the
gloomy prognostications so often pronounced by Jewish communal leaders.
Judging by their pessimism about the future, American Jewish leaders some-

times seem more comfortable seeing the tunnel at the end of the light than they do seeing the light at the end of the tunnel. There has long been a marked tendency to see the glass as half empty rather than half or even three-quarters full. Consequently, the transformationalists argue, projections of demographic demise, anti-Semitic attack, and an atrophying community are often the norm even where there is empirical evidence to the contrary.

This pessimism and sense of impending catastrophe is nothing new. In his seminal essay, "Israel: The Ever-Dying People," Simon Rawidowicz explored the phenomenon that, from early rabbinic times on, each generation of Jews has assumed that it was the last, and that with its demise Jewish learning and adherence to fundamental Jewish values would end or, at the very best, diminish markedly. This demise would result not from an attack from without but because of an internal atrophy, most particularly the diminution of Jewish learning.[17]

Silberman and some of the other "transformationalists" may have chosen to accentuate the positive because they sensed a tendency on the part of Jewish leaders to ignore the strides made in the last 20 years and to wail instead at the dire fate awaiting American Jews. There are those who argue that this tendency toward pessimism was and is essentially a mode of prompting Jews to enhance their level of Jewish observance—the Jewish community is assimilating; therefore you must become better Jews and be more mindful of tradition—or to increase their monetary support of Jewish causes.

Those who are more pessimistic argue that, irrespective of the positive developments, the rate of intermarriage, assimilation, and lack of affiliation are so high that gloom is the only proper response.[18] They believe that the optimists have seriously overstated the positive and ignored some dire developments. Chief among the critics have been Marshall Sklare and Charles Liebman. Their concerns have also been echoed by Arthur Hertzberg, Samuel Heilman, and Jack Wertheimer, who interpret the significance of current sociological trends very differently.[19]

The fundamental disagreement between the optimists and the pessimists concerns the barometer by which to gauge Jewish "sufficiency." An act that may constitute a strong expression of Jewish identity in the eyes of some may be a weak, virtually meaningless act to others.[20] Those who believe the Jewish community is undergoing a transformation contend that the significance of the cultural revival should not be measured simply by its qualitative aspects but rather by the fact that it reflects the Jewish laity's willingness to proclaim openly what it had previously tried to camouflage. What is significant about raising money for Jewish PACs and attending meetings is that these are public activities reflecting comfort in publicly identifying as Jews. No longer is Jewish identity considered a stigma or an obstacle to one's professional stature or advancement as a public figure. These developments represent a significant change in the American Jewish community's *Weltanschauung*.

Participation in a Jewish PAC may also reflect the participants' desire to interact socially with others who share similar attitudes and concerns. In other words, these are individuals seeking a Jewish community and, to use Zuckerman and Goldscheider's terminology, areas for Jewish interaction.

But for those who are pessimistic about the Jewish future, interaction and public proclamation of Jewish identity, though significant, are not enough. Their skepticism concerns the *quality* of the so-called renaissance, which they believe is a mile wide and an inch deep. Their most serious contention is that those activities cited by the optimists as evidence of renewal are often devoid of any serious Judaic content. They may be "consciousness-raising" activities, but they leave the participants with little sense of the meaning of their Jewish affiliation, other than to protect Jews and Jewish causes against danger.

Here we come to the heart of the matter and probably the greatest challenge to those who wish to enhance the quality of Jewish life in America. One can only praise the great emphasis on community and maintaining a Jewish public identity. But something critical is missing from this revival: an understanding of distinctive Jewish values, a sense of mission and unique purpose.

The nearly exclusive emphasis on building and maintaining a "sense of community" sacrifices emphasis on specific and normative Jewish values. I do not mean to suggest that all Jewish values are ignored. Great emphasis is placed on several of them. *Tzedakah* (literally, "justice" used to mean charitable giving), in whose name the idea that "we are one" is generally invoked, is a normative communal value—perhaps *the* value. So too is the idea of *kol yisrael areivim zeh ba'zeh,* all Israel is responsible for one another, which is often cited as an operating principle of Jewish life. It was on these two concepts that the Soviet Jewry and Ethiopian Jewry movements were built. But these guidelines or values seem to have at their base the notion of community and the challenge of building that community rather than a complex and profound system of beliefs and practice. A religious civilization rooted in shared beliefs, values, and culture has been transformed into an amalgam of emotions. There is no genuinely spiritual aspect present. As Arthur Hertzberg has observed, there is little to indicate that those undergoing this "revival" have "any sense of the deep religious meaning of chosenness as the source of moral and social conscience."[21]

This is not meant to denigrate the importance of community as a normative Jewish standard. The need for a *minyan* to perform certain basic Jewish rituals indicates the importance that Jewish tradition places on the concept of community. It is fundamental to the notion of building a religious civilization. But for American Jews living in the closing years of the 20th century, community has been transformed from a means into an end in itself. Too often Jewish leaders—both lay and professional, religious and secular—speak of building community without focusing on the hard question: What kind of community should it be?

If one of the critical functions of religion is to help its adherents determine ultimate values, to help them differentiate between what is ultimately right and wrong, then the connection between this ethnic revival and a genuine religious renewal becomes increasingly tenuous. The celebration of the revival has focused much more on Jewish interaction than on Jewish conscience.[22]

These concerns have been expressed in many quarters. They have been voiced by those who were and are seen to be part of the celebratory camp. Steven Cohen, whose work was so important to Silberman, acknowledges that the "values that American Jews live by are no longer genuine, authentic Jewish values as they are commonly understood."[23] Leonard Fein, whose magazine *Moment* once figured prominently in the "revival," acknowledged his concerns: "A Judaism that knows neither denial nor affirmation, that is exclusively about togetherness, must become a vestigial category."[24]

Interaction and public proclamation of one's identity are certainly significant, for without them it is much harder to produce a vital culture or religion. However, they neither delineate specific norms of behavior nor impose sanctions on Jews who do not adhere to those norms. In the enthusiasm over the renewed interest in Jewish communal life there has been a tendency by religious and communal leaders, as well as some analysts of the scene, to "sanctify" whatever the prevailing standards of behavior and observance happen to be.[25] Civil religion can produce a situation where anything done collectively by Jews *as* Jews becomes an expression of religious identity.

A sense of belonging to a community is extremely significant. Jews cite this as one of the main reasons why being Jewish is important to them. But many suggest it is not enough. Hertzberg argues that "activism can work as a substitute for faith for no more than one or two generations." Can support of Israel, Jewish social service, and anti-defamation provide a strong enough motivation for maintaining a multigenerational link with the Jewish community, not to mention Jewish tradition? Hertzberg notes that for individuals who were the pillars of American Jewish communal life at the beginning of this century and who built an array of organizations including the American Jewish Committee, the Jewish Theological Seminary, and the Joint Distribution Committee, the communal/charitable link—as opposed to the spiritual/religious one—was not enough. "Today one could not fill the boards of directors of [these] organization[s] with the descendants of their founders. Many of their great-grandchildren simply do not want to be considered Jews."[26]

One of the questions that must be asked if one wishes to assess the nature of American Jewish *religious* life is to what degree existing patterns of interaction and a sense of cultural and ethnic identity implant in Jews a set of moral and cognitive values—values universally shared by Jews that determine their behavior and help them differentiate between right and wrong. Moreover, what is the staying power of these values? Has Judaism become, in the words of Harold

Schulweis, a "wonderful hobby"? In a society where significant emphasis is placed on quality leisure time, it is not uncommon for people to tire of one hobby and turn to another, particularly if the atmosphere becomes less conducive to the practice of that hobby.

Certainly a few segments of the American Jewish community do demand adherence to specific values, but they are a distinct minority. There is little that can cause a Jew to be read out of the Jewish community, with the possible exception of rejecting the legitimacy of the State of Israel. Questions remain: Can these patterns of interaction and this sense of community possibly implant standards and values? Can the sense of community become a means rather than an end? If not, then Jewish communal life will probably proceed in the direction Donald Feldstein predicted a few years ago. There will be two groups, one that is knowledgeable about Judaism and Jewish matters and another that is

> largely uneducated Jewishly, less involved and less identified and dependent upon their store of Jewish 'capital' for their survival as Jews. They will still be vulnerable to being lost from the Jewish people, but still Jewish enough to have their attention captured in a crisis and to be worked on towards winning over their sons and daughters to the other group.[27]

Yet another aspect of this renaissance should be considered, particularly if one is trying to imagine how events will play themselves out in the next 30 years. On the popular level this renewal is an articulation of the current American Zeitgeist that has made expressing one's ethnic and religious identity acceptable. Had ethnicity not become a legitimate arena for individual or group expression, it is doubtful whether this renewal would have gained much momentum. Questions must therefore be asked about the durability of the American ethnic revival. Should the social and political climate change and ethnic expression no longer be a desideratum, would the vitality of the revival dissipate as rapidly as it evolved? If the society at large no longer considers a particular "hobby" as healthy to its well being, as has become the case, for example, with smoking in public, then society may well begin to censure the practice of that hobby. If no distinctive values and ideologies are implanted within those Jews who have been part of this revival, it is possible that they will feel compelled to find another hobby with which to occupy themselves.

Even if there is no backlash against ethnicity, various social critics have raised questions about the "hollowness of ethnicity as a form of self-definition."[28] As John Higham observed:

> The American ethnic group is an amorphous entity, difficult to define and in the great majority of cases very incompletely separable from other elements in the population. Except for unusual instances of great internal discipline or external resistance, ethnic boundaries are vague,

fluid and indeterminate. An ethnic group fades out—like a magnetic field—as the distance from its center increases. Its history is one of the energy it generates and the direction in which it moves.[29]

Even if Jews were able to evolve a strong self-definition from their sense of ethnicity, it does not naturally follow that the recent revival will allow this to happen. After all, in its more substantial formulations this revival is mainly an elite phenomenon. It is limited in great measure to Jewish communal professionals, the Orthodox community, a small core of the Conservative, Reconstructionist, and Reform movements, day school students and their families, communal leaders, Jewish studies faculty, members of the rabbinate, and a very limited portion of the Jewish public at large. It certainly does not encompass the majority of the American Jewish community.

The positive developments that have occurred are dramatic and surprising. Only two decades ago no one predicted them. But the often shallow nature of their Judaic content and the fact that they are in so many ways a response to the American Zeitgeist leaves one with the impression that their lasting impact may be weak at best.

Whether one accepts or rejects contentions about the limited qualitative nature of the renaissance (if it deserves to be called a renaissance at all), avenues must be found to enhance the spiritual aspects of American Jewish life and to strengthen the realm of private or personal Jewish activities. History has demonstrated the fallacy of believing that it is possible to be a Jew in one's house and an individual in the street. Conversely, it has also demonstrated the impossibility of being a Jew in the street and an individual at home. Neither formulation allows for a multigenerational continuum of Jewish identification and belief.

One of the first arenas in which a concerted effort must be made is education. *Torah lishmah* (Jewish learning for its own sake) must be implanted as a value. Ira Silverman observed that "we have the highest levels of wealth, occupational status and general education but the deepest levels of Jewish ignorance."[30] The most critical and fundamental area of Jewish ignorance is that of Hebrew. Over 80 percent of American Jews cannot comprehend our sacred texts. Samuel Heilman echoes a similar concern. The fact that these texts are accessible through translation alone removes "the People of the Book . . . from the roots of their being, for language in general and Hebrew in particular is the source of Jewish culture."[31]

Some "leaders" of the American Jewish community seem to have come to recognize the limits of their knowledge and are actively seeking means to fill the lacunae. This is demonstrated by the popularity of certain educational programs that mix text study, history, and Jewish values. But the participants in these programs are generally the lay elite of the community. In no way has this phenomenon of study become a communal standard or an expectation for leaders. Moreover, close analysis of their materials indicates that they too are shallow and relatively simplistic. Even so, they are a quantum leap ahead of what most of the participants have previously experienced. Many of the individuals involved in these programs seem to be seeking the mantle of Jewish "authenticity." The challenge that faces the Jewish community is to develop programs that not only meet an intellectual but a spiritual need, that challenge participants to examine the nature of their Jewish lives and transform Judaism and Jewishness from a wonderful hobby to the all-encompassing system that it truly is.

If no serious efforts are made to enhance the revival or, depending on one's view, to stop the serious attrition from Jewish life, then the changes we have witnessed over the past two decades will evolve into sentimentality and ethnic chauvinism. This will certainly be the case as future generations of Jews move farther and farther away from those foundation stones on which much of this revival was built: a link with an Eastern European immigrant experience, however romanticized; a personal knowledge of survivors of the Holocaust; and a memory or understanding of the nature of Jewish life prior to the establishment of the State of Israel.

Because Judaism has always had multiple meanings, no single all-encompassing, substantive definition of what it means to be a Jew will be possible. But if the Jewish community—or any sector of it—wishes to lay the foundation for a qualitatively thriving Jewish life in, say, the year 2008, then it must be willing to determine specific behavioral norms and to impose sanctions on Jews who deviate. More important, it must be willing to say that our American and Jewish identities do not mesh so easily, that the American emphasis on individualism and self-actualization may conflict with traditional Jewish values.

There is nothing wrong with celebrating some of the communal accomplishments of the past two decades. In many cases they mark a real break with the past and point to a healthier sense of Jewish identity and community. But even as we celebrate we must recognize the limits and deficiencies inherent in this revival and in the broader community. These shortcomings can only be alleviated if we are willing to grapple with them seriously.

A Response

Michael Paley

I start not with my own perspective on the future but with two stories from my present. Every afternoon and on erev Shabbat I attend what I consider a cultural miracle. Daily at Columbia University in New York City, on the third floor of Earl Hall, 90 or so students gather to say *Minchah*. They do not think of this as special; they have done it all their lives On the other side of the *mechitzah*, the partition between the sexes, sit the women, comprising about half the students. On erev Shabbat the number swells to 300, the service is led by students, and the dvar Torah is generally of high quality and always triumphalist. It is given in Teshiva Loshen—English dotted with Hebrew and Aramaic that only insiders can follow. I have yet to hear a dvar Torah in which the Torah is anything less than perfect or the Jews are not the best. All the students are between 18 and 24, for the most part elegantly dressed, and carry a distinct air of genuine sophistication and sense of self. On Simchat Torah more than a thousand such Orthodox students turn out, women with long sleeves and men with their names carefully embroidered onto their yarmulkes.

When I was growing up it was common wisdom that Orthodoxy was dead. All that remained were a few European-accented Jews with yellow beards and open hands. During my own college years 15 years ago, I remember only two students who wore yarmulkes—and that was at Brandeis. It is in this context that I find such a gathering significant. When I mentioned to one of the students at the minyan that I was writing about the Jewish future, he looked at me confidently and said two things: "After 3,500 years you think that 20 or 30 years more will make a difference?" and "The future is ours." That student is 24 years old, and he has two children. I'm not sure he is wrong.

Second story. At Columbia part of my work is connected to supporting community action projects like shelters and soup kitchens. The students who work at such projects are overwhelmingly Catholic and Jewish. They often describe their involvement to me in terms of the ethic with which they were brought up. Like those in the minyan upstairs, the Jews in the group have powerful Jewish feelings. The group is committed and excited and warm, and carries no hint of triumphalism. It is both a learning and teaching community that accomplishes the work in the projects. Whereas the Catholics who participate seem to retain the components of both service and worship, most of the Jews feel that the work they do with the poor and the hungry is enough. They generally have no other connection to the Jewish community at the university. Deborah Lipstadt noted Arthur Hertzberg's argument that activism can work as a substitute for faith for no more than one or two generations. The Jewish students work hard together and become friends, but their work is not anchored in a language or a tradition. They are wonderful and committed, but where will they be in 30 years?

I want to project these two groups into the future before I respond to the question of optimism or pessimism concerning our Jewish future as set in the American context. My student friend may be right about 3,500 years of Jewish tradition, but I think that he is wrong about 200 years of American tradition. Something is definitely changing. I do not say this lightly, cautioned by a variation on Rawidowicz's "ever-dying people." At the end of every millennium, whether determined by the Christian, Muslim, or Hindu count, there arises a fear that the world is being destroyed. But I think the signs are serious.

In 30 years my fellow baby boomers and I will be in social-security land. My students will be in midcareer, paying for this package. Though certainly a delayed birthing phenomenon is going on, my generation will present the next with an abnormally large pool of single, elderly people without natural children and with siblings. With added longevity as a result of medical advances, the financial pyramid will be even more precarious. Even if we start to plan now, we will be facing an incredible financial crisis that will make our current debt problems look inviting. Of course the ethical questions will also be paralyzing. The ecological crisis will continue to show the consequences of indiscretions during the middle of our current century, from ozone depletion to polluted oceans and thinned rain forests. We will move from the fight to protect exotic species from extinction, to trying to save the staples that we now take for granted. World hunger and disease will reach numbing proportions and a change in the world order will no doubt result. When a single hot summer can make a major impact, consider what real and long-lasting change will mean. I am not prepared to say that there will be a one-world government, as Arthur Green predicted in his essay, but I am clear that the way we see ourselves and our world will undergo a radical transformation. Scarcity and priority setting will rule the day.

When we think of the issue of tradition and religious practice, it is usually in terms of whether or not religious particularism can survive in an open society with as tempting a set of fleshpots as ours. The open society has defined the idea of freedom not in the medieval sense of knowing one's true and unique path, but rather through the concept of an actualization of possibility. For us, the open society means that we have great latitude in our choices and desires and that we will not be discriminated against because of race, religion, creed, or sexual preference. I want to turn the question around. My question is whether the society that finds itself in both fiscal and ecological crisis in 30 years will have the desire or even the luxury to remain open. Will these groups continue to live and let live when their own well-being is affected?

Before I return to Jewish identity, I want to spend a moment on this question. The idea of the open society is in some ways based on the notion of ever-expanding resources. In a closed system, if one person has more, it follows that another has less. The birth of the open society was wedded to the idea that expanded populations increased a nation's wealth. In America the concept became connected with the idea of chosenness. Our land was broad and empty, and the early settlers saw themselves as chosen to live in it in equality. Equality would be derived from upright action, a notion of commandment. This quasi-deuteronomic perspective insured that tolerance would be a central theme. People would be rewarded for their upright action and therefore would not need to dominate others. There was finally enough to go around.

There is another underpinning for the belief in tolerance. It is based in the post-17th century explosion in scientific knowledge. Until the 16th century it was commonly believed that the world was finite and that the earth was at the center. All heavenly motions were spherical and harmonious. This meant that the world was clear and predictable and under the watchful protection of the divine. In the 12th century an Islamic astronomer named Al-Biruni looked at the model of Ptolemy and observed that it would be simpler if the universe was pictured in first a heliocentric way and then finally in a centerless way. However, Al-Biruni refrained from public expression of this view because he felt that if people thought that the earth was but a clod of dust winging its way through the heavens, they would destroy it. Therefore he coded his understanding in esoteric Sufi text. In the 18th and 19th centuries, just such a picture of the universe entered the public mind. Al-Biruni's prophecy seems to have come along with it. The past century has seen unprecedented pollution of our environment, and an almost total loss of the ability to see the earth as sacred.

Our modern scientific picture has continued to have a great impact on the way we see and understand our society. In 1922 Edwin Hubble theorized that the universe was not finite but infinite and expanding. Our imagination and consumption followed suit. But our open, expanding society, filled with technological marvels, has begun to show signs of wear. We are no longer dazzled by technology and the politics and science of expansion. We have turned away from doctors, mired in ethical problems, as our high priests, and now look back toward myth makers and sages. I believe that in the next 20 or 30 years we will no longer turn to scientists to solve the problems that they helped bring on. Instead, those movements that provide *definition, context,* and *restraint* amidst our relativism will carry the day. The fact that astronomers like Stephen Hawkings are now revisiting the "collapsing universe" and writing complex best sellers is a sign for the future. Science and society travel together.

It is against this background that I revisit the two student communities, to imagine these exceptional students at midlife in the context of what the world, and our conception of it, will look like, and to take a position on whether to be optimistic like Charles Silberman or pessimistic like Samuel Heilman and others.

Since Deborah Lipstadt focused principally on the non-Orthodox community, I want to comment first on the group of Secular students at the soup kitchen. Arthur Hertzberg has noted the fundamental change in post-Enlightenment Judaism. He claims that until the Enlightenment we were a corporate community whose laws and structures had an impact on the lives of all Jews. Short of painful apostasy, those born Jewish died Jewish, and in general lived in communities apart. The modern world has changed all that. Jews are now granted general mobility (with certain exceptions) and if they want to assimilate are free to do so without pain or problem. As Hertzberg has noted, the vast majority of world Jewry is a voluntary community. Its voluntary nature includes those in the State of Israel as well as the Orthodox. The Orthodox are so because they want to be. This represents a real change for the Jewish people.

Another distinction is suggested by Harold Bloom in his essay, "Jewish Culture and Jewish Identity." Bloom proposes that there are three areas of Jewish identity today: Israel, the Diaspora, and the United States. In Israel the fact of sovereignty and power has so dramatically altered the Jewish culture that its connection with the Diaspora past has been nearly obliterated. Bloom goes on to comment that though there is still a Diaspora, American Judaism, no matter how it is seen from Israel, is different from any Diaspora community since the Hellenized Jewry of the third century B.C.E. in Alexandria.

Bloom rejects the Israeli logic that the Jewish alternatives are limited to complete assimilation amounting to another Holocaust or to life in Israel. Instead he embraces the idea that America, like Hellenistic Alexandria, is an eclectic culture, of which American Judaism is a part. In fact, Judaism's very distinctiveness is its liberating factor. Unlike Europe, America is full of religions that have become peoples. If Mormons, Quakers, and Calvinists are to embrace America as the resting place from their exile, then they must be prepared to accept Jews as well. Even the notion of "chosenness" is so prevalent in America's religious traditions that our Jewish sense of election does not radically distinguish us.

This notion that American Jewry does not constitute a Diaspora is, I believe, correct; it will have a great impact over the next 20 to 30 years. If America were indeed a single society, I would be pessimistic about the Jewishness of our soup kitchen volunteers in 30 years. Only through language and texts does a community stay together, and the secular American Jewish community shows no signs of committing itself to learning that language other than from quips on television or at the deli counter at Zabar's. But I do not see a single American society now, and I see a less unified one in the future. In the year 2018, more than a third of Americans will be Spanish-speaking, with no real intention or need to learn English. At the university I see separatism as the dominant perspective of blacks, Asians, and Hispanics. Integrationism does not seem to be the wave of the future. As the limited society overtakes the expansive society, group identity will become ever more precious. I do not think that there will be a new rise in anti-Semitism. On the contrary, our nation will have to cope with the boredom of McDonald's-brand homogeneity and so individuals will crave uniqueness. The issue will not be "Jew in the home and man on the street" but rather a deep critique of the street itself.

America, in a resource-poor, imperiled future, will begin to look more like Andalusian Spain during the Jewish golden age. Spanish society encouraged both strong religious communal identity and a deep sharing between those corporate communities. It was a society that produced particularistic philosophy and law and at the same time poetry celebrating the mingling of all. Spain before the *reconquista* was rich with traditional images but also broad in educational perspectives that trained its elite to live in more than one culture and to know more than one vocabulary. We still have scholars with that ability: their work appears in this volume. Certainly there were problems such as the lower status accorded to the Jews, the *dhimmi*. Still, Spanish society can serve as an illustration of the possible, even if the reality did not completely fulfill its promise.

Like Spain, America will be a society in which religious and ethnic identity will be generally cherished. It will be understood that tradition is the best way to bring meaning into otherwise dimensionless lives in overpopulated urban centers. If the transformationalists are optimistic because formerly reticent Jews are now publicly proclaiming their Judaism, they are missing the general American trend, with everyone proclaiming an ethnic identity. These proclamations by themselves would certainly not be enough, but as we move into the future the society in general will encourage deeper learning and creativity in its ethnic communities. Higham's *Ethnic Leadership in America* is now ten years old, and by the turn of the decade it will be out of date. All one has to do is look at the ethnic clubs at universities to see that the next generation is recapturing the world of our ancestors.

One final observation from the soup kitchen. Lipstadt quotes Hertzberg as saying that the current Jewish revival has no "sense of the deep religious meaning of chosenness as the source of moral conscience." When I read Lipstadt's essay, I was startled by this comment. With my great admiration for Kaplan resting heavily on my heart, I want to report a soup-kitchen conversation. Remember these are generally secular Jewish students who come from the social action movement and not from a religious framework. I reported Hertzberg's claim to the students and asked them how they saw chosenness. The immediate responses were what I had expected: "We chose God, not the other way around," and "everyone is chosen" were popular. However, one of the volunteers was from a traditional background, and he asked the question, "if you don't feel you are chosen and therefore don't think that your religion is the best, what is the point of being Jewish, what is its mission?"

The other students began to respond with answers like "Judaism is a source of values," "It's an ethnic identity," even "It makes my parents happy," but the traditional student was relentless. "Why these values rather than others if they did not come from God? If we are not chosen, why don't you simply become an American? If we are not chosen, why care about continuity? If you do not feel chosen, do you really think you have a deep bond with me?'' It was a disturbing conversation, raising questions about Jewishness that neither I nor the students could answer.

I also found the question difficult to answer, partly because I do feel the uniqueness of Jewish tradition and the Jewish people. The question of the nature of the postchosenness mission of Judaism is an important one and must be addressed. That is one of the central challenges of postmodern Jewish thought.

Finally, I want to return to the first story, the story of the minyan. It is easy to say the story is unrepresentative. One can point to demographics that show how small the Orthodox yeshiva world is and also predict the eventual assimilation of those students. One could claim that they are the children of Holocaust survivors and that once they lose their European connection they will collapse under the weight of the modern world or even their own arrogance.

I do not think so. The future may not be theirs, but that is where society in general is heading. Our perspective on the world will have to start to cope with the ethic of restraint. The oil crisis of 1973 was a short glimpse into this world; the next 30 years will bring it closer and closer. All people, religious and secular, will have to learn how to make choices without sacrificing meaning and intimacy in their lives. There is no community better schooled in this than the minyan upstairs. From kashrut to Shabbat to the palpable sexual tension of *Nigean* (restrictions on physical contact between men and women), boundaries exist for these students, as does the idea of the forbidden. They are separatists, the most committed of any group at the university and hated as such. They are self-reliant and self-protective. They are text-committed and have a clear sense of mission. Lest you think that they are closed to the modern world, let me remind you that this minyan takes place at Columbia University, which is saturated with the ideas and practices of modernity. For example, on the first Friday of the month they have to clear out the minyan fast because the gay and lesbian dance needs set-up time. The Jewish students take the Western Civilization core curriculum and recently organized a lecture on the ''Effects of Proton Decay on the World View of the Rambam.''

Yet this is a community that believes that the Halakhah will stand up against the perils of the future better than any other system, that the Halakhah is, in fact, essential for preserving the universe both because it serves as a divine channel and for practical reasons.

As noted, the students tend to be the children or grandchildren of Holocaust survivors. Without doubt, this community therefore sees itself as comfortable but not at home in America. The Holocaust was the impossible that happened; they will never feel at home in its shadow. This creates a community apart, integrated and intimate within itself but contemptuous of those outside, embracing myth and symbol but rejecting advice or even affection from the other side of the lines they draw. However, in a world that lives with the possibility of total destruction, the Orthodox community becomes more attractive because it has a clear sense of having coped with destruction and having survived. It has survived with texts and with songs, with friendship and with boundaries. As it becomes more confident and as our need for Jewish answers grows, its potential for survival as "teacher" also grows.

The challenges that face us—as Jews, and as members of a world community—are urgent. If we fail to address the problems of the world we live in, then it will be doom and gloom not just for Judaism but for all of humanity. But then maybe I just have the end-of-the-Second-Christian-millennium blues.

A Response

Everett Gendler

Though we at times feel beset by the uniqueness of this unprecedented open society in which we find ourselves—whether by accident or assignment, happenstance or *hashoachah* (providence)—for the most part we are, I think, blessed by the need to integrate new elements and adapt to new surroundings, thereby yielding freshness and growth of an invigorating variety.

Let me begin by noting a special problem for consideration: the very term *Jewish*, so often invoked as a measure of authenticity, has itself shifted from a relatively impermeable to a relatively porous predicate. Such words immediately evoke the image of Judaism as a cell, with a protective membrane and pores that permit entry or exclude substances from the outside. It is fair to say that during most of our existence as a people we have been relatively impermeable cells.

Has anyone lived so charmed a life that he or she has been spared a classic Yom Kippur rabbinical student sermon that goes something like this: When his shipmates asked Jonah, "Where is your work, from where are you coming, what is your country, what is your nationality," he replied simply to all four questions, "I am a Hebrew." That is Jonah, the quintessential Jew, impenetrable by other influences, all of whose being can be expressed by that single predicate, Hebrew.

We should not, of course, exaggerate our cellular purity in earlier times. There was always some penetration, some interchange. North Semitic residues can be found in Psalms, the heart of our devotional life. The late Saul Lieberman's learned works, *Greek in Jewish Palestine* and *Hellenism in Jewish Palestine*, illustrate clearly some degree of surrounding cultural influence on Jewish thought and practice. Yet never before has there been such availability and congeniality of external material as in our open society.

Let me be specific. In my ripening middle years I'm becoming acquainted with some Bratslaver melodies; they are significant for my spiritual life. But Beethoven also contributes to my spiritual life, and from long ago Bloch, but also Bartok, who stands as a moral figure of impressive dimensions. Milhaud's Shabbat Morning Service I find deeply affecting, but Mozart's music is simply divine! (If my theology permitted the singling out of one human being as the supreme incarnation of the divine, the birthday I would celebrate would be January 27th, Mozart's, rather than the more widely observed December 25th.)

Moving from scores to texts, canon—Bible and Talmud—is certainly central, but the Declaration of Independence and the United States Constitution are profoundly significant as well, not only in regulating my life but in shaping my worldview. "We hold these truths to be self-evident: that all men are created equal . . . " No text in Torah states with greater emphasis this stirring spiritual truth, and its clarity in the Bill of Rights compares favorably with that in the Torah.

Moving from texts to role models, prophetic street theater (see, for example, Jeremiah or Hosea) has certainly inspired some of my all-too-meager involvement in various nonviolent, direct-action projects, but so have Thoreau, Gandhi, and King.

Examples from poetry, literature, philosophy, reflections on science, and other disciplines could and should be added to this list. The salient fact is that in our age, even for the most Jewishly identified among us, our world and our lives are fed from many sources. The predicate *Jewish,* insofar as it significantly defines our inner being, is unprecedentedly porous. This spiritual fact alone presents a challenge that is also an opportunity: to achieve a more inclusive unification of these various compatible elements. I emphasize compatible because pores are selective, with electrically charged linings that invite the entry of some substances and deny entry to others.

Societal and social factors also affect tradition in our place and time. One is the significant cooperation across religious lines on societal matters that often involve a spiritual affirmation or expression. Let me cite examples.

— Havurat Shalom of Somerville, Massachusetts, founded by Arthur Green in 1968, is joining with several churches to celebrate the birthday of Martin Luther King Jr.

— Project Ezra: On Christmas Day many members of my temple and other temples filled positions at hospitals, clinics, soup kitchens, and other agencies so that our fellow citizens who are Christian could celebrate their sacred day. From Shabbos goy to Christmas Jew, one might say.

— The U.S. Interreligious Committee for Peace in the Middle East brings Jews, Christians, and Muslims together to join in applying the teachings of our various religious traditions to that strife-torn area of our planet.

— Witness for Peace is a nonviolent interreligious effort to protect lives and further human rights in El Salvador, Guatemala, and Nicaragua.

— Interreligious projects in every city for the homeless, the hungry, AIDS victims, etc.

How can our sense of who we are and how we are, our relation to God and purpose and mission, not be affected by these experiences? How shall we not strive
to give religious expression to these discoveries? We need only consider the version of the Alenu in the new Reconstructionist prayerbook to see an appropriate
liturgical response to this aspect of our open society:

> to ascribe greatness to the world's Creator,
> Who made a world filled with many nations and tongues,
> All of them blessed with knowing God's ways,
> Nations that act kindly and turn from evil,
> Call to God in their own tongues,
> And their prayers are heard.

Such an inclusive version of an historically exclusive prayer is eloquent testimony to the mutual respect and acceptance prompted by our open society.

Socially there is also a marked change from earlier periods. Common
schooling, a shared general culture, and socializing across traditional religious
lines have resulted in many interreligious marriages. This is a subject unto itself,
but in this context we must recognize that in many, perhaps most, synagogues
and temples, many member families include more than one religious tradition.
How do we respond to this? Are the social tone and religious atmosphere of our
places of worship such that the universal relevance of Judaism can be felt and
appreciated by all who attend a service, whatever their religious background or
affiliation? Is breadth or narrowness of spirit the norm? Do we include or exclude those religiously different from us who find or place themselves in our
communal midst?

The questions stem from more than mere courtesy. Make no mistake: those
who attend seek the spiritual as well as the social, for despite the rich potential
sources of spirituality in our society, many thirst after the spiritual and do not
know how to find it. Perhaps one needs the training of a traditional religion to
discern the spiritual within the aesthetic. Whatever the explanation, seldom
have the words of Isaiah been more applicable than to our age and place (water,
wine, and milk being understood as spiritual fare):

> Oh, come to the water all you who are thirsty;
> though you have no money, come!
> Buy and eat;
> Come, buy wine and milk without money,
> at no cost.
> Why spend money on what is not bread,
> your wages on what fails to satisfy? . . .
> Pay attention, come to me;
> listen, and your soul will live.

[55:1–3]

Though a cliché, it is nonetheless true that we are overfed and undernourished, stuffed but unsatisfied. There is a great spiritual hunger and thirst as people increasingly discover that this is less a consumer society than a consuming society. Do I misapprehend the situation? Let me give just one example in support of this reading of the mood today. At our temple this year, one Friday evening each month is devoted to learning a Bratslaver melody and exploring some of the teachings of Reb Nachman. We've done it twice now, and each time I've noticed something unusual. People have stayed at the informal Oneg Shabbat after the service much later than on any other occasion. The service generally ends around 9:15 P.M., and by 10:00 or so most people have headed homeward. On both these Reb Nachman evenings, people lingered until 10:30 or 10:45. Why? I believe that the combination of melodies and teachings touched their souls in such a way that they, and I, were reluctant to leave that special space.

Parenthetically, this availability of Reb Nachman's music even to the non-Bratslaver is but one instance of another development in our age. Parallel to the earlier-mentioned riches of secular Western culture, we find a bountiful harvest of Hasidic and Kabbalistic material of great practical interest and utility for the spirit. Along with Western and also Eastern sources, new Jewish resources are ours to embrace.

One further spiritual resource, of which I am reminded each time I recite the Grace after meals, is a special inheritance of this particular open society. When thanking God for this lovely, productive, and spacious land (*eretz chemdah tovah ur'chavah*), the words "O beautiful for spacious skies, for amber waves of grain" come immediately to mind. Nature is present and available to us here in the United States in a way not experienced since the days when Hasidim wandered the Carpathian mountains and valleys and infused their religious life with those natural gifts. Why should we do less?

There are stirrings. Consider the growing number of Tu B'shevat seders throughout the land, increasing environmental awareness, conservation projects in religious institutions, and so forth. The organization Rural Jews of Vermont/ New England, which Michael Paley helped form, is evidence of some Jews actively returning to the land, a development found in other areas of the United States as well. People seem to want more of nature in their religious lives. When asked for significant personal religious experiences, many refer to experiences of nature: a sunset, a seascape, a storm. Aren't there many for whom outdoor services at a summer camp remain memorable?

Why do we not celebrate the seasons in our synagogues, temples and havurot—not just as aspects of the traditional pilgrimage festivals, but in their own right? After all, in Jewish folk tradition the *tekufot*, the turnings of the seasons, were observed throughout the centuries. Heschel speaks of the Sabbath as a cathedral in time. Are not the seasons a series of spatial temples in time, temples whose visible and olfactory and tactile changes surround, penetrate, and inspire us with a sense of time made palpable? Do not the seasons, at once spatial and temporal, bring true *yichud,* unification to disparate time and space?

How might we respond to these new developments and opportunities presented by our open society? Let me confess that I evaluate the phrase "Judaism as a wonderful hobby" differently from some who use it. It is not enough in itself, but don't knock it, for insofar as it includes the element of play, it is essential for the next stage in the development of our Judaic religious civilization.

I use *play* as did the distinguished Dutch cultural historian Johan Huizinga in his *Homo Ludens, A Study of the Play-Element in Culture.* There he asserts that "civilization is, in its earliest phases, played. It does not come *from* play like a babe detaching itself from the womb: it arises *in* and *as* play, and never leaves it." Affirming "the supreme importance to civilization of the play-factor," Huizinga characterizes play as an activity involving the irreducibles of mind and fun; a voluntary, free activity; a stepping out of ordinary life and into a temporary sphere of activity with a disposition all its own; creating order and establishing a sphere, secluded and limited and distinct from ordinary life, with its own rules; of no material interest but utterly and intensely absorbing of the player; adorning life expressively; and retaining its magic beyond the duration of the individual game for those who were "apart together."

Does this immediately bring to mind associations with ritual? Huizinga draws explicit comparisons with ritual, noting the similarities involved in marking out a playing field or a sacred spot spatially separated from ordinary life, and says "archaic ritual is thus sacred play, indispensable for the well-being of the community, fecund of cosmic insight and social development but always play."

Does this sound too laudatory, an exaggeration of the creative function of play? If so, we would do well to reread Chapter 8 of Proverbs. There Wisdom, *chokhmah,* proclaims her companionship with God before the earliest of the divine works, before the earth was formed or the depths of *tehom,* before springs or mountains or hills or heavens, and continues:

> I was with him forming all things:
> delighting him day after day,
> ever at play in his presence,
> at play everywhere in his world,
> delighting to be with human beings.
>
> > [8:30–31]

In this biblical account Wisdom at play contributed importantly to the formation of the world as we know it. We, in our developing religious civilization, are again at an initiating stage where we must play our way to new integrations and new insights, where the performative, beyond words and beneath concepts, may again prove "fecund of cosmic insight and social development," as "the feeling of being 'apart together' . . . retains its magic beyond the duration of the individual game'' or ceremony.

Concrete examples of how we might reintroduce play into our Jewish religious civilization abound. In the societal sphere, nonviolent actions, whether about nuclear issues or Soviet Jewry or Israel or the environment, have very specific ludic elements, such as their ritualized methods of confrontation. In the area of newly available mystical resources, the play of head and neck movements combined with sounds and directional orientation are the only way to receive whatever the medieval Kabbalist Abraham Abulafia may have to offer us. As for the liturgical appropriation of nature elements within the synagogue service, seasonal poetry and songs combined with the ceremonial turning of a Judaic Sun Wheel around the time of each solstice and equinox have proved to be of lasting appeal. Finally, for the integration liturgically of our Judaic and American civilizations, the weaving together of Native American and Kabbalat Shabbat–Maariv themes at the post-Thanksgiving Friday evening service has proved to be deeply satisfying to many worshipers.

So here we are, in an unprecedentedly open society, surrounded by societal, social, and spiritual challenges, opportunities, and resources—Jewish, Western secular, and Eastern spiritual. We are at a stage of self-awareness where we can appreciate the need to play our way, not solemnly but yet in utmost seriousness, toward the next stage of our development as a religious civilization. What new shape we shall assume I do not know, but I find the prospect both frightening, by virtue of its unfamiliarity, and enticing, by virtue of its novelty.

Whatever the outcome, I am also convinced that no previous generation in the long history of our people has had more reason than we to recite with conviction the traditional words of the morning service:

How fortunate we are!
How goodly our portion,
how pleasant our task,
and how beautifully abundant
our inheritance.

Section II

Culture and Education

3

Jewish Education: Crisis and Vision

Jonathan Woocher

Imagine:

— The Samuels family is finishing its preparations for Shabbat dinner. The Kaplans and the Grants, their regular study partners in the synagogue Family Learning Experience program, will be arriving shortly. Nine-year-old Tammy is busily reviewing the worksheet on this week's Parashat Hashavuah, which the family worked on together Wednesday evening after supper. Twelve-year-old Brian is rehearsing the Kiddush, which he will chant this week. He also checks the notes he took on Tuesday at the community "Judaic learning center" at the JCC on the concept of *kedushah* in Judaism. The "Torah tutor" there had been a real help in suggesting some interesting questions he could ask about the different prayers and rituals that all have "KDSH" as part of their title. He hopes that his father's weekly class with some of the other lawyers and businessmen downtown hasn't covered this. In fact, he thinks he has enough interesting material to lead a minilesson at one of the monthly retreats where all of the families in the Family Learning Experience program come together. The doorbell rings and the Kaplan and Grant families come in, with Jessica proudly carrying the challot she baked at the synagogue after-school program.

— Steve Rubenstein looks up from the papers he's correcting. His 11th-grade class on Government and Politics will be arriving any minute. Today the class will be dealing with the clash between majority rule and minority rights. The excerpts from the *Federalist Papers,* several U.S. Supreme Court decisions, the Talmud, and two early medieval responsa are all ready to be distributed. There are a few phrases from the responsa that he may have to translate for the students, but otherwise they should be able to handle all of the texts fairly easily. When the new integrated, bilingual curriculum for social studies, literature, and *machshavah* (that really sounded better than "philosophy") was introduced four years ago at the Bernstein Hebrew Academy, there was a lot of skepticism, but Steve was a true believer. Of course, it wasn't easy for him to learn how to teach it well. But when the Academy recruited him (after he received his M.A. in political science), they promised that the special training program supported by the Kravitz Foundation would provide both the academic background and ongoing supervision he needed, and it had. Being part of a team with other teachers in other cities using the curriculum, and spending the whole summer together with them in Israel, also made a real difference. The school was certainly pleased; enrollment was at an all-time high.

— When Betsy, Shoshana, Nancy, and Rina are settled on the bus they begin to jabber, mostly in English, but with a little Hebrew thrown in. Three weeks ago they didn't even know each other, other than through computer messages sent back and forth between youth groups. This trip to Israel was working out just as the group leaders had hoped. The kids were mixing well, though it was a shame the American teenagers didn't speak Hebrew better. But meeting face to face and traveling through Israel together certainly made the "twinning" project come alive. The Israeli teenagers are full of questions about American Jewish life that are challenging the American participants. They give as good as they get, however, thanks to the seminar they all took on Israel and Contemporary Jewish Identity. Of course, nothing could compare to the impact of Israel itself, and the Israeli and American *madrichim* were all skilled at maximizing that impact. The American youngsters would have a lot to contribute when they returned to their community service assignments, and they were already looking forward to working on the program for the visit the Israeli teenagers would be paying them during winter break.

— Jeff Siegel dumps his schoolbooks and sits down in front of his computer, with its attached videodisk player. He has only 45 minutes before soccer practice, but he wants to finish the "trip" they started in Rabbinics class at the day school today. The class is studying *mishnayot* dealing with Sukkot, and the teacher has started them looking through the material stored on the videodisk showing how the holiday has been observed throughout the ages. Jeff is especially interested in the pictures and stories about the sukkah itself. When his family puts up this year's sukkah next Sunday, he will have lots of improvements to suggest. Even though he is far from the hardest-working student in the class, he has to admit that the new "hypermedia" system almost makes studying fun. This disk on the holidays has so much information, he could never explore it all: There are passages from the Bible, Midrash, Talmud, and other rabbinic writings, including commentaries, of course; pictures of all sorts (even cartoons); stories, games, quizzes—the best thing being that he can control it all! Or maybe it is controlling him? Last night he'd wanted to review some of the laws of the lulav and etrog for the test on Friday, and before he knew it, he was looking at pictures of beautiful etrog holders from different countries where Jews had lived. It was like having a museum at home.

— The synagogue parking lot looks almost like the High Holidays. It's the first Sunday of the month again, and that means Community Day. The congregants and their children are familiar with the routine. The different corners of the auditorium are marked with signs: the cantor will be teaching a new tune for *musaf* in one; the rabbi will be telling a Hasidic story in a second; one of the congregants is preparing the projector to show slides from his trip to Eastern Europe and Israel; in the fourth, materials are set up to make challah covers. Adults and children intermingle, picking a corner for the day's first activity. Forty minutes later the announcement is made: it's time to go to study groups. Now the participants divide up by age groups—the children and adults have their own "classes," though they often study the same material. Today, the theme for Community Day is Tzedakah. Later, it's time for the community meetings. Although the younger children aren't involved, everyone age 12 or above is entitled to attend one of the meetings. Today, as usual, several of the synagogue committees will be meeting. There will also be a special meeting of the synagogue Tzedakah collective to discuss how to allocate the money it has collected this year. Having the meeting as part of the Community Day gives everyone a greater sense of involvement, and having young people there seems to make the discussions "a lot more Jewish." As the parking lot empties again, the Community Day planning committee sits down to lunch to ask, "What do we do next?"

Are these visions of the future of American Jewish education? Fragments, perhaps, yet these fragments and others we might add to them point toward a vision that is more than the sum of its parts. It is the vision of a holistic pattern and structure of lifelong Jewish learning, a seamless continuum of educational experiences that fit naturally into the life of the Jew and of the Jewish community. In this vision Jewish education is not merely an instrumental means toward some other end, such as Jewish survival, but what Jewish tradition has always seen it to be: a self-validating goal, an intrinsically rewarding activity that constitutes the very core of Jewish living. In this vision Jewish education takes place not only in schools, but in the home, the synagogue, community centers, in Israel, alone in front of computer screens, and with others at meetings and on trips.

This vision is not unfamiliar today. Yet we must admit that we are still far from fulfilling it, at least in the lives of most American Jews. Jewish education is for the majority an intermittent, indifferently pursued avocation of uncertain impact. We invest in it heavily, yet are skeptical in valuing and evaluating it. It mostly serves the young, and only occasionally their elders. Jewish education is by no means the abject failure it is sometimes presumed to be. Indeed, I would argue that the quality of education available to American Jews—young people and adults—has never been higher. Yet Jewish education is not the shining beacon of success it might and should be, given the dollars we spend on it, the creativity of the people involved in it, or our professions of commitment to it.

If there is a crisis of Jewish education today, it is a crisis of unfulfilled potential. Many today do have a glimmering that Jewish education could be, should be, something much more than it is. I am not among those who believe that American Jewish education stands on the brink of catastrophe. But I am very much among those who feel the frustration of the "not yet" and the "what might be." The fragments of a vision that I shared above are within reach. The question is, How do we reach them? What will it take to transform present vision into future reality?

Three things are required: First, there is the vision itself. It must be sufficiently clear, broad, and compelling for us to mobilize our energies around it. "Without vision a people perishes." Without a shared vision of what we want Jewish education to be, Jewish education will remain sadly ineffectual, with islands of excellence surrounded by a sea of uncertain achievement. Second, there must be an honest analysis of where we are and what holds us back from reaching our vision. What accounts for the variegated landscape of Jewish education today? Why do we continue to fall so far short of our potential? Finally, there is the need for a strategy of change. Even a cursory reading of the literature of American Jewish education confirms Koheleth's observation: There is nothing (or at least little) new under the sun. Both the cries for change and the elements of a vision of where to go have long been with us. How, this time, do we make sure that change actually takes place?

Though I cannot provide definitive answers to all these questions, I offer some observations, primarily about where we are in Jewish education today, in the hope that others can tie them securely to a powerful vision and a potent strategy for change.

All three requirements—vision, analysis, and strategy—are interwoven, because what we are really talking about are the body, mind, and soul of contemporary American Jewry. If we can understand ourselves—who we are, why we are what we are, where we can go—we will have our answers. It is perhaps a truism, but worth stating clearly: The problems of Jewish education in America today are primarily problems of American Jewry itself. In its strengths and weaknesses, Jewish education is a reflection of Jewish society, of how American Jews define themselves and of what they want for themselves and their children. Not Jewish education alone, but the Jewish community must change if any bold vision of what education might be is to be realized.

Is there, can there be, an American Jewish community and culture in which Jewish education "makes sense"? That is the central issue for Jewish education today. Education cannot function in a vacuum. It requires a community and a culture to nurture and sustain it with more than the provision of material and financial resources, though they are surely important. Education also requires a community and a culture from which to draw its mandate and goals. Who empowers our teachers to teach? Who will tell them what is important to transmit, and will guarantee that they will not be embarrassed (if they are successful) by students who conclude that what they have been taught is in fact worthless? Education requires a living community that can share with it the dual tasks of enculturation and instruction, of initiation into a group and its way of life, and of transmission of the knowledge, skills, practices, and attitudes that enable one to function effectively and satisfyingly within the group.[1] Education requires a community and a culture in which one lives out and tests what one has learned. Where the testing reveals a gap between the ideal and the real, education requires a community prepared to be critiqued and transformed, to say, as we are told God once did, "My children have bested me!"

It should be obvious that what Jewish education most sorely lacks today is precisely the vibrant community in which visionary education can be meaningfully and successfully pursued. There is nothing original in this diagnosis. Yet I am not sure that we take it seriously enough as we examine the litany of shortcomings in our educational system today. Virtually all of the oft-cited symptoms of the contemporary "crisis" of American Jewish education are attributable largely to the lack of a vibrant Jewish community. Whether it be the lack of clear educational goals, the confused state of curriculum, the absence of standards for achievement, the short span and limited hours of instruction, the persistent shortage of quality personnel, or the self-destructive fragmentation of the educational system itself—all of the ills besetting Jewish education today can ultimately be traced back to the fact that it too often floats in a vacuum, with no community prepared to embrace it, shape it, use it, and be permeated and transformed by it in order to pursue *its* Jewish vision and vocation as a community.

Confused Educational Goals

If Jewish education is vague, unfocused, and often over-ambitious in its goals, it is primarily because those concerned—parents, professionals, institutional leaders, religious authorities—can rarely agree on what is important to achieve. What do we want our educational efforts to produce: A Jew who prays? One who can speak Hebrew as well as an Israeli? One who can read a *blatt* of Gemara? One who will give to the UJA? One who won't intermarry? All of the above, or none of the above? Without consensually validated goals education becomes a medium of mixed messages, and nothing gets accomplished.

Curricular Confusion

Since we are not sure why we teach, it is no wonder that we are not sure what to teach. The day is short, and the work is great. Shall we try a smorgasbord approach, a little Hebrew, a little Bible, a little history, and a few religious concepts and skills? Shall we aim for mastery of one area? But which one, and how to do it in a few hours a week? What will truly serve the needs and wants of our students, of their families, of our institutions? Are those needs and wants the same for each group?

Low Standards

What expectations does the community set for an "educated Jew"? That he or she be able to perform at a bar or bat mitzvah without causing embarrassment to self, family, or community? That expectation, virtually the only one ever enforced, is usually met. But the lack of any other expectation means that there is no effort to measure achievement. Hence, Jewish education operates without standards.

Short Span and Limited Hours

Jewish education is by and large elementary education because apparently nothing further is needed to function as a Jewish adult. Jewish education is important, but so are many other things that seem to relate far more directly to being a mature, competent, fulfilled human being. Since adults seem to get along quite well without much involvement in Jewish education, the closer we get to adulthood, the less of it we evidently need.

The Personnel Shortage

One can make a decent living as a full-time Jewish educator, but why would one want to? Educators are not community leaders; they appear rarely on podiums; their advice is not sought on important issues; they work all day with children. Meanwhile, too many educators cut themselves off from the community they serve. They are knowledgeable Jews; the community is comprised of *am haratzim*. Best to be left alone to do one's job, free from the meddling of board members and parents. Until one finds oneself being asked to leave.

Institutional Fragmentation

Jewish education belongs not to the Jewish community, but to the institutions that provide it, and they can be jealous owners indeed. In a fragmented community, Jewish education cannot help being fragmented, too. Countless opportunities for reinforcement, for sharing, for creating a powerful "plausibility structure," a social base for Jewish education are lost because we cannot get our act together.

To be sure, the fraying of the thread that should tie Jewish education to the active life of a sustaining community is not the sole problem. But the weakness of that link, and especially the inability of Jewish education to ally itself with an adult world in which education is visibly valued, is the Achilles' heel of Jewish education today. "The crisis in American Jewish education," writes Sheldon Dorph, "consists in this very loss of an educated adult Jewish community and life-style. . . . Without such an image of cultural and communal Jewish adulthood, the direction, purposes, and methods of Jewish education—schooling or otherwise—become unclear."[2] Barry Chazan suggests "there is no general con-

Extending the Educational Life-Cycle

Increasing the number of settings where Jewish education takes pl[ace] have its maximum impact only if the range of Jewish involvement in educa[tional] experiences also increases. This means, above all, extending the educat[ional] life-cycle—a primary objective on the current agenda for Jewish educati[on]. There are already signs of significant growth in early-childhood education, an[d] a new emphasis on education programs for teenagers, families, and adults. The aim of this effort should be clear: to build a full continuum of educational experiences, utilizing the complete range of settings and methods available to us.

The development and expansion of programs for segments of the Jewish population that are rarely involved in Jewish education is a synergistic process. Each element can build on and reinforce the others. New options for young children can draw their parents into the educational system. Family learning can inspire adults to intensify their own studies. The model of adults who take Jewish learning seriously can give a new cachet to Jewish educational programs for teenagers. Building a cradle-to-grave educational system, and recruiting substantial numbers of participants for it, is a massive undertaking requiring unprecedented combinations of educational, Judaic, and marketing expertise. But even the acceptance of this as our goal represents an enormous step beyond the too-common conception of Jewish education as a vaccine given to the young to protect them against the disease of "assimilationitis." As we struggle to extend the educational life-cycle, we will inevitably transform the institutions to which Jews of various ages are attached.

Establishing Educational Accountability

In recent years the American Jewish community has tended to invest Jewish education with the awesome responsibility of insuring the continuity of Jewish life. It has rarely, however, sought to hold educational institutions accountable for achieving demonstrable results in this respect. That is fortunate, since what is being asked of education is (at least today) far beyond its capacity to deliver. But the concept of accountability, which is now beginning to find its way into the vocabulary of Jewish education, should by no means be discarded. On the contrary, if a serious effort can be made to establish objectives for which educational institutions and programs will be held accountable, and if agreement can be reached on measurements of success or failure, Jewish education will have a far greater chance of achieving those objectives.

Accountability implies that there is a community prepared to set educational objectives and to insist on their realization. For any institution, undertak[ing] ing a process of goal-setting and accountability is both a community-buildi[ng] and consciousness-raising venture. Educators should welcome and encour[age] such a process. It can only increase understanding of the problems educ[ators] face and validate their efforts to create quality programs with serious sta[ndards] of achievement.

ception of what a graduate of American Jewish education should know or do, beyond the sense that he/she should 'feel Jewish.' "[3] The Jewish community provides no clear, consensual model of Jewish adulthood that embraces more than this same minimum.

This is perhaps too harsh and too general an accusation. Positive examples of Jewish living can be found outside the school's walls, and it is to Jewish education's discredit that it has failed to take greater advantage of them. And there are subcommunities in which Jewish education is tangibly valued, and even rewarded. There are places where the ethos and worldview that Jewish education seeks to instill receive validation and support. But these contexts are frequently limited, isolated, and at times lacking in respect for one another.

Until recently, the settings for Jewish living—the home, the synagogue, communal institutions—have either failed to acknowledge or lacked the competencies to undertake an educative mission. Thus Jewish education has been thrown back on its own resources, and these inevitably have proven inadequate to fulfill what must ultimately be the task of an entire community and a thriving culture. As a result, Jewish education remains a kind of stopgap, thrown into the breach by a community uncertain of its future in order to stem the tide of assimilation, but never able to exert its full life-transforming, life-enriching potential.

But isn't this just what most American Jews want? The answer is largely yes. As Susan Shevitz has argued in analyzing why there is a perpetual personnel crisis in Jewish education,[4] and as Ronald Reynolds has demonstrated in assessing the effectiveness of supplementary schools,[5] the Jewish education we get *is* more or less the Jewish education we want—unthreatening to accustomed values and life-styles, institutionally sustaining, a benign endeavor limited in its impact. Nor is this analysis applicable only to the supplementary school. Are people eager to see the day schools produce dramatic behavioral and attitudinal changes? How many parents want their child's trip to Israel to result in a commitment to aliyah? For all of the popular denigration of Jewish education (it is difficult to find Jewish adults with anything nice to say about their own Hebrew school experience), surveys indicate that the vast majority of parents are pleased with the Jewish education their children receive.

Does this mean that there is no hope for substantial change? We have suggested that the reform of Jewish education rests on the transformation of Jewish society. But how else can we initiate and steer a self-conscious process of social transformation except through education itself? The limitations of Jewish education—especially the fact that it is largely pediatric and divorced from the realities of community life—define the very conditions that education must itself change. The community and culture that Jewish education needs to be effective do not yet exist; hence, Jewish education must create them. Yet, afloat without the necessary community and culture, education lacks the power to be a generative force. We seem to have come to a Gordian knot we cannot cut through.

Perhaps. But the ends of this knot are already beginning to unravel. For the paradox I have described—that the transformation of Jewish education can be effected only by a Jewish community itself transformed by education—is becoming increasingly evident to many in positions of educational and communal leadership. The diagnosis is now readily accepted, and even the desired treatment is widely agreed upon. What is required to initiate the therapeutic process is a suspension of disbelief, an act of faith, if you will. We must act as if there were a vibrant community and culture ready to support a visionary model of Jewish education. We must behave as if Jewish education were an unquestioned end in itself, a multifaceted, never-ending spectrum of experiences, taking place wherever Jews are working, playing, or living. We must, in short, act as if we already are what we hope to become.

This is possible, I would suggest, because Jewish education already involves a massive suspension of disbelief for many American Jews. We will join synagogues in order to enroll our children in Sunday school, though we are confident we have no need of a synagogue for ourselves. We will start performing rituals at home we have never done before and aren't even sure we believe in, because we think our children should experience them. We will pay hefty tuitions to send our children to day schools to learn texts we can't understand and may not care to, because we think it makes them—and us—better Jews. To be sure, we rarely act out of pure motives. The reservations, hesitations, and limitations are there, but so too are the commitment, and at some level the openness, to yet further possibilities of engagement.

The American Jewish community of today is not the community of 50, 25, or even 10 years ago. It is a community with more Jewish day schools, more Jewish preschools, more JCCs involved in Jewish education, more young people traveling to Israel, more American-born and American-educated teachers, more federation dollars being expended on Jewish education. Perhaps these changes have taken place because of fear—fear of intermarriage, fear of assimilation, fear of loss of identity. Perhaps these changes are not even effective in fighting against those things we fear! What these changes do provide, however, is the spur for a communal and cultural transformation that may never have been consciously intended, but that might, with a little gentle prodding, acquire a momentum of its own.

There is a public agenda for Jewish education in America today. That agenda has not emanated from a single deliberative process, nor can it be implemented in a comprehensive, coordinated fashion. It is being articulated in diverse places by diverse groups and individuals: by professional educators, by federation study committees, by national bodies, and by local activists. The breadth of interest in this agenda in itself holds the promise of fashioning a public for Jewish education more encompassing than we have seen before. What is more, each of the elements of this agenda points beyond the Jewish education

enterprise in its narrow sense. It *is* an agenda for community transformation, not just educational reform. It cannot be effected by educators alone, and those who are advancing it understand this. Nor can it be effected solely by changing educational institutions—and this too is understood. If this agenda can be successfully implemented over the next decade or so, then what was imagined at the beginning of this essay might well become commonplace, and far bolder, more exciting visions can emerge to fire our imaginations and aspirations.

The agenda I see being widely articulated today has five components:

1. Expanding the educational canvas.
2. Extending the educational life-cycle.
3. Establishing educational accountability.
4. Developing new human resources.
5. Creating a true Jewish educational system.

Expanding the Educational Canvas

Education is not the business of schools alone. Today's agenda has embraced the concept of expanding the educational canvas to include a range of settings and methods. "Formal" and "informal" education are now widely accepted as necessarily complementary elements in a total educational experience. Increasingly, the educative potential even of institutions whose primary purpose is not educational—a Soviet Jewry committee, an old-age home—is being recognized and affirmed.

A by now commonplace effort is underway to broaden the scope of Jewish education and to involve more actors in its implementation. Though some may, not without justification, bemoan the loss of rigor implicit in defining almost any Jewish experience or activity as "Jewish education," the sacrifice will be worthwhile if education is again seen as part of the fabric of community life. Jewish education can take place at a ball game, or at a demonstration, or during the synagogue service, or at a museum, or through a film. As long as the unique contribution the school can make is also recognized and endorsed, Jewish education has far more to gain than to fear from an expansion of educational opportunities.

New settings and approaches need not undermine traditional educational forms and methods. In matters of Jewish identification, the rule in recent decades has been "the more, the more," that is, the more Jewishly identified and active a person is along one dimension (for example, in religious life), the more likely it is that he or she will be identified and active along other dimensions as well (for example, in support of Israel). There is reason to believe that the same holds true for Jewish education: the broader the educational canvas, and the more accessible the educational experience, the more likely it is that those who become involved in one rewarding experience will seek out others.

Developing New Human Resources

The fourth item on the public agenda for Jewish education has for decades been a staple of prescriptions for improvement: increasing the numbers and improving the quality of the people involved in education. Today we still hear of the need to recruit more teachers and administrators; the importance of enhancing professional training; the demand to provide better salaries and benefits; the call to restructure positions to create more opportunities for full-time employment in Jewish education.

All of these important components have proved frustratingly difficult to implement in the past. But now two other elements have been attached to the agenda that are, if not entirely new, then at least potentially newly significant. The first is a new interest in the role and contribution of the "avocational" educator. No one suggests that Jewish education can do without a larger cadre of talented, trained, committed professionals. Yet, if we are faithful to our vision of a far more pervasive educational endeavor, it is difficult to imagine how all the new roles could possibly be filled exclusively by professionals. Nor would this necessarily be desirable. The presence of those who are not professional educators can advance the goal of bringing education into a more organic relationship with the community it seeks to permeate.

Some, undoubtedly, will see this as a particularly suspicious form of lemonade making. Stuck with a shortage of trained professionals, we will now make a virtue out of the necessity of making do with amateurs. I would suggest, however, that we not rush to judgment. Amateurs who bring a genuine love of Jewish learning and teaching to their avocational work can also master the skills requisite for success without becoming full-fledged professionals. The challenge is to turn what is now indeed a sad necessity into a planned desideratum—the carefully structured and supervised involvement of large numbers of caring Jews in the work of teaching and guiding other Jews. Creating an educational system of, by, and for the Jewish people without sacrificing standards of performance will be difficult, but beleaguered professionals should welcome new allies.

The second new element is the creation of a lay leadership cadre for Jewish education. Lay people have, of course, always been involved in educational decision making and governance. An honest appraisal of their role and impact, however, must conclude that Jewish education has belonged primarily to its professional practitioners. Whether through abdication or disempowerment, lay involvement in Jewish education has been primarily custodial, rather than substantive. Those involved have constituted a relatively small elite, frequently isolated from other leadership segments in the community. The parochial atmosphere of much of Jewish education has further discouraged the involvement of many powerful and prestigious volunteers. Jewish education has suffered grievously as a result.

It is critical that lay leadership assume ownership of Jewish education—if not as sole proprietors, then at least as partners. To exercise a constructive role, they too will need training. Nevertheless, the emphasis on the need to recruit a new group of volunteer leaders who will lend their energies and resources to that endeavor is not misplaced. For educators, this is a valuable opportunity to mold and mobilize a leadership cadre that will be truly conversant with educational issues and will assume responsibility for the achievements of the system.

Creating a Jewish Educational System

Jewish education today is a system without order, without interdependence, without coordination. That is to say, it is no system at all. It is a collection of parts that generally do not work together, that even at times work at cross purposes. The flow of resources is not planned or organized in a rational fashion. A child may attend a school, a camp, a youth program, and an Israel trip—even ones sponsored by the same denominational movement—and experience virtually no connection among them. The asystemic character of Jewish education is not limited to programming. There is no coordinated mechanism for dealing with personnel needs—recruitment, training, and placement; for disseminating educational information and resources; for funding or evaluating new projects.

In this, of course, Jewish education once again mirrors the community in which it is embedded. This dysfunctional state of affairs is now becoming evident to those fashioning Jewish education's agenda. Coordinated and systematic action is necessary if we are to expand the educational canvas, extend the life-cycle, establish accountability, and develop new human resources. Slowly but surely, those who have thus far been concerned with education only as it has been expressed within their individual institutions are beginning to talk to one another. They are recognizing that no single institution or set of institutions has the ability to carry out the full range of tasks required to reinvigorate Jewish education.

Plans resulting from new ventures in community-wide educational planning are not necessarily promising. The plans are noteworthy, but by themselves plans change nothing. Rather, it is the creation of a new community constituency for Jewish education that makes change conceivable. The effort to plan together can itself generate a more cohesive, united community, one which may discover that Jewish education is both the vehicle for its communality and the focus of it.

Are the ideas laid out here a vision, or pure fantasy? The historical record of Jewish educational reform in America warrants a healthy skepticism about the prospects for genuine transformation. Clifford Geertz has compared maintaining religious faith to hanging a picture on a nail driven into its own frame. Perhaps my suggestion that current efforts to strengthen Jewish education can induce the communal and cultural transformation that in turn can enable the educational changes to take hold is such a vain hope.

I am convinced that at least two major caveats are in order: First, major transformation is impossible unless we recognize explicitly the depth and dimensions of the transformation required and accept no less as our goal. We can initiate a process more far-reaching than we intended, but luck and good intentions cannot complete it. The character of our community will determine the effectiveness of our education—it is the community, and not the educational system alone, that must be changed.

Second, the process of transformation must eventually touch many thousands, perhaps millions of Jews who today have no part and little interest in the efforts under way. I don't believe that we shall ever see the day when all, nearly all, or even a substantial portion of American Jews live what we might define as full Jewish lives. But there will have to be a solid minority of Jews actively participating in the community and culture of American Jewry. I do not pretend to know how many are required—how many families must study together, how many students must attend day high schools, how many synagogues must revitalize their educational programs, how many young people must experience Israel in a profound way—but I know that it is many more than we have today. We should not, however, despair at this prospect. Three-quarters of our children already receive some Jewish education at some point during their youth. That is surely a base large enough on which to build.

Despite these caveats, I remain cautiously optimistic. I believe that having successfully fought the struggle for adjustment and (thus far at least) the struggle for survival, American Jewry is ready for a new challenge, the challenge of creating a true Jewish community and culture. What we envision for Jewish education and what we do to realize that vision are at the heart of this challenge. If we will it, it need not remain merely a vision.

A Response

Kathy Green

In responding to Jonathan Woocher's essay, I would like to focus attention on two obviously interdependent areas. These constitute the overarching concern of all of us who think about Jewish education: first, the absence of an ideology, philosophy, or theology to provide a raison d'être for non-Orthodox Jewish education, and second, non-Orthodox Jewish education's relationship to the larger Jewish community of which it is a part.

The vignettes that introduce Woocher's essay bring home the sense that Jewish education may well wither in the 21st century as a result of boredom. The problem is lack of passion. Involvement in Jewish educational experiences is nice, professionally structured, and generally child-centered. Woocher details experiences that reflect tremendous achievements in competence, albeit without passion. One never has the sense that, to recall some past models, learning or study can be an expression of intimacy (as in the yeshivahs described by Samuel Heilman), an act of subversion or defiance (either of ancient Rome or modern Russia), a manifestation of communion with the sacred (as described in rabbinic and kabbalistic sources), or even a strategy for repairing the universe or bringing messianic redemption (as seen in kabbalistic and Hasidic sources). Woocher's vision of 21st-century Jewish education, though practiced with profound professional élan, seems emasculated, bereft of significant root meaning, devoid of passion.

Perceiving a need for rationale, we search for passionate meaning. We realize that orthodoxies (whether religious, Zionist, secularist, communist, or whatever) benefit from the ability to evolve systems of logical consistency. Orthodoxies, whether led by a Lubavitcher rebbe or Vladimir Jabotinsky, have the advantage of being able to supply ready answers to questions that begin with "why." Such systems tend to provide a critique of the present situation, offer a method for salvation, and identify enemies who stand in the way.

We who stand outside of orthodoxies are both the beneficiaries and the victims of our embrace of ambiguity and ambivalence. As Jews we are challenged to create nonfundamentalist ideologies, to evolve a sense of nonfanatical mission that includes our commitment to the Jewish educational enterprise.

We are sometimes told that funding agencies understand Jewish education as a tool, an instrument for Jewish survival. Let us be very clear about what such a phrase means. Were we to try to list the five most powerful agents for survival of Jews as Jews, Jewish education per se might very well not find a significant position on the list. Surely anti-Semitism would. Though obviously not recommending anti-Semitism we wonder: at its most cost effective, is Jewish education the most efficient tool for Jewish survival?

It seems clear that this Jewish survival is cultural and that what is being sought are Jewish schools that socialize children to communal norms and traditions, thus trying to insure the survival of cultural symbols and institutions within the community. That is why our schools tend to reflect mainstream social values and why, as Norman Newberg and others have observed, our schools aim for mediocrity and achieve it.

It is currently in vogue to speak of schools as agents for change. This potential mandating of educators as change agents is fraught with difficulty and imbued with exciting potential. As Sherry Israel has pointed out, our teachers' professional training has not prepared them either as change agents in the adult community or as family educators. In fact, Israel has noted, teachers often self-select because of their talent in interacting with children, not because they are skilled in talking to adults. Even if the problems of recruiting and training change agents could be overcome, an even greater challenge would remain: change to what? Surely we can advocate change to increased Jewish (and Hebrew) literacy, for such advocacy is about as controversial as was advocating motherhood and apple pie in the 1950s. Given the effort necessary to achieve basic literacy, such advocacy is merely lip service, not unlike sedentary people's commitment to exercise. If the basic change we advocate is to increase commitment, is that commitment to Judaism? to God? to the Jewish people?

What we seek is passionate vision, which, of course, need not necessarily be "religious" or find expression in theological language. Of course, we are acquainted with secular dreams of Jewish renewal (from Yiddishists, Hebraists, Socialists, Labor Zionists, and so on), but it seems much more likely that Jewish secular vision can survive in Israel than in the United States.

Those of us who stand outside of orthodoxies in the United States seek redefinition, new visions, renewed connections to old passions. We look to our collective past for inspiration. Our rabbis taught that the world survives on three pillars: Torah, *avodah* (prayer), and *gemilut chasadim* (acts of loving kindness). The genius of this statement becomes apparent when we realize the social context from which it emerged. While seeing themselves as receivers of Torah, the rabbis were confronted by the need to redefine Judaism after the destruction of the Temple and the termination of temple sacrifices. While in no way negating the importance of *avodah* and of *gemilut chasadim*, they located the central devotional act of Judaism in talmud–Torah. I would venture that in different historical periods, one or another of these three pillars has dominated as the metaphor defining the age. Very recently in America we were defined as a religion, one of the three great denominations: Protestant, Catholic, and Jew. The larger American society told us that the most acceptable mode of expression for our Judaism was prayer, worship in the church of our choice.

Even more recently we have seen our sense of extended peoplehood and of our somehow extended citizenship in a Jewish state manifested both in our concern for Israel in 1967 and in our intense reactions to the Law of Return and who is a Jew issue in 1988. We have also seen the development, so well catalogued by Woocher, of American Jewish civil religion most readily found at home in our federations, where we hear articulated commitment to values of *gemilut chasadim*.

What do these observations about American Jewish life tell us about our relationship to Torah, *avodah* or *gemilut chasadim?* Ironically enough, our communities' commitment to supporting Jewish education even at its worst reflects our primal, residual memory of the importance and power of learning, of talmud–Torah.

Also ironically, some of the strongest elements of our heritage serve to create barriers for Jews today. We are a people of memory, of tribal memory, but the tales and wisdom of our ancestors are no longer passed on primarily by communal elders. They are preserved in print. The history of our triumphs and tragedies, our encounters with the sacred, our responsibilities and our techniques for fulfilling our obligations, our poetry and our pilpul, all have been written down. This vast treasure trove is closed to most American Jews because they cannot read Hebrew. This barrier leads Jewish adults to express their Jewish commitments where their education and talents can be appreciated and where their Jewish literacy is not an issue: in the board rooms of federations, in *gemilut chasadim*.

We are currently witnessing the growth of non-Orthodox day schools. There is not yet enough data to allow accurate speculation as to the potential influence of this small but better-educated element of our population. We must acknowledge that day schools are plagued by problems in recruiting qualified Jewish studies teachers. We might dream, however, given this cadre of day school graduates and given immigration from Israel to the United States, of a growing, bilingual segment of our population, a segment capable of dreaming in Hebrew.

We are not pressured to develop a learning theory; Piaget and others have done that for us. We *are* compelled to develop an ethic for Jewish living that includes study. We are compelled to evolve a new theology of talmud–Torah, paralleling the creativity with which the rabbis responded to the end of their hopes of rebuilding the Temple in 135 C.E. Gershom Scholem has told us that these early rabbinic thinkers reinterpreted their relationship with revelation to include all new rabbinic dialogues and debates as somehow having been revealed at Sinai. Thus they understood themselves not as creating new interpretations, but rather as discovering old. They forged a living link with Sinai that was solidified in the process of study as sacred act. Our task is to redefine, to articulate a new theology of talmud–Torah, not purely as an instrument for survival, but as a response to our adult needs. Only when the passion for Jewish learning and participating burns in adults can there be a flame to pass to our children. Understand that the educational needs of children are very different from those of adults, but the need for passion spans the generations. We respond in developmentally appropriate ways to the needs of children, but our task is not simply to develop more effective techniques for socializing our children. The future of Jewish education rests on our dreaming of new ways of standing in dynamic relationship to our heritage and the sacred while seeking to be most fully human.

Our task is not saving Judaism but rather saving ourselves as Jews. Our task is no less challenging than that which confronted our ancestors in the first and second centuries of the common era.

For us to imagine Jewish education in the 21st century means that we must dream, and out of our dreams weave myths that give meaning to our learning and studying.

A Response

Joseph Reimer

At the heart of Jonathan Woocher's convincing presentation lies his linking of the problems of Jewish education in America today with the problems of American Jewry and the insistence that "the Jewish community must change if any bold vision of what education might be is to come to realization." For, as Mordecai Kaplan once argued, it is not schools, but communities that educate. Jewish education can be only as powerful and effective as the sponsoring community allows and wishes it to be.

Central to formulating the Jewish education of the future are the questions, for what and for whom? As my fellow respondent, Kathy Green, addresses "for what," I will address "for whom." Who are the "students" whom Jewish education addresses? How broadly shall we conceive the clientele for these educational services?

Woocher argues elegantly for why we need to abandon a "pediatric" conception of Jewish education in favor of a "life-cycle" conception. What I wish to add is some background to his argument and some consideration of what it means to adopt that conception.

One salient fact about the clientele is the concentration of students in the 8–13-year age range. Jewish education is primarily education for the young; it is pediatric in that sense. And while it is a blessing that a majority of American Jewish children get some form of Jewish education, it is alarming to realize how precipitously participation in any form of Jewish education falls off from age 13 through the rest of the life cycle.[6]

Of the many reasons for this pattern of participation and withdrawal, I wish to focus on two. The first is a historical factor: the origins of the supplementary school movement in the earlier part of this century during the period of the great migration. Following Margaret Mead,[7] I wish to suggest that it is common in immigrant society for education to be identified with schooling for the young. The assumption behind this identification is that whereas adult immigrants will remain as they are—part foreign and part new world—the children represent the future. They are the ones who can become more wholly assimilated into the new culture, and insofar as that is a desired outcome, schooling is viewed as the means to the end. Since the parents cannot embody the new world for their children, they look to the schools to play that role and support the schooling process even though its values may differ from their own.

For most American Jewish immigrants, it was the public schools that played this role. But the supplementary schools, modeled on the paradigm of the public school, also played a role. They could teach children an American rather than an East European Judaism. Insofar as the parents wanted their children to practice an Americanized Judaism different from their own *yiddishkeit,* these schools made sense as agents of socialization into the new world of Jewish living.

What made no sense in the immigrant context was for the parents to see themselves as clients of Jewish education. They had their Judaism, and though they realized their children would practice differently, they were on the whole comfortable to remain immigrant Jews. Since Jewish educators had their hands full contending with a second generation of quickly assimilating Jewish Americans, they were also content to leave the parents to the Jewish ways of the old country. To everyone's immediate benefit, there arose an understanding or conception of Jewish education in America as giving children the minimal knowledge they would need to function religiously as Jews in America. The rest they could learn at home or in the neighborhood.

We clearly are past the immigrant moment in history and no longer live with an old-world Judaism in our homes. Yet the resilience of the initial conception of Jewish education—an imparting to children of minimal knowledge—is surprising. To understand this resilience, I suggest we change frames and consider a psychological dimension that may be operating to keep Jewish education pediatric in concept.

In most American Jewish families today, the children coming for a Jewish education are the children and grandchildren of American-born adults. These adults themselves received only a minimal Jewish education, and that during their childhood. Mommy, Daddy, Grandma, and Grandpa are not much more Jewishly knowledgeable than are Joshua or Jennifer. Then why are the adults sending Joshua and Jennifer to learn while they remain in their relative state of ignorance? Given no old-world *yiddishkeit* to preserve, why are they not also part of the future, of the learning community?

Some observers respond that sending children to Jewish school has become a regular, ritualized part of the Jewish life cycle. Jewish families tend to respond to the children's coming of school age by looking for some Jewish education for them that will culminate in a bar/bat mitzvah. This ritualized activity does not "by tradition" include adult education, so there is no inherent cultural push for the parents and grandparents to ask "why not us, too?"

Though there is power to that explanation, I wish to suggest a parallel possibility that I learned from systems theory in family therapy.[8] I put it forward as a hypothesis aimed at describing a dynamic that may operate within our Jewish educational system.

From this perspective we might ask: What is the meaning or function of the decision to keep investing so vast a majority of our energies in servicing only the childhood stages of the life cycle? Does this decision represent an over-investment rather than a wise investment? Could it be that this over-investment in children's education serves as a collusive technique to avoid notice of the adults' issues? Could it be that the really embarrassing issue for us adults is that we do not know how to handle our own conflicts over being Jewish, and that instead of facing the pain of that conflict, we turn our attention to our children and worry about their Jewish identity?

What worries us most about our children is often what remains least resolved for us as adults. The dilemma of the American Jewish family is that the adults do not know how to resolve their own Jewish identity issues: Ambivalence remains the dominant emotional tone. How can parents transmit what they love about being Jewish without also confronting what they hate or resist? How can they transmit knowledge that is only dimly remembered or even happily forgotten? Parents want to transmit "Jewishness" to their children, but do not know how to work through their feelings about Judaism and their lack of Jewish knowledge. Being stuck over this dilemma, they turn to the Jewish school for a solution, but they present their dilemma as if it were the children's problem. My question is why the school and community buy into the deal.

When Jewish families present their children to us as having the problem of needing a Jewish education, why do we routinely respond, "Send us your child, and we will treat the problem"? Why do we allow them and ourselves to believe that we *can* treat that problem? Would it not be better to respond by saying, "We are very happy that your family wishes to learn more about being Jewish and we are ready to serve the family's need to know more"?

When I pose this question to Jewish educators, many agree in theory; they know schools cannot transmit an identity unless the family is integrally involved. But some ask, "What about the many parents who will say thanks but no thanks?" When the idea of life-cycle learning or family education meets resistance, when parents refer back to their pediatric conceptions, educators often feel defeated. Why does familial resistance feel so defeating?

One answer is that we are still working with a historic conception of Jewish education as Jewish public school. The public schools also strive to involve parents in children's education, but they do not insist upon parental involvement or remove the child when parents are not involved. So how can the Jewish school take a stand stronger than theirs?

Here is where the analogy to the field of mental health may be helpful. Though Jewish education is not to be equated with the search for mental health, it may be helpful to follow the lead of that field in terms of a shift in paradigm. For as long as we continue to think of ourselves as being in the business of educating children, and of simply asking the parents to partner our efforts, we will find their resistance defeating. It may be that only when we reconceptualize our task as educating the family at every point of its life cycle can we begin to develop a new understanding of our work and our contract with our students.[9]

This reconceptualization must emerge from the leadership: from the rabbis and the lay leadership of synagogues, federation, and other communal agencies. What is at stake is not the definition of Jewish education in its narrow sense of school for children, but its broadest sense of life-cycle education. Only to the extent that the community, through its leadership, seizes upon communal participation as an occasion for Jewishly educating people of all ages will we let go of the collusive aspects of the pediatric conception of Jewish education and embrace a wider vision of education as that which the whole community engages in as part of its raison d'être.

4

Creativity and Community: The Jewish Artist's Experience

Marcia Falk

A couple of decades ago, when as a graduate student I began formally to study Yiddish, I undertook to translate into English a number of poems by the Yiddish-American poet Abraham Reisin.[10] I was motivated not just by the relative simplicity of Reisin's vocabulary but by the challenge of translating his regular metrical forms and simple balladlike rhymes into English verse. As a student of verse translation, I had come to believe that the "simple" work of art is often the hardest to translate well: making a folksong or a nursery rhyme come alive in a new language, for example, is at least as difficult as rendering more complex or intellectually sophisticated texts. For, in the journey that is the process of literary translation, it is harder to keep alive the heart—the *neshomeh*—than the mind. The simpler, the more accessible the art—and Reisin's poetry is nothing if not accessible to Yiddish readers—the more it relies on movements of the heart to sway its audience.

After considerable effort, I was pleased with the results of one of my attempts to translate Reisin into English. A little poem called "A Gezind Zalbe Acht" had found its way into my voice, emerging in English as:

> *Family of Eight*
>
> Only two beds
> for a family of eight.
> Where do they sleep
> when the hour is late?
>
> Three with the father
> and three with the mother—
> small feet and fingers
> entwined with each other.

And when it came time
to prepare for the night,
then Mama starts wishing
her death were in sight.

And what is the wonder
she'd rather be gone?
The grave's narrow too
but you lie there alone.

I was particularly moved by this poem when I first read it in Yiddish because it evoked stories I had heard from my mother about *her* mother's childhood in Warsaw. My mother herself was raised in Harlem, in a small flat behind
a tailor shop, where her immigrant parents worked by day. This three-room
apartment in Harlem, which sounded quite modest to me, was considerably
larger, my mother would remind me, than the one-room flat in Warsaw where
my grandmother was raised.

Like many of her generation, my mother grew up bilingual, speaking Yiddish to her elders and English to her peers. By the time she was herself a
mother—living in a small two bedroom house on Long Island, which must have
seemed to her a mansion—she spoke English almost exclusively in her daily life.
Still, about once a week I would hear her talk Yiddish on the telephone with
family members in distant parts of the world like the Bronx. And I was informed
by many a cousin and great-aunt that my mother's Yiddish was particularly
fine—rich and expressive, and adaptable to all occasions (''Poilisheh'' when
speaking to her mother's kin from Warsaw, ''Litvishe'' when speaking to her
father's Muscovian side of the family). I often wished that I knew my mother's
Yiddish more intimately, wished she would speak it to me directly.

In my twenties, a graduate student in comparative literature, I particularly
regretted not having learned more Yiddish from my mother's mouth; instead, I
had to study it out of a textbook, in one of America's most genteel and gentile
of academic institutions. Three thousand miles from my mother's house, I sat
under a pomegranate tree in the backyard of my Palo Alto cottage, translating
Abraham Reisin and wishing that I didn't have to work so hard at what should
have been mine without effort at all. But all these stories of homes and moves
and displacements are leading me astray from the story I started to tell you. Let
me return.

Having completed the translation of ''Family of Eight'' just a few days before my mother's birthday, I decided to send it off to her as a birthday present.
Her reaction caught me by surprise.

''Did you like it?'' I asked in our regular Sunday morning phone call.

''Oh, yes,'' she replied, ''I liked it very much. When I read it, I recognized
it right away. Only—'' She paused, and in the silence it almost seemed she was
embarrassed.

"Only what?" I pressed.

"Well," she finally went on, "I didn't realize it had been written by a famous writer. I always thought it was grandma's folklore—you know, passed down from generation to generation."

"Family of Eight" had in fact been written in Warsaw in 1899; my grandmother's generation (along with Reisin himself) had imported it with them to America. The poem was not much more than a decade old when my mother was born, yet in that time it had acquired the status of folklore. Like many of Reisin's poems, it had even been set to music and sung, passed along like a popular folksong. What irony that I had had to go off to graduate school to learn it—a work by a "famous writer"—from a textbook!

Since experiencing my mother's reaction to my translation that day, I have often wondered what being a poet must have been like for Abraham Reisin. To have one's work be so central to, so enmeshed in, the experience of one's audience that, in your lifetime, you see it (no, *hear* it) become folklore—can an English-language Jewish-American poet even imagine this?[11] Not just Reisin but several Yiddish poets of the early immigrant period—Yehoash, Morris Rosenfeld, David Einhorn, and others—were popular to a degree that may seem unbelievable to the American poet today. Indeed, these poets were so identified with the community out of which they came that a rebellious move toward individualism was spawned among their descendants, the Yiddish poets of the next generation. Mani Leyb, Reuben Iceland, Zishe Landau, and others of *Die Yunge*, the Young Ones, proclaimed their individual identities as poets and aesthetes even as they pursued their livelihoods as shoemakers and housepainters. They were not the folk heroes that their antecedents had been; their work was far less celebrated and understood by the masses. And yet they too expected recognition from their audience; they too were tied to the Yiddish-American community with cords that would not be severed, and they expected that community to know its poets:

> I am Mani Leyb, whose name is sung—
> in Brownsville, Yehupets, and farther, they know it:
> Among cobblers, a splendid cobbler; among
> poetical circles, a splendid poet.[12]

Mani Leyb was certainly known to Yiddish readers in Brownsville, if not in "Yehupets" (Shalom Aleichem's fictional name for Kiev); and he found camaraderie, support, and stimulation in "poetical circles," such as the cafe society of the New York Yiddish poets.

Of course, the situation of Yiddish culture in America has changed significantly over the last decades, and the modern Yiddish poet may not quite share Mani Leyb's confidence in his own fame. As the Yiddish-speaking population in America has died off—with no new generation to replace it in America or anywhere else on the globe—contemporary Yiddish writers have understandably been prone to envy writers of English, whom they see as having a much larger and potentially lasting readership.

The Yiddish-American poet Malka Heifetz Tussman, for example, who died in 1987, spoke at times of her decision to write in Yiddish as a kind of sacrifice. As a sixteen-year-old immigrant from Russia eager to adapt to her new home in the United States, Malka Heifetz had written her first poems in English. But early in her development as a poet, a trusted mentor urged her to return to her mother tongue. His advice to her is recorded in her memoirs: "So many poets in America! So many write English. Some good, some not, but we have so few writing Yiddish. Stay with us. Write Yiddish poetry. Write your own way, even if it is hard to get into print. Even if it is not to the liking of some established literati."[13]

While not admitting explicitly to regrets about her decision to return to Yiddish, Heifetz Tussman nonetheless reveals a certain wistfulness in recounting the story: Had she written in English, might she not have found it easier to get into print? Might she not have found the greater audience that her work amply deserves?

Part of what Heifetz Tussman was feeling, I think, was the marginality imposed on her as a Yiddish writer in an English-speaking country. Yet she may not have been fully aware—or she may have taken for granted—that she was part of a vital group, a whole generation of modern poets writing in Yiddish: Jacob Glatstein, Rachel Korn, Kadya Molodowsky, Aaron Zeitlin, Melech Ravitch, and many others. Within Yiddish circles, these poets were far from marginal; they were published, read, reviewed, and known. Moreover, and perhaps more important, many of these modern Yiddish poets knew each other; there was a real sense of what we might call society (*chevreshaft*) among them, if not always friendship. Thus one can, I think, speak meaningfully about the role of community in relation not only to the first generations of Yiddish poets in America but to the moderns as well.

Like the Yiddish writers, many contemporary Israeli authors speculate about their own position in relation to writers of English: If they only wrote in English, Israeli writers suppose, they would achieve broader recognition than is available to them in the Hebrew-speaking world. And yet, the situation of the Israeli writer, like that of the Yiddish writer, is hardly one of isolation. From Bialik and Tchernikovsky to Uri Tzvi Greenberg, Abraham Shlonsky, and Yocheved Bat-Miriam; from Natan Alterman and Leah Goldberg to Amir Gilboa, Abba Kovner, Zelda, Chaim Guri, T. Carmi, Yehuda Amichai, Dan Pagis, Dalia Ravikovitch, Natan Zach, Yona Wallach, and Meir Wieseltier, to name only a few—the 20th-century Hebrew poets enjoy a readership and a following whose size and devotion might inspire envy among any of their Jewish-American peers writing in English.

For the truth is that both Yiddish and Hebrew poets have an idealized vision of the reality of the English-language writer in America, and especially of the

English-language poet. Today, the English-language poet in America is hardly guaranteed an audience at all; poetry is barely read by the general population. As for the Jewish-American population, the situation is not much different. Though Jewish readers are said to affect disproportionately the best-seller lists, they haven't catapulted any poets into that category in recent years.

Indeed, some of the finest Jewish poets in America are unknown to most Jewish readers. One case in point is the late Charles Reznikoff, hailed by the critic Abraham Chapman as "the dean of modern Jewish-American poets," who went largely unnoticed during his long and prolific lifetime. Reznikoff, like the earliest Yiddish-American poets, was a spokesperson for the working class. In his two volumes of verse entitled *Testimony,* he documented the lives of poor and working people in all regions of the United States. Reznikoff was interested in Jewish-American life in particular, and he wrote movingly about the Jewish immigrant experience. In many poems, he testified eloquently to his own feelings about Judaism and Jewishness. His volume entitled *Holocaust* was a documentation—based on actual testimony from the Nuremberg trials and the Eichmann trial, rendered into lines, with little commentary and no embellishment—of that most unspeakable of all Jewish experiences.

Born in 1894, Reznikoff was the contemporary of Jacob Glatstein and Malka Heifetz Tussman, Uri Tzvi Greenberg and Abraham Shlonsky. Yet Reznikoff was far less known to Jewish audiences than any of these authors. Although admired by many (among them the critic Milton Hindus and the poet George Oppen), Reznikoff was not widely appreciated by circles of readers, and certainly not among consciously Jewish circles—nothing that we might call Jewish community.

Where, we might ask, *is* the Jewish-American population in relation to the Jewish-American poet? Do Jewish-American readers read Jewish poets? Do they buy their books, attend their readings? Do Jewish-American newspapers and journals (with the notable exceptions of *Response* and *Shirim*) regularly publish poetry—more than a token poem per issue? Do Jewish-American foundations fund the writing of poetry? Do Jewish parents recite bedtime poems to their children? Do Jewish schools encourage pupils to find their own voices as poets of the next generation? One cannot say "never" in answer to these queries—but neither can one say "often." Why?

Though one may speculate about reasons for the general lack of popularity of poetry in the United States, it is somewhat harder to account for the Jewish-American population. What has become of the audience for poetry in the Jewish-American community, the audience that was once so responsive to Yiddish verse? Why are its English-speaking peers and descendants not equally responsive to poetry, especially Jewish poetry, written in English? Is it just the endless barrage of media in contemporary culture that has threatened to make extinct the reading and recitation of poetry? But if the lack of interest in poetry among Jews today is simply a sign of postmodern times, why is this not the situation in Israel? The popularity of poetry in Israel has not declined since the time of the founding of modern Israeli culture. What accounts for these differences between Jewish-American and Israeli culture, and between Jewish-American and Yiddish-American culture?

The Yiddish-American community, especially in its first two generations, was united by many bonds: first, the language—Yiddish in an environment where English was dominant; second, social and economic conditions of hardship, and thus common struggles; third, a common experience of displacement and exile, or the memory of this within a single generation. The Eastern European Jewish immigrant community constructed an elaborate support system in the new world of America—and poetry, it seems, became part of that system, a medium to express the shared sorrows and triumphs of a people already united in many ways.

Quite a different situation existed in the young, emerging State of Israel, whose immigrant population came from a wide variety of backgrounds. The fervor of building a new state ignited the country for years with a common cause. For many Israeli Jews, Zionism was the new religion. Poetry had an important role to play in this concept: It was the voice of an incipient culture, a culture in formation. The enthusiasm for poetry in Israel somehow did not wane over the ensuing decades, despite increasing disillusionment with the Zionist dream. Instead, poetry in Israel today reflects the diverse passions of a people in struggle and conflict; the broad lyric range of Israeli poetry encompasses a variety of styles, voices, sentiments, and opinions. In the midst of wars, upheavals, and internal dissension, the Israeli population reads poetry, even seems to look to it for a measure of salvation. The Friday (Sabbath) editions of the major national newspapers all feature literary sections, in which poetry plays a prominent role. Old and young, Ashkenazim and Sephardim, Israelis of all classes and vocations know the names of the Hebrew poets, are curious about their lives, sometimes turn them into national heroes. The role of the poet in Israel today is vital and even central to the ongoing life of the society.

But in today's America, no common tongue, no common struggle or oppression, no unified socioeconomic class, no shared revolutionary dreams distinguish and unite the Jewish population. Indeed, it is not at all clear to me what we mean by the term "Jewish community." Where is this community? Who defines it? Who is in it? What are its expressions? Whatever it is, it seems to have little positive relationship to the Jewish poet. The Jewish poet in America speaks, for the most part, like other American poets—as an individual, often isolated, in an atomized world.

Indeed, one might argue that Jewish culture does not exist in America today—that, as for Jewish culture, to paraphrase the Israeli novelist Amos Oz, Israel is a stage, America a museum. I think that this is to some degree true. For example, I know of few (there are some, to be sure) Jewish artists in America who see their work as primarily Jewish, or who are able to articulate the connection of their work to Judaism or Jewishness. At worst, Jewish artists in America will label as "Jewish" the nostalgic or sentimental aspects of their work. Any poem about Bubbee or Zaydee, or even about Nana and Grandpa, is "Jewish"; any mention of Israel, especially romanticized Israel, immediately qualifies a work as "Jewish," as does reference to "Shabbos," "Shabbat," or even the Protestant-sounding "Sabbath." Thus begins the trivialization of Jewish art, the turning of art into souvenir, the relinquishing of authentic vision.

But if Jewish culture is faltering in America, it is only partly the responsibility of Jewish artists. The amorphous American-Jewish community—that term I have resisted using because I think that today it represents a kind of mythological thinking (perhaps we ought merely to speak of the Jewish population?)—whatever and wherever it is, does not provide much support to stimulate and sustain the making of serious Jewish art. Indeed I would say that, although lip service is paid to the arts, and Jewish artisans and craftspeople are enjoying a resurgence of popularity today, the daring and courage of real art are not, for the most part, valued or embraced.

Except in one arena. There is one area of Jewish life in America where creativity seems to be nourished, where the making of Jewish culture is visibly happening. That area is the "new spirituality." In the blossoming Jewish renewal movement, in small pockets of Reconstructionist and other *havurot,* in the emerging lesbian and gay Jewish communities, and in the many manifestations of the Jewish feminist movement, the creative revival of Judaism is going on. In communities that might be thought of as the fringe rather than the establishment, in networks of people united by shared visions of change, authentic art is being born. This art emerges out of a dialectic, an interplay between the individual and the community, and it feeds on the forces that surround it, on context and on history. If you want to see where Jewish culture is happening, culture that is not trivial, art that is not trivially Jewish, look first to the emergent "alternative" communities in American Jewish life.

And now it is time for me to tell my own story because my story is part of this larger one.

As I suggested at the outset of this piece, the practice of literary translation has engaged me as a poet for a long time. In particular, translating Hebrew and Yiddish texts into English has allowed me to make Jewish traditions my own in a way that is more satisfying than any other mode I have experienced, including that of academic study. To make a text come alive in my own voice, not only to engage with the tradition but to enter and become a part of it—this has inspired me. Not to "observe" tradition but to make it, to be one who hands it down, shaping it ever anew with my own hands—this is what I have wanted to do. For tradition is a live, organic thing, or it is nothing, ossified, dead.

As the translator of the Song of Songs as well as of a number of modern Hebrew and Yiddish poets, I was seen, virtually from the time I began to publish, as a "Jewish poet"—an identity that felt natural and comfortable to me. I was also fortunate in that what I offered was well received by its audience—an audience comprised, at least in part, by the new Jewish communities of which I have been speaking. I think that one reason for the enthusiastic reaction to my translations was that they were bringing Jewish sources and texts into a contemporary medium, enabling people to have more direct personal connection with tradition. Whatever the reasons, this reception was very encouraging to me. What moved me most was hearing of how my work took on a life of its own in the hands of others—when, for example, I would hear my version of the Song of Songs sung to melodies by composers and folksingers, or see it dramatized by actors, or hear it recited ritually in *havurot* as part of Pesach celebrations. This response to and use of my work made me want to keep writing.

Then came the time when something changed in my own journey as an artist. It was the result of a convergence of things—turning points are never single-faceted—and it is hard to say exactly when it began. At a certain point, translating texts as a way of engaging with tradition was no longer sufficient. Although there was much that I loved in Jewish texts, there was also much that I found painful. I had always thought of my work with texts as an artistic endeavor rather than a religious one, but theological issues were becoming more and more crucial to me. I saw how theology colors everything in our lives, everything in Jewish tradition, whether or not we think of ourselves as "believers." I saw how deeply theology is itself art—metaphor-making on a grand scale. And I saw how the metaphor system of Judaism is embedded in all our literature, and also how deeply that system affects who we are in the world.

I began to take the traditional words of Hebrew prayer more seriously. Through too much familiarity, they had lost their impact; I had related to them for years as a kind of mantra. Now, hearing them fresh, seeing the images they painted as though for the first time, feeling the arrangements of power and dependency that they constructed and maintained in the world and inside myself, my spirit enflamed. I who cared so much about words and images—how could I use them to perpetuate lies? The old images ("lord," "king") were no longer serving our vision; why did we pretend to pay them homage? Could divinity not be conjured in a thousand different ways? It was time for the artists of Judaism to draw new pictures.

It was not long after that realization that I first began to adapt and then to write Hebrew prayers. This had not been done much before, at least not in this century. Although people had been experimenting a little with the English versions of the liturgy, the Hebrew words of prayer were left largely untouched. Was it an act of chutzpah to change the Hebrew? Yes, perhaps—but then, no, not really. For although the old words were hallowed by time, they too had been written by human beings—poets, in fact (although the term generally used is "liturgists"). I stood at a moment in time when numbers of Jews were struggling to articulate a new vision of the world. My vision, I knew, was part of that moment; my own, yes, but also nourished by sources all around me, as well as by those that had come before. As a poet, I had the skills to give voice to this vision through the medium of words. With the old texts still echoing in my ears, while the thrill of new creation stirred within me, words sprang to my pen. I wrote with an eagerness that had been dormant in me for some time. Not since my work on the Song of Songs a decade earlier had I felt so powerfully connected and engaged.

The connection flowed in both directions. My blessings—for that was the form I had chosen to write—came back to me in the voices of others, those praying in *havurot* and synagogues and homes across the United States. Once again, it was the network of new communities, Jewish seekers uncomfortable with the forms of establishment Judaism, that provided the first burst of response to my work. My prayers traveled in many vehicles: printed in journals and newsletters and handmade "alternative" prayerbooks, woven into challah covers and *tallitot,* set to music and sung, discussed on public radio. Were my new blessings becoming, like Abraham Reisin's poems, part of the public domain?

As it turns out, the price of acceptance by segments of the Jewish population was a backlash from others that I had not anticipated. Most astonishing to me, my new blessings were attacked as "un-Jewish," and use of them was censured. In my own mind, these prayers were Jewish to their core, as well as on their surface: In the process of their composition, I had grappled with every aspect of my relationship to Judaism—as literary culture, as ethical system, as theology, as communal practice. To that grappling—that turning of text and context—had been added invention, something my own, something to make it new. How else does an artist create, I wonder?

Of course, implied in my blessings is a deep critique of the imagery of the Hebrew liturgy; yet this critique grew out of an understanding and embracing of Judaism's own conceptual principles, including the fundamental monotheistic idea. Thus the critique is a critique from within, and the new liturgy is a reconstruction of Jewish prayer from a feminist perspective. Both critique and reconstruction were—and continue to be—labors of love. When my blessings began to emerge from within me, after years of waiting inchoate, they appeared the way all poems do—as gifts.

What I would have liked to see from Jewish critics, in response, was a critical dialogue centered around questions that stimulate further creativity—issues more fruitful than whether a work is Jewish. As for my new prayers, I would like to hear what is meaningful in them rather that what is permissible.

Liturgy scholar Lawrence Hoffman has spoken about the "limit game" that is played in Jewish religion.[14] First we decide what the limits of Judaism are; then whatever crosses a predefined limit we label "forbidden" or, at the extreme, "un-Jewish." The game is a way of controlling the topography, a way of denying movement and change. It is a way of keeping power and authority in their place—and keeping the disempowered in theirs. It is also a way of stifling art—because art cannot play the limit game. The limit game stifles organic process, dampens creativity.

Jewish civilization has been characterized as an interplay of *halakhah* (law) and *aggadah* (lore, the realm of the imagination). There is an inherent tension between the two tendencies, which—given a respectful coexistence—can be stimulating and creative. However, when *halakhah* tries to control the realm of *aggadah,* when steely cages of authority attempt to restrain the imagination's flow, when limit-setting efforts dominate the critique of culture, the results are not so fruitful. Although halakhic disapproval may not entirely squelch the aggadic impulse, it can certainly encumber the path to its expression. Censure is wearing on the artist's spirit; it siphons off where replenishing is needed. An artist's consciousness—or even subconscious inkling—of the dominance of the limit game can be profoundly alienating. If Jewish artists are not interacting meaningfully with Jewish communities today, the apprehension of the limit mentality may be part of the reason why.

What is it that artists do need in order to keep practicing their art? What kind of response will replenish creative energy and bring Jewish artists into vibrant relationships with Jewish communities?

If American Jews want to think of themselves as supporters of the arts, they must do more than buy pretty pictures and nostalgic retellings of old stories. They must also do more than sponsor intellectual debate about what constitutes Jewish art. They must nurture the aggadic impulse, which finds and makes meaning in the world by breaking boundaries and challenging limits.

This may explain why creativity is flowing today from "marginal" sectors of the population—sectors that themselves test the limits. Once, in the days when the Jewish population as a whole experienced itself as marginal in America—in the days when the term "Jewish-American community" still made sense—Mani Leyb had a context in which to call himself, with pride, a poet. Today, it is the fringes of the Jewish population that honor the identity of the artist and encourage the making of real art. For it is the fringes that appreciate the subversive, and it is the subversive that regenerates culture.

And so, if you ask what it is ideally that I would like, as a Jewish artist, from the hypothetical American-Jewish community, it is this: that it have the courage to remember its own marginality—what it was like to be a stranger in the land—and once again act upon the impulses of that marginality.

A Response

Richard A. Siegel

The artist in the American Jewish community is quite different from the artist in the Yiddish community or from the artist in Israel. This is not because the nature of the artists differs, but rather because the communities, the environments in which the artists function, differ. As Marcia Falk articulated in her essay, "in today's America, no common tongue, no common struggle or oppression, no unified socio-economic class, no shared revolutionary dreams distinguish and unite the Jewish community." Or as she expressed in positive terms, "the Yiddish-American community was, especially in its first two generations, united by many bonds: first, the language . . . ; second, social and economic conditions of hardship, and thus common struggles; third, a common experience of displacement and exile, or the memory of this within a single generation."

I would like to look at these three conditions—language, societal flux, and shared experience—a little more closely, particularly as they relate to differences between Israel and the United States, and in terms of their implications for a creative revival in the American Jewish community.

1. Language. The impact that not having a separate language has had on the development of an American Jewish culture is incalculable. The use of a special language, as with Hebrew in Israel or Yiddish in previous generations in America, both defines a community and insures a basic commonality of experience. Members of the community read the same newspapers, listen to the same songs, attend the same plays. In such an environment, an artist knows who the audience is and what vehicles to use to reach that audience.

Even more important, language in the hands of an artist is an instrument to play upon: The language is itself an aspect of creative energy. This is particularly clear with Hebrew. In 1989–90, we celebrated the century-mark in the revival of Hebrew. Hebrew is the major cultural achievement of modern Israel. It is not just a means of communication; it is a reflection of the values, history, traditions, wanderings, and longings which underlie the state. Its grammar, nuances, and resonances are the materials with which Israeli writers and poets weave their stories and songs. It reacts to them and they react to it. The language is a living organism, and it grows with each use, addition, coinage, allusion, and play of words.

Not too long ago the National Foundation for Jewish Culture sponsored an intensive encounter between Israeli and North American Jewish writers, critics, and scholars. There was no communication problem. Everyone was more or less comfortable speaking in English. In fact, at the one session where we arranged for simultaneous translation, three of the four Israeli panelists preferred to speak in English. But while there was no communication problem, there *was* a language problem. English is not a Jewish language; Hebrew is. The Israeli participants rightly challenged the Americans that if we are to seriously engage Israeli culture, then we must become more serious about learning Hebrew.

Where language is concerned, we resemble most other Americans, but not Israelis or earlier generations of American Jews. Our Jewish community is not defined or identified by the use of a particular language. The newspapers we read, even the Jewish ones, are in English; the plays we attend, even the Jewish ones, are in English; the songs we sing, even the Jewish ones, are in English.

Artists share the problems created by the diffusion of the American Jewish community with others who seek to influence it, be they advertisers or visionaries. American Jewish artists, however, suffer uniquely from having to operate in an English-language environment: English is not an instrument of Jewish creativity. Not having a uniquely Jewish instrument means that in order to convey Jewish sensibilities and sensitivities, a greater burden must be placed on content, the most obvious and superficial dimension of creative work. The artist is thereby stripped of one of his or her greatest tools, subtlety and nuance. It is the truly brilliant artist who can plumb the linguistic nuances of English in a uniquely Jewish way—by inflection, the subtle references to literary traditions, the exquisite word plays on other texts. Given this limitation, we are confronted with what Irving Howe recently described as "a crisis of subject matter."

II. Social flux. Israel is a "hot" society; the United States is not. Israeli artists have a power that American artists lack: When Israelis have something to say about burning issues, they command the most powerful media for conveying their messages.

I remember a writer friend of mine from Boston once saying rather wistfully that "at least in Russia, they imprison their writers." (This was obviously before glasnost.) At least someone was listening and took words seriously; at least the creative act generated a response. In Israel art generates a response without the context of restricted expression. In America, neither in the Jewish community nor in the larger American society can an artist expect to be heard.

In Israel, where even bus-shelter advertising can become a national issue, the artist has incredible power. Yehoshua Sobol's play "The Jerusalem Syndrome," produced by the Haifa Municipal Theater as part of a 40th-anniversary festival of original Israeli theater, was fiercely debated in the Knesset in the spring of 1988, during the height of the Intifada. The play provoked street demonstrations and newspaper editorials, and eventually was closed; it led to the resignations of both the playwright and the director from the company. I attended a performance of another of Sobol's plays, "The Palestinian Woman," at the Cameri Theater in Tel Aviv, where the production was disrupted for 30 minutes by a group of right-wing protesters chanting *"teatron tzioni"* ("Zionist theater"), while an ad hoc group from the audience shouted back *teatron democrati* ("democratic theater"). The ideology and values of the state are being debated in the halls of the theater. It is hard to imagine any such scene taking place in an American venue. The role of the artist here is different, more subtle.

III. Common experience. The creative artist stands in relation to a community or society—imitating it if a panderer, reflecting it if a critic, or pushing against it if a visionary. Although from one perspective Israel is a highly heterogeneous society reflecting a broad diversity of ethnic groups, socio-economic experiences, and political ideologies, compared to America Israel exhibits a high degree of homogeneity; at least among its Jewish population, such homogeneity is bred in its history, its still operative founding mythologies, its language, and its centralized institutions. An artist can both tap into this common reservoir of experience and stand clearly in relation to it; that is, the artist can have a perspective.

The Jewish community in America lacks those elements of cohesion. We no longer share an immigrant experience or refugee status; the younger generations have no active memory of European Jewry destroyed or of Israel reborn. Rather, our Jewish community is more elusive, a composite of subcommunities broken down by religious affiliations, regional proximities, and political-intellectual orientations. We may possess a variety of ways to reach these subcommunities—newspapers, journals, congregations, community centers—but they are all decentralized, fragmented. It is difficult to gain a clear or comprehensive perspective.

So what does it mean to be a Jew and an artist in contemporary America? There seem to be two options, although they are probably more like points along a continuum. For lack of better terms, I will call these options the "artist-as-Jew" and the "Jew-as-artist."

The artist-as-Jew identifies first with his or her particular creative muse. The artist-as-Jew inhabits the theaters, concert halls, journals, and galleries of American culture; reads *Variety,* or the *New York Review of Books,* or *Dance Magazine;* and relies on professional agents and managers to handle the business side of the arts. The Jewish identity of these artists is often quite pronounced, but is normally seen as a background influence on personality, character, and values, or as occasional stimulation for particular artistic creations.

There are many examples of such artists, and, significantly, the numbers increase as we get farther away from the immigrant generation: for example, Steve Reich, a contemporary minimalist composer, whose "Tehillim," based on intensive study of Jewish texts and sources, has been performed by major orchestras around the world and has been used as the basis of new choreographic work by at least three prominent contemporary dance groups; Elizabeth

Swados, the multitalented playwright/composer/director, whose "Haggada," "Jerusalem Cantata," and "Esther" stand beside her "Runaways," "Alice-in-Wonderlands," "Nightclub Cantata," and "Rap Master Ronnie"; choreographers like Ohad Naharin and Liz Lerman; writers like Max Apple and Rosellen Brown; visual artists like Irving Petlin and Tobi Kahn. There are dozens more, representing a new synthesis of artist, American and Jew. They are neither escaping from old-world or immigrant insularity, nor seeking refuge in their Jewishness. Rather, they are able to participate fully in the culture of America while affirming their identities as Jews.

Many of these artists are considerably uncomfortable within the normative Jewish community because they rightly resist being described as "Jewish artists." This label is a limitation; it cannot encompass the breadth of their creativity nor the complexity of their identities. They may be extremely proud of being Jewish and use Jewish sources or experiences in some of their work, but they do not want to be pigeon-holed.

The other option for integration is the Jew-as-artist. Here, Jewish identity takes precedence over artistic identity, and the focus of creative energy is directed toward the Jewish community. Marcia Falk rightly questions whether there is anything we can call "the Jewish community" in America. The concept may be appropriate on a socio-political level, but in reality what we have are subcommunities. The Jew-as-artist, therefore, must choose or create a subcommunity he or she can relate to, be it the Yiddishist community or the Syrian community; the Boro Park community or the Venice, California, community; the National Federation of Temple Youth (NFTY) community or the *havurah* community. The problem is that these subcommunities are so small that they are easily saturated, and the artists quickly become overexposed. Only the most powerful artistic vision can cross over many subcommunities and perhaps approach the outer reaches of that nebulous construct, the American Jewish community.

I must disagree with Falk at this point, however. She writes, "If you want to see where Jewish culture is happening, culture that is not trivial, art that is not trivially Jewish, look first to the emergent 'alternative' communities in American Jewish life." Unfortunately, with very few exceptions, I do not see great art or even great artistic intent emerging from the Jewish renewal movement. What I see too often is self-congratulation and dilettantism. Though it may not be trivially Jewish, it is artistically trivial. The visual arts are decorative; the writing is shallow; the music is repetitive; and there is virtually no theater or dance.

I have never understood why some of the artists I mentioned, like Reich and Swados, have not been integrated or even invited into this community. They can be extremely important to us, and we can be extremely important to them. They can revivify us with their vision, their aesthetics, their depth, their groping for new integrations of Jewish and contemporary American consciousness. And we can demonstrate to them that there are other ways to be modern Jews than those with which they grew up, by revealing the unanticipated depth and beauty of Jewish tradition, and by giving them the tools and resources to enrich their lives as Jews and as artists.

We in the Jewish renewal movement have never taken the arts seriously, either as subversive activity or as instruments in the shaping of our consciousnesses—certainly not in the way we embraced Hasidic teaching, group dynamics, or intellectual debate. We have been content to accept art as *hiddur mitzvah* (beautification of ritual objects). In so doing, we have overlooked its potential as *shvirat kelim*—the breaking of the vessels of our limited consciousnesses so as to explore different ways of being Jewish in the world.

Hiddur mitzvah is fine. I even accept a certain amount of responsibility for having promoted it as a concept. It was a revelation when we discovered it 20 years ago, and it still has the power to inspire some delightful creations. This year, our family used hand-dipped candles in the chanukkiah instead of the usual ones we get in the mail from some yeshiva in Cleveland. They made the lighting more pleasant, and everyone commented on how much nicer they looked. On a less trivial level, I recently had the experience of serving as a judge for a Chanukah arts festival at the Ansche Chesed synagogue in New York City. This festival now draws hundreds of people on Saturday night and all day Sunday. The craftspeople are supposedly some of the best in the country, or at least in the East. I was pleasantly surprised with the quality of some of the work. There was certainly a general improvement in the field since the last time I had checked into the Jewish crafts scene, but even the best work was hardly remarkable or exceptional. It could not begin to compare with the quality found at the annual Holiday Crafts Fair just a few blocks up the street at Columbia. This experience reinforces my feeling that if we want exceptional crafts, we need to stimulate the interest of exceptional craftspeople in the forms of Jewish ceremonial life.

I do not want to minimize art as *hiddur mitzvah.* A burgeoning cadre of calligraphers, ceramicists, weavers, and woodworkers now form a growth industry. We can now pray wrapped in hand-woven, multicolored *tallitot,* cut the Shabbat challah on carved wood boards inlaid with mother-of-pearl, and drink from glazed ceramic kiddush cups. Our lives are enhanced, made more pleasing and pleasant. However, even with art as *hiddur mitzvah,* we have not fully explored the aesthetics of the prayer environment or the performance dynamics of *tefillah* (prayer), to mention but two areas where we could benefit from the insights and talents of the art world.

But what about art that disturbs, that challenges, that provokes, that inspires? What about art as *shvirat kelim,* the light of creation that breaks the vessels of complacency and redirects the light toward new and unanticipated universes?

Let me conclude with a brief thought about the programmatic implications of this critique. While we would want to continue to encourage the Jew-as-artist within our midst, there is much greater potential in reaching out to the artist-as-Jew. It is far easier to help an artist discover Jewish depth than to expect that Jewish identity will lead to artistic talent.

If we want a future agenda in this area, I would recommend programs such as that undertaken by the Reconstructionist Rabbinical College several years ago. Six outstanding American Jewish poets were brought together there with six Jewish scholars to teach each other and to learn from each other. The National Foundation for Jewish Culture has developed a variety of programs—conferences, festivals, symposia, and special events—for the involvement of playwrights, choreographers, writers, and composers. I can envision other formats, subjects, and participants, as well; this seems to be a fertile area for further nurturing. Let us create opportunities to involve the outstanding artists-as-Jews and bring them into dialogue with our "alternative" Jewish community. Let us do this for their sake and for ours.

A Response

Omus Hirshbein

When I was invited to contribute to this volume, I was pleased to be seen as a Jew in the world of the arts and not only as a general arts administrator.

The comfort that I feel being here certainly comes from the work that I do currently, but perhaps more so from my childhood. My father was the noted Yiddish playwright, author, journalist, and world traveler Peretz Hirshbein. In California, where I grew up, our home was filled with writers, actors, and intellectuals from within and without the Yiddish speaking world. I remember Maurice Schwartz, Sholem Asch, the poet Rosenblatt, the actor Elihu Tennenholz, the writer Y. Y. Schwartz (who wrote the American novel *Kentucky*), and perhaps the greatest Yiddish poet of our times, Itzik Manger. As World War II had already started, this was the end of the golden period of Yiddish.

I disagree with Marcia Falk about the popularity of Yiddish poetry in Eastern Europe and America, and I believe that she does not sufficiently acknowledge or discuss the real force that the spoken word had and still has, ethnically, through theater.

Further, poets in Europe and America became known to the populace not so much through books, but rather through a kind of daily newspaper different from those we are accustomed to in this country. Yiddish newspapers—for us in America, the *Forward*, the *Morgen Journal, Die Freiheit,* and most centrally, *Der Tog*—published all kinds of literature, poetry, essays, parts of plays, serialized novels. The populace did not have so very many books published by institutionalized publishing houses. And every Jew on both sides of the Atlantic was a poet. Let's remember that the central part of this literary history is to be found between the world wars, certainly before the Holocaust.

I believe that there is also a misconception about the popularity of poetry altogether. Though the Poetry Center of New York's 92nd Street Y may be thought to be "wildly successful," as a *New York Times* magazine article put it, it is a small program with 1,100 members, the success of which can be attributed in no small part to the inclusion of prose writers and playwrights in its program. The Yiddish Culture Club in Los Angeles, which I attended almost weekly, like *shul*, from 1941 to 1959, when I left for the confusing life of New York, was also "hugely successful," although in retrospect the audience of 250 on any given evening was really a tiny, loyal constituency. The club belonging to *die linke,* the left, was even smaller. By this time Zionism had taken hold, and there was a gradually growing disaffection with the promise of communism by Zionism's Soviet sympathizers. (My father wrote off the Soviet Union as a healthy place for Jews back in 1927, in his novel *Red Fields.*)

The decline of Yiddish culture in America is attributable to the ease with which Jews were able to enter the mainstream culture. Among those cultivated or cultured Jews, Yiddish continued to be kept alive, but it was an increasingly small percentage who recognized the language as the purveyor and vehicle of a cultural and political identity. The Holocaust killed the potential of a continuing infusion of Yiddish language into the Jewish-American culture, and the Soviet repression was successful in erasing the Yiddish/Hebrew cultural canvas; 1953 spelled the end, with the murder of the Yiddish writers, some of whom foretold their undoing. In 1943, when I was nine years old, three writers came from the Soviet Union on a lend-lease mission to visit my father and mother in Holly-wood. Itzik Feffer, Chaver Paver, and Solomon Michoels worried about what would happen in the Soviet Union when the war was ended and Stalin would turn his attention to the Jews. Indeed, they foretold their doom. (There was one survivor, Ilya Ehrenburg, and he remained a tool of the Bolsheviks.) Recently there has been only one post–World War II journal of the prewar quality, and that is *Die Goldene Keit* (The Golden Chain), published and edited by the last Yiddishist giant, Abraham Sutzkever, in Tel Aviv.

Poetry, prose—these were for the literati. The newspapers helped to spread the word, but there was nothing like the theater, indeed, there *is* nothing like the theater to inspire the masses. They flocked more to *Schund* (Vaudeville), but many also went to the art theaters of Maurice Schwartz and Jacob Ben Ami, and in Russia to the Habima theater of Nathan Zemach. It is in theater that ideas have really come alive. Most of what has been popular lately has been what contemporary Jewish writers have grown up with: home, domineering mother, exhausted father, young love—in short, kitchen dramas. But there is a new wind in the air. It is felt ever so strongly in the work of the Haifa theater and in some smaller Israeli theaters. Even the Habima is trying to catch up. Here in America there is a gifted director who cares passionately about a Jewish theater of ideas. At the 92nd Street Y Michael Posnick created the Mosaic Theater. This theater explored theology, politics, history, art, and culture, proving that by its very Jewishness it could be universal in its examination of various human conditions. Theater can be a very powerful educational tool in our present Jew-ish communities.

''Pure'' music is harder. The search for Jewishness tends to breed stereo-types. The visual arts remain what they are—either a palette for honest artists or a money pit for charlatans.

It troubles me that Falk would have us believe that Jews came here to suffer, having come from conditions of greater ease. Let us not forget that America was *Die Golden Medine* (the Golden Land), and that we Jews made good here. Unfortunately, our will to integrate and assimilate has placed us outside the community of minorities when entering college or the workplace, or when applying for scarce arts funds. Falk does recognize with vigor the vibrancy of the Israeli literary ferment. Oddly enough, it parallels quite strongly the Yiddish secular cultural experience before and between the wars, both in Europe and America—newspapers printing poetry and literature. To quote Falk, "Israelis of all classes know the names of the Hebrew poets."

Now let's be very clear. What Falk described—the Yiddish-speaking or -appreciating communities of America and Europe and the community of Israel—are homogeneous Jewish communities. We do not have that in America today. (Except for the Orthodox, but they have never counted where the notion of art is concerned. Apropos the Orthodox, neither I. B. Singer nor his brother I. J. ever told their rabbi father that they wrote for a newspaper, but rather that they sold newspapers.)

Falk intertwines the notions of theology and art, and she insists that the new Jewish "creativity is flowing today from 'marginal' sectors of the population—sectors that themselves test the limits," and that "Today, it is the fringes of the Jewish population that honor the identity of the artist and encourage the making of real art. For it is the fringes that appreciate the subversive, and it is the subversive that regenerates culture." She speaks of *halakhah* trying to control the realm of *aggadah,* but has it not always been that way in theology? Art is different. We can individually say that a work of art is good or bad, but not sinful or against *halakhah.* In the arts, no "steely cages of authority attempt to restrain the imagination's flow." Finally the academy is dead.

I am afraid that Falk confuses art and theology to the extent that I feel unable to comment fairly or with a sense of comfort. The best in art is made by individuals, not communities. It is an individual playwright who can create a play that is relevant to the Jewish community, or rather to Jewishness. It is the individual poet, painter, composer, or choreographer who transcends limits with equanimity. People can like or not like; critics can laud or lambast; but it is not sin—art is not like that. We do not have to choose to live by art as I think we may choose to live a theology. I was a concert pianist. I am the son of a great Jewish writer. I am a member of the mother church of the Reconstructionist movement, a synagogue in New York City led for years by one who has left the Reconstructionist movement. I make my living as an administrator of arts and humanities at a secular Jewish institution. I speak and read Yiddish fluently. I am a Zionist who wishes to defend Israel. My mother, Esther Shumiatcher, has five published books of Yiddish poetry to her credit. With all of this as my background, I am confused by what it is that Marcia Falk means when she mixes theology and art.

5

Jewish Literacy: Will More and More Be Known by Fewer and Fewer?

Hillel Levine

At the outset, I must confess my very limited success in making predictions. My one experience with futurology nearly ended in disaster. In the early 1970s I spent a week driving through the Rocky Mountains with Herman Kahn, who was lecturing at the Air Force Academy missile bases and executive seminars. We almost missed his most important lecture. He was planning to reassure America's captains of industry conferring on the *angst* of the day, the recently published Club of Rome report on the "Limits of Growth." The great futurologist, on a treacherous mountain road as he was rehearsing a spirited defense of his claims that global resources were actually expanding, ran out of gas.

The words of Amos—"I am not a prophet nor the son of a prophet"— haunt us as they entreat us to modesty in our efforts to imagine the Jewish future 30 years hence. But the call of the prophet is a call to responsibility—and to responsiveness. For some of us, imagining springs from vision, for others from statistics. The best planning is to try to assess the contradictory trends of the present, to conjure up images of a desired future, and to face that future with a realistic assessment of our competence and endowments. We can plan with a perceptive grasp of those elusive forces beyond our direct control with hope and prayer, and with a vague design for muddling through. How well we do this as a community is of some question. Also a question is whether it is plausible, or even safe, to assume a surprise-free future—the only future for which this type of planning makes sense.

Traditional thinking, the *Zeitgeist*, and the genealogical claims of many American Jews should lead me to start with some dour prognostications. What might we expect of a generation that will be 30 more years removed from Sinai? While the attention that some crotchety cultural commentators have received of late is quite remarkable—not to mention their book sales—it may be more appropriate to begin with the good news. That may not be quite as interesting as the bad news, but please bear with me—I will get to that as well.

The good news is that, after all, there is a good deal of Jewish literacy. Although it is not at all evenly distributed among Jews of different countries and origins, across denominational, age, gender, or socio-economic lines, it is impressive by any expectations of 30 years ago. Two dramatic examples come to mind: *lernin* (yeshiva-style text study) and scholarship.

The renewal of yeshivot in Israel, North America, and now in France following the devastation of the centers of traditional learning during World War II caught everyone by surprise. Who could have imagined that yeshivot, represented to us by tea bags and jars of honey before Rosh Hashanah, *pushkah* (charity) boxes on kitchen refrigerators, and *yahrzeit* glasses, would now be situated on sprawling campuses? In Israel alone there are estimates of twenty thousand yeshivah *bachurim* (students) based on the number of military exemptions. The actual number is probably larger. (According to an estimate I have not been able to verify, the government of Israel provides an annual subsidy of $350 million for its yeshivot, but only $250 million for its universities. This allocation is likely to increase in favor of the yeshivot.) We have no statistics for North American yeshivah attendance, only impressions of a considerable number. Eastern Europe in its heyday did not have as many students. I will not make any evaluation of the quality of study, nor of the seriousness of the students. To be sure, the elimination of the draft in the United States did not, as some expected, close down the yeshivot. And I suspect that in Israel, as well, a range of motives, including pious ones, prompts students to stay in the *bet midrash*.

The results remain to be seen. Will this unanticipated expansion in the ranks of learned Jews generate increased competitiveness and new modes of study, much as the crowded academies of medieval *Ashkenaz* encouraged *pilpul?* Will the intensity of study of traditional sources result in a proliferation of halakhic insights focused on areas heretofore outside the domain of Halakhah? Our late teacher Abraham Joshua Heschel would ask, "How can you kosher an atomic bomb?" Will the *poskim,* the halakhic adjudicators, of 30 years from now, question the kashrut of junk food and junk bonds? Will they be ill at ease with the religious sensibilities manifest in the young stockbroker charged with trading on inside information who, as a result of plea-bargaining, agrees to record surreptitiously the incriminating boasts of deal-making made by his fellow religious stockbrokers over Shabbos dinner? Will it matter that he went to great pains to clarify that the recording equipment was neither turned on nor turned off on the holy Sabbath? Will the grappling of New Age *masmidim,* the truly learned, with worldly issues unanticipatedly allow into the house of study "the light of day"? Will this cadre follow the Jesuit/Lubavitch model of ever-widening networks, infiltrating the houses of worship and the marketplaces—of commerce as well as of ideas—reinvesting with some combination of higher spiritual purpose and obstructive normative restraints what religion centuries ago surrendered to the mundane? The new triumphalism in the world of ultra-

Orthodoxy will certainly lead to crude efforts at religious control. But the "swing to the right" may have unanticipated consequences. Out of the tens of thousands of those involved in *lernin,* there will always be a few learned defectors who will contribute to the spiritual and intellectual development of other Judaisms. Moreover, it may precipitate an ideological renewal of militant Jewish secularism, as well as a full spectrum of more moderate religious communities. What are the conditions under which the ultimate beneficiaries of an apparently inevitable Kulturkampf would be those who want to combine religion and democracy, Zionism with universal moral concerns, nurturing communities with rigorous individualism? These issues should be of concern to those who want to think now about three decades hence.

Another example of Jewish literacy is the dramatic rise of university-based *Wissenschaft des Judentums* (scientific study of Judaism) in North America and in Israel during the last two decades. This study harks back to the birth of modern Jewish scholarship: the publication by Leopold Zunz of his *Etwas uber die Rabbinisch Litteratur,* followed shortly thereafter by the organization of the *Verein,* a circle of German Jewish intellectuals including Heine, who wanted to imagine their Jewish futures.

Before we celebrate what is now, we bow our heads to what existed in Europe before World War II. Yet who could have imagined that the survivors of Berlin and Breslau, of Odessa, Vilna, and Frankfurt would have sired a second, even a third, generation of many hundreds of disciples, who are now researching every nook and cranny of the Jewish past, and teaching thousands of courses at universities. A conference of the Association for Jewish Studies held several years ago featured hundreds of scholarly papers, many "made in America." The International Congress held in Jerusalem every four years illustrates the same richness, multiplied several times over. Again I make no assumptions about the quality, historical significance, or spiritual import of this development, other than to say that in its quantity and scope, it is very impressive and quite unexpected. Without being irreverent toward the past or arrogant toward the future, it is fair to celebrate the fact that we have come a long way. Yet we must examine academic-based Judaic studies in terms of its contribution to the larger quotient of Jewish literacy.

Like the commentaries and supercommentaries of traditional Jewish *lernin,* the Judaic studies that entered into the North American academy some two decades ago carried with it traces of the earlier stages of *Wissenschaft des Judentums.* While aspiring to define the role of Judaism in the larger setting of world history, social patterns, political forces, and cultural influences, it never fully eschewed searching in the past for some normative essence, an abiding character, for the meaning if not the theology of Judaism. Emerging in the 1960s after Jewry had given up hope of such a revival of high culture, Jewish studies benefited from the promotion of ethnic studies while ardently and correctly trying to differentiate itself from them. The study of Judaism, if not of Jews, made an unspectacular exodus from the divinity schools, but rarely got beyond departments of religion.

The marketplace of ideas is just that; it is by no means immune to fads and fashions. The receptivity to Jewish scholarship in the contemporary academy may not prove to be enduring, notwithstanding the endowed chairs, centers, and departments, whose number is still on the increase, and successes at fudging the import of class enrollment statistics. Jewish futurologists should definitely start worrying. Universities have ways of reallocating resources. The dramatic and rapid growth, the success with which we have "classicized" modern Jewish scholarship, should not make us overly confident. What will ensure the viability of Judaic studies, as well as its relevance to the educational experience of all students, is its integration within the major disciplines of the humanities and social sciences. Moreover, given the war between those trying to restore the preeminence of Western civilization, as expressed in the renewal of core curricula, and those trying to impose mandatory "Third World Studies," Judaic studies is intellectually and organizationally at great risk.

With all the show of intellectual force of Judaic studies on campuses in recent years, it is still possible, as it was in the days of Columbia University's famous Western civilization curriculum, to construct a multisemester course with woefully little attention to Jews or Judaism after the biblical period. Not to mention that one can still study patristic literature at Christian seminaries without resort to rabbinics; the classical world at universities without looking at ancient Israel; medieval Spain, early modern Poland, modern Germany, France, England, Russia, and certainly America, without looking at the Jews. Shockingly enough, even in Israel the study of history and that of Jewish history are less than fully integrated. Moreover, if not for our vigilance, even greater academic respectability would be given those historians who promote the study of the Holocaust without the Jews. With the well-trained and respected representatives of Jewish scholarship positioned on American campuses, now is the time to be concerned with the future memories of Judaism—with the role to be ascribed 30 years from now to Jews as shapers of Western civilization.

The shift in the practice of Jewish scholarship from rabbis who no longer have either the expert knowledge or the leisure to devote themselves to Jewish studies on a level commensurate with modern requirements, to professional scholars, largely university- rather than seminary-trained, raises the question of the extent to which this new practitioner will contribute to the increased tempo and vitality of Jewish communal life. The contribution of academic Judaic studies to Jewish communal life 30 years from now will be determined, in part, by the extent to which rabbis concern themselves with these new bodies of knowledge and scholars make themselves available to Jewish communal life. The contribution of academic Jewish studies to Jewish literacy will be measured by a new generation of sophisticated Jews who have greater expectations of the public rhetoric of Jewish communal life and who are willing to appropriate more complex images of the Jewish past to serve the communal needs of the present. To what extent will Jewish communal leaders—lay and professional—become important consumers of Jewish scholarship and Jewish culture? To what extent will scholars deem it honorable to be popularizers, and to which journal pages and lecture tours will they have access?

It is precisely the indicators of literacy that make the larger picture so incomprehensible, so vexing, and ultimately so bleak. For it is not clear whether the developments that I have described point to larger trends with the potential for some sort of ripple effect, or whether both *lernin* and scholarship represent the activities of elites, confined and confining in their influence. Again using the recent past as a standard, are we becoming more or less Jewishly literate?

Some two decades ago, in one of the periodic efforts of the organized Jewish community to foster Jewish revitalization, a high-level commission was convened to study the future of Jewish identity. Abraham Joshua Heschel attended the opening meeting of 50 distinguished leaders. At a critical moment, Heschel made an appeal resonating with tones of Yochanan ben Zakkai and Bontsche Schweig: "It would be a great accomplishment for this commission to establish a new and innovative institution in which teachers for Jewish schools could be trained." The commissioners were shocked. An impressive group of leaders had come together to plan the spending of a hundred million dollars on Jewish education and culture and the great visionary, Abraham Joshua Heschel, has nothing more to propose than the training of teachers! Though American Jews are spending literally billions of dollars on Jewish education and identity, it is questionable whether three decades from now there will be a sufficient number of teachers of Jewish studies in any Hebrew school, synagogue, or community or day school. We want our children to be at home in multiple cultures, yet we do so woefully little to enable them to develop cognitive bridges. I shudder at the thought of this lost potential as I commiserate with the boredom of my children. Perhaps, as Heschel tried to do, we should surrender grandiosity and focus our discussion of the Jewish future on Hebrew school teachers and their training.

One small town in Poland shortly before World War II had three Yiddish and two Hebrew dailies as well as several weekly journals affiliated with the different Jewish political parties. Its total Jewish population at no time exceeded 900. Contemporary Jewish communities with close to three million Jews cannot rival that. The papers Jews read seriously might be the *New York Times* and *Ma'ariv,* but there are issues pertaining to Jewish literacy that are not to be found in either source. To be sure, most Jewish newspapers are not Jewish, nor are they newspapers—they are little more than an embarrassment. A retired editor of a Jewish newspaper in Boston, the Athens of America, recently described a typical workday: The pictures from federation dinners and other Jewish celebrations of ephemeral accomplishments—rather than Jewish news and thought pieces—that he was under various sorts of pressure to publish were piled so high on his desk that he had to stand in order to see his associate at the next desk. This may foster Jewish activity but not necessarily Jewish literacy.

The creative and entrepreneurial involvement of Jews in the media and the arts is almost of the magnitude that our enemies assume. This is one of the great success stories of postemancipation Jewry. Contrary to what our enemies think, Jews concerned with fairness or free markets have not necessarily learned to "control" those media for Jewish interests. We cannot discuss here the multiple and at times conflicting responsibilities of Jews in the media who must both inform the public and profit their shareholders. What is clear is that Jews have not chosen to utilize those powerful instruments of modernity to promote Jewish knowledge and values. For example, Al Jolson's *Jazz Singer* was not only a milestone in the history of the cinema but an emblem of Jewish involvement. The dissimulating jazz singer returns to the synagogue at the last moment, but ultimately fulfills his ambition and is rewarded for bringing his "Mammy," and even less admissible mammies, to Broadway.

The failed efforts of several Jewish federations, organizations, and individual entrepreneurs to establish Jewish cable television programs are by now well known. With a few exceptions such as *Heritage: Civilization and the Jews,* which reportedly reached some 52 million viewers, we do not have the quantity or quality of films and videos that can serve our educational and documentary needs. Important efforts in Jewish theater, music, and the arts require the involvement of Jews as patrons, consumers, and critics. These endeavors are receiving little communal support. Neither do they benefit from serious discussions of aesthetic and educational standards. Opportunities for stimulating Jewish knowledge and literacy are being squandered.

In *Humanities in America: A Report to the President, the Congress, and the American People,* Lynn V. Cheney, Chairman of the National Endowment for the Humanities, reminds us of the paradoxical situation of the humanities in contemporary America: All indicators point to declining interest and enrollment in the humanities in formal education, including at the universities. Yet public participation in cultural events—from attendance at museum exhibitions to viewing of Shakespeare productions on public television—has exceeded all expectations. In fact, in recent years Americans have spent more money on these leisure-time activities than on sports events.

These successes of the humanities in filling private time and public spaces with the arts have significant implications for thinking about the future of Jewish literacy. Indeed, the one Jewish institution that may rival budgetary commitments to the renaissance of Jewish swimming pools and athletic facilities is the Jewish museum. It will soon be the civic pride of every Jewish community, perhaps every synagogue, to have a museum of sacred artifacts, of local Jewish history or Jewish art. This development is somewhat independent of the proliferation of Holocaust museums and commemorative exhibitions, a phenomenon that raises other issues. Will the educational potential of these very expensive media be realized? How do we, the descendants of those souls standing at Sinai who were warned against graven images, encounter the *object?* Will Jewish museums continue the universally significant idol-smashing efforts of Abraham, fostering a Jewish visuality that penetrates the surfaces and seeks the numinous dimension of objects, as it calls to mind those who made, used, and loved *kley kodesh,* the utensils of holiness? Will the exhibits bind us to the past and therefore bind us to each other? Or will Jewish museums excel in cabinetry and display technique, training individual-universal eyes of spectators upon impermeable surfaces, expressing aesthetic, demonstrative, even apologetic ideals to Jews and to whoever else might wander into these vaults of ethnic curios? Concerns for the future of Jewish literacy must focus on uncertainties of method and limits of media as well as content. As the report of the National Endowment for the Humanities reminds us, a different type of learning results from watching film or drama than from poring over a text. Successes in one area need not ensure successes in the other.

We can no longer avoid defining what it is that we mean by Jewish literacy. Perhaps the controversy over E. D. Hirsch Jr.'s *Cultural Literacy: What Every American Needs to Know* can be instructive here. If it has not appeared already, I am sure there soon will be a book called *Jewish Cultural Literacy: What Every Jew Needs to Know.* It will include the measurements (metric) of Noah's ark and suppositions as to whether its lighting system was energy-efficient; Haninah ben Dosah's weekly diet and whether it was nutritionally balanced; the *dagesh kal* in its essence and manifestation; what Balaam's ass really said to Franz Rosenzweig on that famous Sabbath, and whether it addressed him in *hochdeutsch,* and the like. I tend to agree with Hirsch that, more than surface meanings of words, we must understand a cultural context and share background information. The concept of cultural literacy is particularly apt if we are to determine the salience of Jewish modes of knowledge by standards of what strengthens our communities and *klal Yisrael:* the emphasis upon knowledge that socializes and integrates rather than knowledge of seemingly antiquarian or technical value.

Yet learning lists without knowing the interrelationship between ideas turns knowledge into trivia. We need both history and social studies. A culturally literate Jew must know not only who Napoleon was, and who he was to the Jews, he or she must understand why Napoleon, who smashed the ghetto gates in one place, was received by Jews in another with heckles of ''napol tipol Napoleon'' (down with Napoleon.) We must be mindful of Judaism's internal dialectics.

In the hope that Joseph II's 1782 Edict of Tolerance would benefit Jews, Naftali Wessely, one of the early advocates of Jewish Enlightenment and educational reform, asked what knowledge Jews would require to qualify fully as "*adam*" (ordinary people). Curricula that pander to fashionable universals, separating between *Torat Ha-adam* and *Torat Ha-Elohim*, between ethics and piety, as Wessely attempted, invite reaction and prove to be superficial. The future of Jewish literacy must be oriented to *shamor* as well as to *zachor*, to action as well as to contemplation. The presentation of *Halakhah* has always been a dialectic between terse, action-oriented codes and expansive legal discourses and commentaries presenting both the legislative history and the rationales of particular observances. Culturally literate Jews must have access to both types of knowledge. The competition between the *baki*, the one who has breathtaking, comprehensive knowledge of Torah, and the *ma'amik*, the one who analyzes texts to their depth, has never been finally decided. Again, we need both. Memory is an important cognitive skill, and there is some use for those who retain lists of facts. But the rabbis were prepared to render the skills of the *tannah*—the memorizer and the reciter of rabbinic texts—obsolete, when they audaciously applied available transcription technologies to the "oral Torah." Latter-day memory palaces will not serve the most profound interests of Jewish literacy. Though modern technologies of retrieval should not be ignored, knowledge is more than access to information. The computer can help us learn facts; the video can help us visualize connective ideas. But Jewish literacy entails more than going through the Torah; its most important standard, to recall one of Heschel's favorite quips, is how much Torah goes through you.

Although recent research suggests that we exaggerate the levels of literacy among our East European ancestors, there seems to have been a humanizing, integrative, and enlightening context for knowledge, which Jews not only went through in their ongoing *lernin*, but which went through them in their profound and purposeful living, whether or not they could read and write Hebrew, Yiddish, or the language of the land. The prayers coupled with basic Torah study provided a broad range of shared associations that affected the very modes of thinking of Jews as diverse as the *Tehilim Yid* (the enthusiastic reciter of the Psalms), to the infamous *apikoyres*, defiantly demythologizing Jewish life. Who among those active in contemporary Jewish communal life—rabbis, cantors, teachers, professional and lay leaders, fundraisers, politicos, Hadassah members, and Jewish war veterans—are carriers of such bodies of knowledge? Can we envision a time when one might find in the firmly grasped attaché cases of the New Class, nestled between spreadsheets and computer disks, a *sefer* (Jewish book)? What that *sefer* should be and how it might be studied is the concern of those who try to imagine an exciting Jewish future.

The rabbi of a distinguished community I once visited reflected rather whimsically: "Things are not like what they used to be. You can't hit 'em over the head with a *pasuk* [biblical verse], you can't kill 'em with a *midrash* [rabbinic comment]." That comment indicates a loss of cultural responsiveness to sacred words and a decline of personal authority bemoaned by many. Is the status of Jewish sources in communal life an unlikely sign that our generation has not been endowed with gifted preachers, or does it point to an ironic development in our broadmindedness and tolerance—to borrow from Allan Bloom, the closing of the American Jewish mind?

As we have thought about a phenomenology of Jewish visual experience, so must we think of the "presence of the word" in a tradition that preceded and, we hope, will supersede many forms of literacy. Judaism is a classical culture still committed to the spoken word. That word is more than a unit of communication, or, in its ethical sense, a unit of obligation. The representation of the spoken word in our culture, comfortable with electronic ciphers, must be more than a new gimmick. The visual is a solitary experience. The presence of the spoken word through oral-aural communication enables one to enter into the life and consciousness of others and thereby into his or her own life. It relates the sense of one's presence to one's self, to other people and to one's sense of God's presence. However modern media might enhance communication and memory, however well we may adjust to the succession of difficult and often traumatic reorientations of the human psyche that accompany the adaptation of those media, when we lose the world of voice and sound, we lose religion. With it we lose love, decency, and all good things.

Individuals need no longer journey to the four corners of the earth to encounter one another. The past has never been as present, as a result of the accumulation and storage of historical and other knowledge to which we have instantaneous access. We have constant awareness of urgent problems around the world. But we avert our eyes from the street people and deflect our attention from the dangers of nuclear war. The weakness is in the human being, who can take in only a limited amount of stimuli. The presence of the Jewish word—the representation of that *pasuk* and that midrash—must strengthen us, the weak link.

One need not be a prophet to predict that Jewish words could be present in Jewish homes within a decade. A casual reader of electronics catalogues will bear witness to an imminent future in which, on a few disks resting on the family computer, we might have access to the entire content of the Judaic Reading Room of the National and Hebrew University Library in Jerusalem or the Hebrew College in Boston, or to Harvard's Widener Library and the Library of Congress. Yet what might be available 30 years from now to equip the Tents of Shem, from the Japanese–Satmar collaborations in the production and marketing of technological wizardry, is beyond the imaginative powers of most bearers of visions or statistics.

The computer and the video will never replace the compassionate teacher, the guide, the role model. The educational film will not substitute for the presence of the Word. The multilevel textuality and the intergenerational dynamics depicted on one *blatt* of *Gemarah* might, better than the blinking lights of the computer screen, enhance our decision-making capacities by training us how to keep variegated and complex factors in our fields of vision and how to balance variables. For some Jews admitting the beauties of the larger world into the Tents of Shem will be more substantial than kosher pizza, more fluid than pareve milk, and more subtle than Hasidic rock music. For those Jews there is much to be done to face the challenges of the future. And if we cannot plan strategy, let us at least learn to recognize opportunity.

A Response

Rela Geffen Monson

As I understand them, these are the main points of Levine's essay: 1. There is a good deal of Jewish literacy in America today bifurcated into trends toward yeshiva *lernin* and *Wissenschaft*. 2. Knowledge has shifted from rabbis to professional scholars (I would argue that there was always a class of rabbis who were the scholars and that a majority of Jewish studies professors—at least in classical rabbinics—have rabbinical degrees). 3. We know little about lay leaders as consumers of Jewish culture. 4. Jewish mass culture as represented by newspapers is a weak link. 5. The media are underused by a group that contains many experts in the media—but, at the same time, the presence of a live teacher and that teacher's relationship to the student are essential to conveying Jewish learning. 6. Museums celebrate dead civilizations and do not facilitate live culture. 7. We don't have adequate definitions of Jewish literacy anyway, but surely literacy implies both action and contemplation, comprehensive and in-depth knowledge. An ongoing thirst for knowledge would be such that the "ideal" lay person would have a *sefer* hidden in his/her attache case. 8. Finally, we should not romanticize the past and overgeneralize about the level of learning, particularly in Eastern Europe.

A few comments are in order. First, although learning is qualitatively different for the vast majority of Diaspora Jews today than for those of yesterday, it is clearly a more available and positive experience for women than it has ever been in the past. Some men may know more and some less than in previous generations, but just about all of the women with any formal learning know more than their ancestors did.

Second, *Wissenschaft* affects the students as well as the professors. Levine focuses on the academics rather than on their tens of thousands of students and where they go after their studies. The upgrading of continuing education for those off the university campus is a crucial need for the near and distant future.

Third, we should not underestimate the contribution to literacy of the federation young leadership programs around the country. They "turn on" the best and brightest—but who will take over from where the federations stop? They are not in the Jewish education business, so unless all those who consider themselves Jewish educators work with them, there will be no payoff in the long term for this pioneering enterprise. In one community a federation director told me that he offered the lists of those in young leadership to the synagogues, as well as money to subsidize classes for them, and was turned down. This is one piece of the puzzle, but it needs other pieces fitted to it. We should not always try to reinvent the wheel but rather to rearrange the existing pieces in such a way that we can see what we really need to focus on.

Fourth, moving from adult to children's education, specifically with regard to the issue of teacher training, we can learn from the Orthodox. If teachers of children and young adults lack the proper social and economic status in the community, then we will not be able to recruit qualified people unless they are idealists or masochists. It must be considered valuable and honorable work to train the next generation. Engaging in *chinukh* (Jewish education), whether in formal or informal settings, should be considered a desirable occupation for any Jewish boy or girl.

Fifth, Levine is correct in pointing to the currently untapped potential of the Jewish newspaper. However, he leaves out the host of excellent periodicals available to the American Jewish community—whether (forgetting politics for the moment) it is *Commentary* or *Tikkun, Reconstructionist* or *Hadassah Magazine, Moment* or *Sh'ma, Present Tense* or *Conservative Judaism* or *Tradition.* The issue is not their existence but their dissemination to the various publics out in the Jewish heartland (which might be Nassau County or Elkins Park, Des Moines or Dallas).

Sixth, Levine has left Israel out of the equation altogether. I suggest that this is not possible or desirable. Granted that Jewish literacy is not and should not be equated with living vicarious Jewish identities through Israel; still, Israel surely has a great role to play as a generator of modern Jewish culture, whether it be in literature, music, or the arts. Moreover, trips to Israel and familiar links lead to the desire to study, which then must be nurtured.

What is Jewish literacy anyway? To ask the question properly one must further specify the terms. Are we referring to children or adults, to culture or religious ritual, to rote or in-depth learning? What follows is one attempt to define what we might mean by, and through what vehicles we might achieve, Jewish literacy at two levels—that of minimum competencies, and that of intensive knowledge at various ages or life-cycle states. A list of minimum competencies might include:

1. Be able to say Kaddish and Shema
2. Be able to follow a service in the movement of one's choice
3. Be able to participate in home rituals of Shabbat, Chanukah, Pesach
4. Be able to read Hebrew phonetically
5. Be able to participate in life-cycle rituals
6. Know basic benedictions
7. Read popular articles about Judaism or the Jews regularly
8. Know the basic timeline of Jewish history

9. Be able to name great Jewish books
10. Be interested in acquiring Jewish books and ritual objects for one's home.

More intensive knowledge competencies might include:

1. Be able to study classical Jewish texts
2. Be able to participate in and/or lead a service
3. Be able to follow a service in any country
4. Understand and be able to transmit a knowledge of Jewish history
5. Be able to read and understand a Hebrew text with a dictionary
6. Be able to lead a Passover Seder, a home Shabbat or Chanukah service
7. Set aside regular periods for study
8. Create and use a home library of Judaica

The following chart details the possible means of achieving various levels of competence:

	Minimum	*Intensive*
Child	Supplementary school, summer camp	Day school, committed home
Adolescent	Youth movement, trip to Israel	Day school, youth group, home, trip to Israel
Young Adult	Jewish studies course, Hillel services, arts, Jewish periodicals	Jewish studies major, work in Jewish community, year in Israel, role model
Adult	Leadership training courses, sermons a few times a year, lectures, Jewish news-papers, "Jewish" news in secular media, Home rituals, synagogue and/or organiza-tional membership	Overnight conferences, *havurah* membership, regular synagogue goer, home rituals, repeat trips to Israel, build home library, attend classes regularly

Of course our ideal should be to nurture and then foster as many maximally competent or literate Jews as possible. But it is not wrong to anticipate levels of competence and it is surely abdicating our responsibility as planners and implementers of plans not to try to specify the dimensions of the task we are urging ourselves and others to undertake.

As is the habit of the sociologist, I close with a typology based on a fourfold table. The dimensions on the table, following Levine's idea, specify knowledge and experience as primary dimensions of Jewish literacy. This table yields four types. The Jewish adult with knowledge and experience of Judaism is a prepared and perhaps ideal citizen of the modern Jewish Diaspora world. The one with

		Knowledge	
		Yes	No
		+ + Prepared citizen (Type 1)	+ − Ritualist (Type 2)
		− + Dispassionate intellectual (Type 3)	− − Am ha'aretz (Type 4)

Experience — Yes / No (row labels)

experience but little knowledge is personified by the often-encountered *ba'al te-shuvah*, who has become a ritualist practicing *am ha'aretz frumkite*. The one with knowledge but little experience is the cerebral Jew who observes the others with the cynicism that dispassionate objectivity and analysis often bring (perhaps he is a modern *apikoros*). Finally, the one without knowledge or experience is the am ha'aretz. As in the case of the four children in the Haggadah, different approaches are necessary to reach out to these four types, but that is the subject of another essay.

Section III

Israel and World Jewry

6

Are American and Israeli Jews Drifting Apart?

Steven M. Cohen

Are American and Israeli Jews drifting apart? Unfortunately, the answer is neither obvious nor straightforward. Some evidence suggests that they are more separate than before, some that they are not; other considerations suggest that serious differences have been in the making for a long time and are only now beginning to be felt.

According to one line of reasoning, since the founding of the State of Israel there has never been a time with as many overt signs of strain between American and Israeli Jewries. Since 1977, a date not coincidentally tied to the coming to power of a right-wing Israeli government, several incidents and developments have generated considerable discomfort toward Israel among some American Jews. They include:

1) The hard-line foreign and security policies of the Begin government and its successor, especially with regard to Jewish settlements on the West Bank.

2) The Israeli instigation of the war in Lebanon, which is the only war Israel has fought that failed to provoke a marked increase in philanthropic support for the United Jewish Appeal and Israel Bonds.

3) The election to the Knesset of Meir Kahane, who until his murder in New York in 1990 represented racist and anti-democratic tendencies distasteful, if not abhorrent, to most American Jews.

4) The numerous religious-secular conflicts, sometimes graphically violent, over such matters as Sabbath observance or archaeological exploration, and the frequent legislative maneuvers to strengthen Orthodox rabbinic control of matters of personal status.

5) The tough nature of Israeli military responses—officially sanctioned or otherwise—to the Intifada.

Accompanying all these developments are vituperative and passionate internal Israeli conflicts. These conflicts themselves may have diminished Israel's standing in the eyes of many American Jews.

The American Jewish Committee-sponsored surveys of American Jews I have conducted almost every year since 1981 have repeatedly measured levels of psychic support and active involvement with Israel. They demonstrate that those most disturbed by the rightward political and religious trends in Israel share certain characteristics. They are politically liberal, religiously less traditional, more remote from organized Jewish life, and highly educated.[1]

The available quantitative evidence on Jewish attitudes, however, does not point to any broad trend of alienation (or intensification). In each survey we find that about a third of American Jews are relatively indifferent or even hostile to Israel; about a third claim to feel a strong commitment to Israel; and another third is indeed even more passionately involved with Israel. Among the latter we count the third of American Jews who have been to Israel, who would want their children to spend a year living there, who have relatives or friends in Israel, and who have some minimal knowledge of Israeli society. To be sure, American Jews' ignorance of Israeli affairs is truly startling, even to supposedly "expert" observers such as myself. I was shocked to find that only a third of my nationwide sample of American Jews knew that non-Orthodox rabbis could not officially marry Israelis, and only a third knew that Arab and Israeli schoolchildren generally attend different schools.

One objection to the conclusion that the proportion of American Jews at each level of involvement has remained fairly constant focuses on the fall-off in tourism to Israel in 1988 and the years following. This drop did not reflect political or moral opposition to Israeli policy. It rather pointed to the keen sensitivity of American Jewish travelers to images of terrorism and violence when contemplating international travel. Nor should the protestations of well-known American Jewish public figures be seen as proof of a decline in American Jewish attachment to Israel. Whether these figures represent a large fraction of the American Jewish public is a debatable point. Furthermore, my surveys of the larger public demonstrate only weak to insignificant correlations between caring for Israel and support for Israeli government policy. In other words, criticism of Israeli policies is simply not empirically associated with psychological distance from the Jewish state. In fact, while just under half of those surveyed admit to being disturbed by some Israeli government policies, those who do are more likely to claim strong psychic attachment to Israel than to be apathetic to Israel. Moreover, the vast majority of respondents agreed that "Even when I disagree with the actions of Israel's government, that doesn't change how close I feel toward Israel."

The survey data do point to one significant attitudinal change during periods of heightened hostilities, such as the Lebanon war or the Intifada. In both 1982 and 1988, the surveys uncovered greater anxiety about non-Jewish attitudes toward Israel (and toward Jews by extension). More Jews than in other surveys (1981, 1983, 1984, and 1986) were worried that Gentiles were anti-Israel and anti-Semitic. Though generally supportive of Jews' right to criticize Israel, the minority that demurred from this position jumped between September 1983 and April 1988. Notably, these months followed significant Arab-Israeli violence and public criticism of Israel by Jews and non-Jews alike. To reiterate, the surveys suggest far more stability than decline in measures of American Jewish attachment, involvement, and commitment to Israel during the 1980s.

As constant as American Jews' attitudes appear to be from the survey data, however, such data can often obscure important changes occurring beneath the rhetorical surface. To a certain extent, replies to questions about feelings toward Israel reflect the respondents' sense of what they are expected to say. Not surprisingly, Americans exercise far more regularly and eat more nutritiously on social surveys than they do in real life. Survey answers indicate something, but assuming a one-to-one correspondence between responses and genuine sentiments may not always be prudent. In my 1986 national survey of American Jews, 89 percent of the respondents agreed that "I get just as upset by terrorist attacks upon non-Jews as I do when terrorists attack Jews,"and only 8 percent disagreed. On the basis of this evidence, I am not ready to claim that Jews were in fact equally disturbed by the Munich massacre as they were by the car-bombing of the U.S. Marines in Lebanon. I would be ready to take these findings as evidence of American Jews' public commitment to universalism, and their resistance to publicly expressing overt and blatant particularism, even on a confidential survey that promises anonymity.

Similarly, the apparent stability in commitment to Israel as measured by a decade of survey data may mask some distancing occurring beneath the surface. We may need to look at other sorts of evidence before concluding that positive American Jewish feelings to Israel have remained largely unaffected by Israeli-Arab clashes, the rise of right-wing extremism, religious-secular clashes, and all the rest.

One place to look is at pro-Israel philanthropy, a sphere of American Jewish activity that is both significant in its own right and symptomatic of a larger dynamic. Here several potentially meaningful trends bear noting. First, for over a decade, total contributions to the UJA-Federation local campaigns have been nearly flat in aggregate dollar terms; this means that, adjusting for inflation, total campaign contributions have declined since the mid-1970s. The second noteworthy trend derives from the fact that every local fund-raising campaign decides how much of the moneys it collects will be handed over to the United Jewish Appeal for overseas charities (where Israel's needs play a prominent symbolic role) and how much will remain in the community for local and national allocation. For several years, the overseas proportion has been drifting downward, a tendency all the more notable since change in such matters normally assumes a glacial pace. Given that federation allocation patterns move very slowly, even a small dip over the last few years in the proportions devoted to Israel (and other overseas needs) may well indicate an even more substantial cooling of ardor for Israel on the part of philanthropic decision makers. The positive response to the surge in Russian aliyah embodied in Operation Exodus does not necessarily imply a change in that trend.

In a related area, directors of community relations councils (CRCs) report a lack of enthusiasm and of qualified lay leadership willing to work in their sphere of activity. Prior to 1967, the CRCs were hotbeds of Jewish liberalism. After 1967, for less than a decade the causes of Israeli security and freedom for Soviet Jews came to dominate their agendas. Since the mid-1970s, if the scattered reports of a few informed observers can be trusted, Israel no longer excites the passions of the top (or even middle) rung of Jewish volunteer leadership in the environs of local Jewish federation campaigns.

Another observation worrisome to those interested in strong ties between Israel and Diaspora Jewry is based on even softer, less tangible impressions. Some communal professionals have observed that their prominent lay leaders have chosen to "dis-attend" to Israel-related matters. Dis-attention, as some social scientists use the term, refers to the process whereby people ignore some issues, object, or contradiction that causes them discomfort, rather than deciding to deal with the troublesome matter directly. While prepared to defend Israel's honor against what they regard as unfair criticism, these lay leaders may be choosing to invest their energies in areas where they find less conflict, less ambivalence, and less complexity.

In short, the available evidence, be it quantitative or impressionistic, provides contradictory answers to the question of whether American and Israeli Jews have been drifting apart. But even if they have been, the ostensibly disturbing events listed at the outset may not deserve all the credit (or blame) for the drift. After the supercharged pro-Israel atmosphere of the period from 1967 to 1976, American Jews have been unable to replicate the enthusiasm that we now understand as peculiar to the very unusual decade that began with the Six-Day War.

From Romanticism to Realism

The cause of Israel took American Jewry by storm in 1967. Prior to the Six-Day War, Israel ranked well below other issues on the American Jewish communal agenda. Before 1967, intellectuals writing about their Jewishness hardly mentioned Israel—or, for that matter, the Holocaust. It is clear in retrospect that the dramatic televised events surrounding the Six-Day War came at a time when American Jews were primed to enter a period of ethnic assertiveness. The old liberal coalition was splintering; blacks had challenged the melting-pot conception and given ethnicity a good name; and a third generation of Jews (grandchildren of East European immigrants), more secure in their American-ness and anxious to preserve their families' Jewishness, replaced the second generation as the demographic and political center of gravity within the Jewish community. As a result of the 1967 and 1973 wars, pro-Israel sentiment and activity among American Jews shot upward. The UJA and Israel Bonds experienced significant increases in contributions, reaching levels in the year or two after the wars that were dramatically above those of the years just prior to them. On another plane, American aliyah hit its historic climax in the years between the wars (1968–1972). Jewish travel to Israel also climbed dramatically. In 1970 only about 15 percent of American Jews had been to Israel; by the early 1980s, over a third had been there at least once, and about a sixth had visited twice or more.

As concerns shifted from integrating into America to Jewish survival, Israel became the survivalist cause par excellence (along with memorializing the Holocaust and rescuing Soviet Jewry). Israel and related themes came to dominate philanthropic campaigns, community relations work, electoral activity, and political lobbying, at times to the exclusion of all other matters.

Equally significant was the superinflated image most American Jews held of Israelis. Israelis were heroic, industrious, family-oriented, and peace-loving. In short, they were romanticized and idealized, seen as a better version of American Jews.

Blind romance and unfounded idealization can last only so long. As familiarity with Israel grew, as travel increased, as Jewish leaders developed their relationships with counterpart Israeli officials, and as the internal conflicts among Israelis became more visible, a more realistic and down-to-earth image of Israelis took hold. The emergence of divisions between hawks and doves, religious and secular, Sephardi and Ashkenazi, and Arab and Jew within Israel all served to disabuse American Jews of an ill-informed, primitive, one-dimensional and overly flattering image of Israelis. As the years passed, as more American Jews became increasingly familiar with Israel, the romanticized images began to fade. In this context, it is not surprising to learn that those who had been to Israel became more attached to Israel Jewishly and politically, but less enamored of Israelis personally.

Moreover, the American Jewry that was ready to fall in love with Israel in the late 1960s had become somewhat jaded by the late 1970s. The remarkable events of that first decade had served to reinforce the image of Israeli heroes withstanding the onslaught of the Arab villains. Each year brought another dramatic event that further deepened the image of a valiant Israel under siege: the Six-Day War (1967); the first postwar fatalities of Arab terrorism (1968); the War of Attrition with Egypt (1969–1971); the Munich Massacre (1972); the Yom Kippur War (1973); the Rabat Conference in which the Arab world united behind the PLO (1974); the UN's "Zionism is Racism" resolution (1975); and the Entebbe hijacking and rescue (1976). In contrast, the events since 1976 (with the possible exception of the Baghdad nuclear reactor raid) have sent forth far more ambiguous messages, certainly to non-Jewish Americans and very likely to American Jews as well.

The recent distancing from Israel (to whatever extent it exists) may simply derive from the end of an era of romantic idealism. American Jews could not be expected to sustain permanently an unrealistic romance with Israel. At some point, the glamour had to wear off, the warts begin to appear. With such a perspective, the ostensibly disturbing developments of the last ten years, along with the tension between some American Jews and some Israelis arising from specific issues and disagreements, can be seen as but the evidence of a changing relationship that was bound to become more complicated, ambiguous, and mature, and perhaps more distant as well.

Such a conclusion would, however, underestimate the significance of a series of disturbing events. Although their immediate adverse impact on the pro-Israel sentiments of the American Jewish rank and file may not have been severe, they do bear a deeper import. Even if they have not (yet?) provoked serious and widespread alienation of American Jews from Israel, they may indicate some deeper trends in Israeli society that bear watching. In particular, the troublesome incidents of the 1980s may portend the emergence of a permanently ''illiberal'' Israel (at a time when American Jews show no signs of retreating from their identity as political and cultural liberals). Perhaps even more ominously, the 1980s may well symbolize a widening gulf between the Judaisms of American and Israeli Jews. The 1990s so far have continued that trend. In other words, Israelis may be acting in ways objectionable to many American Jews not only because of divergences in political values, but because of more fundamental differences over what it means to be Jewish. And it is in these trends, on the deeper level of Judaic beliefs, symbols, and values, that we may find reason to believe that American Jewry and Israeli Jewry really are drifting apart.

Two Judaisms in Two Countries

Since their recent forebears left the quasi-traditional communities of Eastern Europe, North Africa, and the Middle East, the Jewries of America and Israel have been compelled to interact with their contemporary environments and with their historical cultural traditions to construct Judaisms appropriate to their needs. The American and Israeli Judaic constructions certainly resemble one another, but they are far from identical.[2]

To be sure, there are many points of overlap between the two communities' understanding of Judaism. Jews in both countries observe many of the same holidays, rituals, and ceremonies; they respond (albeit sometimes differently) to many of the same symbols; they retell many of the same myths; and they share some sense of common origins and common destiny. All of this is not surprising since Israeli and American Jews draw upon a common past, a common religion, and a common civilization.

Fully recognizing these and related commonalities, it is also fair to say that in the reconstruction of Judaism under the impact of highly discrepant contemporary conditions, Israelis and Americans have arrived at varying, even diverging conclusions. This is not merely a matter of saying that more Israelis are Orthodox or more observant (although this is part of the story). Rather, the Judaic differences are so profound and thorough as to separate *dati* Israelis from Orthodox Americans, as well as *chiloni* Israelis from secular or nondenominational Americans. The Judaic gaps between Israel and the United States are not solely or even mostly a function of a religiosity gap. Some differences are truly enormous. Sometimes one community sees as genuinely Jewish that which the other sees as totally irrelevant or even antithetical to Judaism. A few examples of the most glaring differences will suffice to illustrate this point.

In a 1988 *Los Angeles Times* survey, a national sample of American Jews was asked, "As a Jew, which of the following qualities do you consider most important to your Jewish identity: a commitment to social equality, or religious observance, or support for Israel, or what?"[3] Half answered "social equality." The rest were equally divided between the other three options. As one might expect, denominational traditionalism was closely associated with the liberal response. The proportions choosing "equality" amounted to only 18 percent for the Orthodox, but 44 percent for the Conservative respondents, 65 percent for the Reform respondents, and 63 percent for the nondenominational. "Social equality," the progressive, moral, and universalist response, dominated the more traditional and particularist answers of "religious observance" or "supporting Israel."

One cannot imagine that most Israelis, even political leftists, would identify the most important element in their Judaism with such a universalist, politically progressive principle as "social equality." The more traditional Israelis would undoubtedly select "religious observance" as the basis for their Judaism, seeing observance as fundamental and preliminary to other aspects of Jewish life; most of the secular would have little trouble seeing the Israeli state or society as central to their Judaism. Indeed, the Israeli component is so strong that some Israelis allege that "Diaspora Jewish life" is an oxymoron, or at least tenuous and inauthentic. Over two-thirds of our national sample survey of Israeli Jews in 1986 claimed that "it is almost impossible for me to think of what it means to be a Jew without thinking about *Medinat Yisrael* (the State of Israel)." Secular Israelis, even as they reject the legitimacy of the Orthodox rabbinate's authority over certain parts of their own lives, nevertheless recognize *Halakhah* as interpreted by Orthodox rabbis as the authoritative definition of Judaism.

Not only are American Jews politically liberal while Israelis are not, American Jews remain well to the left of the national political center in several key areas, regarding liberalism as central to their Judaism. American Jewish liberalism consists of a package of values: support for social welfare programs, sympathy for minorities, commitment to civil rights, support for civil liberties, and extreme opposition to lowering church-state barriers. Not only do Israelis generally take the opposite points of view on many if not all of these issues; they regard their advocacy as having little bearing on what constitutes a "good Jew." The following observation by Michael Walzer seems perfectly natural, almost innocuous, in the American context, but would seem bizarre, naive, and/or heretical to many Israelis:

> Our ethos is leftist: because we remember that we were slaves in Egypt, because we remember the ghetto, the years of persecution, the pariah years. . . . We have learned, many of us, to part with our money in the name of Justice. . . . It is a simple fact of our experience that . . . radical ideas come naturally.[4]

While the "leftist ethos" may be the essence of Judaism to many American Jews, for many Israelis—especially the more traditional—the same ethos actually has anti-Judaic connotations. In Israel leftist universalism has been associated with movements and parties that advocate curtailing the power of the rabbinate and, more generally, the role of Judaism in the public sphere. But more to the point, not only are Israeli leftists anticlerical, some of them even argue that Judaism by its very nature is antithetical to their progressive, universalist principles. (A few old-line secularists, such as those in the Mapam party, would still argue—to a very skeptical and small Israeli audience—that Judaism and leftist politics are harmonious with one another.)

Not only is a universalist struggle for social equality seen by many American Jews as central to Judaism, but so too have they come to provide universalist connotations regularly to their major rituals, ceremonies, and holidays. Thus, to take some typical examples, Passover is the holiday of liberation for all people, not just Jews; Tishah B'Av is a memorial to utter destruction be it of the Holy Temple or a nuclear Holocaust; and Purim can be shared with merrymakers of all faiths. Philanthropic spokespersons regularly equate the traditional concept of *tzedakah* with the modern liberal concept of social justice. Liberal political activists routinely appropriate Jewish texts and symbols to buttress their claim of the identity of Judaism with a liberal social ethic.

In another departure from tradition and from their Israeli counterparts, Americans have deemphasized the tradition's understanding of ritual practice as obligatory. Instead, the ethos that pervades non-Orthodox schools and synagogues emphasizes a personalist and voluntarist approach to religious practice. Teachers and rabbis urge the Jewish laity to select those practices they find particularly meaningful, or, alternatively, to work at identifying or creating a personal meaning in religious observance. The commercial success of the volumes of the *Jewish Catalogue,* significantly self-described as kits for do-it-yourself Judaism, bears testimony to the power of the personalist and voluntarist side to American Judaism. To Israelis, this personalist voluntarism is foreign, to say the least. Even secular Israelis understand the religion that they reject as constituting a mandatory legal system, and it is one within which the lay person surely cannot choose or improvise (except with the consciousness of committing a sin).

Israelis for their part have also moved in directions that most American Jews would find very strange. If American Jews have universalized Jewish thought and practice, significant particularist strains have taken root and flourished in Israel, especially (but not only) among ardent nationalists and the traditional Orthodox.

Telling examples of these trends abound. In a remark that represents the view of many rather than the idiosyncrasy of an isolated individual, a leader of Jewish settlers on the West Bank stated that there is no place in Judaism for ''a humanistic attitude in determining responses to hostile behavior of the Arab population.'' Another has said, ''Jewish national morality is distinct from universal morality. Notions of universal or absolute justice may be good for Finland or Australia but not here, not with us.''[5] Such particularist statements would be roundly condemned in most American Jewish circles; but in Israel they are part of the landscape, acceptable to a major part of Israeli Jewry, and seen by many as valid expressions of Judaism.

Love of Eretz Yisrael, the land of Israel, is another Judaic concept developed and nurtured among Israeli Jews that has little resonance among American Jews. Few of the latter appreciate the extent to which even secular Israelis attach an intrinsic sacredness to the land of Israel. The widespread fascination with the land's flora and fauna, the national passion for archaeology, the regular hikes and encampments by schoolchildren and youth movement participants, to say nothing of the political inclinations of most of the Israeli right and even the rural Israeli left, all testify to the supreme value the land holds for most Israelis. In fact, in our survey of Israelis, over two-thirds claimed that ''it is almost impossible for me to think of what it means to be a Jew without thinking about Eretz Yisrael.'' Below is a passage from Rav Kook, first chief rabbi of the prestate Jewish community in Palestine. It could never have been written by an American Jewish thinker. Yet in Israel, Rav Kook, as interpreted by his followers in Gush Emunim, is treated with great seriousness and reverence:

> It is the air of the land of Israel that makes one wise. . . . In the land of Israel, one draws upon the light of Jewish wisdom, upon the quality of spiritual life which is unique to the people of Israel. . . . The impure soil that is everywhere outside the land of Israel is thus suffused with the stench of idolatry, and the Jews there are worshippers of idols in purity. . . . Enlightened wisdom is to be found only in the land of light; there is no Torah like that of the Land of Israel.[6]

If the Israelis' passion for their land is foreign to American Jews, so too is their understanding of the Israeli state. The distinction goes beyond the simple fact that the State of Israel and its major policy orientations have become constituent elements in the Judaism of most American Jews. It also extends to the very concept of the relationship of the state to the Jewish people.

The only concept of state with which Americans are familiar is the Western, democratic version. In this well-known model, the state ideally treats all its citizens alike, without regard to race, religion, or ethnicity. Moreover, the state has a corporate interest above and beyond those of the individuals who constitute the country. The Israeli concept, akin to that shared by many Middle Eastern and Asian societies, sees the state as an instrument of a particular people; it is truly a "nation-state," that is, the sovereign expression of an extended clan, tribe, folk, or people.

Two interesting consequences at variance with the Western concept of the state flow from this model. First, the state is seen as truly belonging to one national or ethnic group—in Israel's case, the Jews. Minorities are tolerated but can never legitimately aspire to full political, economic, and cultural equality with the group that constitutes the rightful citizens of the state. Second, the Western model recognizes only individuals; it theoretically ignores the existence of ethnic, religious, or national groups. In contrast, the Israeli state in practice and in theory attends to family-like needs of the Jewish people, to the extent that state interests are often subordinated to the norms of family-like behavior. Personal contacts, special privileges, waivers of rules, never-ending bargaining and bribery without a financial profit motive are rife throughout the operation of the Israeli state. The Anglo-Saxon insistence on clearly stated and fairly applied procedures is certainly an oddity in the Israeli context. Family-like behavior characterizes the Israeli bureaucracy, and family-like concerns often take precedence over state-oriented needs and interests. In short, contrary to what many American Jews may think, Israel is not a state like any other, at least not like any other in the West; rather it has many attributes of the familial (or national) state more prevalent in the Third World. Ben-Gurion's efforts at state building notwithstanding, the signs point in the direction of the long-term ascendancy of familial rather than Western features in the Israeli state.

American and Israeli Jews have developed contrasting, and sometimes conflicting, norms and values of Jewish life. American Jews differ from Israeli Jews in their emphasis on voluntarism, universalism, and liberalism in their Judaism. Similarly, Israeli Judaism is distinguished by unabashed particularism, ritualism, and a deep attachment to the land. The examples described—and there are many others—demonstrate the emergence of some very serious differences between American and Israeli Jews and Judaism at a fundamental level. Are these differences likely to widen? Will the world's two largest and most important Jewish communities continue to produce variant versions of Judaic ideas and values? Only by exploring the reasons these differences have emerged can we begin to imagine whether they will persist or even grow in depth and number.

Israel and American Jewry: The Major Structural Distinctions

Though we can only speculate as to why the Judaisms of Israel and the United States have grown so different, certain factors that appear to be permanent features of Israeli and American Jewish life are most critical.

First, almost all Jews in Israel live in an exclusively Jewish social environment. Most Jews in America have predominantly non-Jewish neighbors and at least some Gentile friends, even though their close friends are usually Jewish. Furthermore, over a third of American Jews who married in recent years married non-Jews.

What Jewish density means for cross-national differences in the understanding of Judaism is not immediately obvious, but the distinctions between American Jews in heavily Jewish social networks and those in less Jewishly dense networks are suggestive. Those with more Jewish friends and neighbors report higher levels of ritual observance, more traditional religious identification, lower levels of political liberalism, greater anxieties about and perceptions of anti-Semitism, greater attachment to Israel, and, most notably, greater commitment to the notion of Jewish family. The causal order here is impossible to disentangle. We can never be sure of the extent to which Jewish density of social networks stimulates these tendencies or the extent to which these tendencies generate greater Jewish exclusivity in choice of spouses, friends, and neighbors. It is reasonable to assume, however, that living among heavily Jewish networks helps maintain, if not stimulate, the Jewish identity phenomena enumerated above.

No comparable data exist for Israelis since nearly all Jewish Israelis confine their social relations to fellow Jews. Closely related to the concept of Jewish friendship, however, is that of cosmopolitanism or parochialism. In America, Jewish friendship may be seen as reflecting one's worldview on a cosmopolitan-parochial spectrum. Using these terms, it is fair to say that Israelis are far more Jewishly parochial than are Americans, and that this parochialism has consequences for Israelis' Jewish identity, undoubtedly feeding their particularistic tendencies.

Not only is Israel more densely Jewish than is American Jewish society; Israel is also a Jewish state. Thus, when the state makes policy, it is Jewish policy; the state's bureaucracy and instruments are by their very nature Jewish; and, as a corollary, Jewish authorities and Jewish ideologies are compelled to take public-policy stands. In Israel, Judaism is a public matter, whereas in America it is more private; some see it as an analog to the model of religious faith provided by liberal Protestantism.

Although both Israeli and American Jews feel threatened by the non-Jews around them, both agree that the threat of Arabs to Israelis is far more palpable and serious than that experienced by American Jews. The perception of threat has greater consequences in Israel. The classic responses of a community under siege and mobilized for defense include heightened levels of solidarity and greater antagonism to outsiders and dissenters. Undoubtedly, the Israeli-Arab conflict has contributed to feelings of Jewish familism in Israel, Jewish particularism, antagonism toward and fear of non-Jews, and cultural chauvinism. Just as surely, these sentiments have worked their way into the Israelis' understanding of what it means to be a Jew.[7]

While Israelis confront a physical threat primarily from outside their state, American Jews feel the insecurity of a minority living in a multiethnic democracy. American Jews seek protection through combating prejudice and discrimination, advocating strict enforcement of civil rights and liberties, supporting separation of church and state, and improving the situation of the most poverty-stricken to forestall social violence. All of this amounts to the domestic liberal agenda. (But not only has their Jewishness made liberals of many American Jews; it has made conservatives of many Israelis.) Many American Jews are "minoritarian"; Israeli Jews are "majoritarian." As the majority in their society, as the controllers of their government, and as a group faced with physical dangers from belligerent outsiders, Israelis have little reason to adopt a liberal political posture akin to that of American Jews. They have even less reason to incorporate the principles of American-style liberalism into their concept of a "good Jew."

American Jews live in a society of religious voluntarism. Not only can individuals freely choose the religious body with which to affiliate; they can choose not to affiliate at all, or they can choose how to interpret their affiliation. No coercive state power is brought to bear to affect these choices. One consequence for American Judaism has been the emergence of non-Orthodox Jewish denominations headed by rabbis and lay leaders who offer alternative models of Jewish authenticity. Just as pluralism is part of America, so too is it part of American Judaism. In contrast, state power in Israel confers exclusive Jewish legitimacy on the Orthodox rabbinate. Until recently, non-Orthodox religious movements have not only enjoyed little active support, but little respect as representatives of authentic Judaism, even from non-Orthodox Jews.

As a voluntarist religious group, American Jews have needed to construct a thick infrastructure of voluntary organizations operating in a variety of functional areas. Schools, synagogues, philanthropies, defense agencies, periodicals, hospitals, old age homes, camps, and fraternal organizations are only some of the more prominent categories of American Jewish organizational life. The purposes served by these agencies are often served, in Israel, by government agencies or by institutions heavily subsidized by public funds. As a result (or at least as a corollary), American Jews have attached great significance to voluntarism as an important part of adult Jewish life, while Israelis, clearly, see the State of Israel as imbued with Jewish significance for themselves personally and for the destiny of the Jewish people generally.

Another feature unique to Israel as a Jewish state is the pervasiveness of Jewish culture in all its variety. The national language is Hebrew; schoolroom texts—even for secular students—include the Bible and other Judaically significant material; the most important holidays of the traditional religious calender are national holidays as well. The diffusion of these and other aspects of Jewish culture means that even the most secular of Israelis are inevitably caught up in the religious tradition, even if they reinterpret it in a secular way. In America, the absence of a taken-for-granted quality to Jewish life can be seen as having two apparently contradictory effects. On the one hand, the voluntary nature of Jewish involvement means that Jews can opt out of participating in religious or communal life if they choose. On the other hand, such participation demands an intentionality that cannot characterize Israelis who partake of Jewish living as a part of their everyday life.

To say that the factors mentioned above are among the most critical is not to deny that society-wide, global factors other than those touched upon here may also be responsible for leading Israeli and American Judaism in different directions. Jewish social density, the state apparatus, state legitimation of Orthodoxy, the Arab threat, and the pervasiveness of Jewish culture all play crucial roles in influencing the nature of Israeli Judaism. Minority status, the voluntarism and pluralism of the larger society, and relative physical security are among the important features that characterize American Jewry.

What of the Future?

The purpose of this essay is to peer into the future, to examine the state of Israeli-American Jewish relations 30 years hence. The discussion above certainly informs speculation about this issue, and may even provide the beginning of an agenda for policy making.

No analysis of current or recent trends can provide an infallible look into the future, however. Even the most accurate, precise, comprehensive, and sophisticated grasp of the present and recent past does relatively little to advance significantly our understanding of the distant future. The most we can say is that if recent trends continue, we will be heading in such and such a direction. Mathematicians have developed "catastrophe theory" to describe and explain sudden changes of events. My own view is that social history develops along the lines of catastrophe theory. We live most of our lives through periods of developmental and gradual change. At certain points that change speeds up rapidly. Wars and social revolutions represent the classic ways of charging up the engines of change. The Jewish community of the United States is still living in a period shaped by the tumultuous American and Jewish history of the years 1967 and 1973. Little has changed since the mid–1970s, but this observation says nothing about the possibility of another period of rapid change lurking around the corner, beyond the horizons of our vision. A Syrian attack against Israel more direct and devastating than the 1991 Iraqi attack, a no-holds-barred Palestinian insurrection, a full-scale economic depression (in the U.S. or Israel), a reemergence of the Christian right or an anti-Semitic left, and other plausible events beyond our ability to predict could significantly alter the texture of American Jewish life and relations with Israel as well.

Speculating on the Jewish future may be an amusing exercise, but it has no policy-relevant value. Accurate predictions are beyond our ability. So, too, is the formulating of plans. At best, we can make plans that take into account our vision of the world 5 to 10 years from now, not 30 or 40 years.

With this shorter time perspective in mind, we can say that policy makers in American Jewish life and Israel do need to confront the challenge of Israeli-Diaspora relations posed by the long-standing processes described here. Israeli and American Jewry have been parting company politically, culturally, and religiously. This does not mean that they necessarily feel any less allegiance to one another; what it does mean is that the objective basis for that allegiance, the Judaic resemblance of one community to the other, has been diminishing. Further, Israel itself appears more fractured and conflicted, making it difficult to project a unified, neat, and orderly image of Israel. More important, imposing a unified sense of what it means for American Jewry to be pro-Israel is more difficult.

These twin developments (American-Israeli divergence and internal Israeli division) have special implications for those American Jews engaged in education, philanthropy, political activity, and cultural activities.

In the past, educators have presented Israeli Jewish life essentially as a more intensive version of American Judaism. They have used Israel-based travel and study solely as a way of intensifying American Jews' understanding of and commitment to one or another version of American-style Judaism. I would suggest that educators need to place more emphasis on how Israelis differ from their American Jewish counterparts, and how the possibilities for Jewish living in Israel differ from those in the Diaspora. Beyond that, educators need to convey an understanding of the wide variety of Judaic choices within Israel, their rationale, and their consequences.

Philanthropic supporters of Israel need to capitalize on rather than resist the pluralization of American Jewish philanthropic support for Israel. The development of alternatives to the United Jewish Appeal ought to be seen as a healthy and positive sign, one reflecting American Jewish interest in associating with specific pieces of Israel rather than a whole, undifferentiated entity.

There are political implications as well. Some Jews undoubtedly feel most comfortable serving as advocates of official Israel's cause in the United States. But demanding that those who feel closer to the Israeli opposition (whether it be of the right or left) support the policies of the party in power is counterproductive. Rather, the development of passionate American counterparts to the full spectrum of Israeli political opinion will serve not only to strengthen Israel's representation in the United States but also serve to strengthen identification and involvement with Israel.

It is in the cultural arena that the growing divergence between Israeli and American Jews and Judaism poses the greatest challenge. Educators, philanthropists, and political activists can easily adjust to an Israel that is culturally at variance with American Jewry. But the growing gap between what is Jewish in Israel and what is Jewish in the United States poses the possibility that Israel will become Jewishly irrelevant to American Jews, and vice versa. It is already the case that the two Jewries do rather little to enrich each others' internal Jewish life. The most notable and admirable features of American Judaism (for example, denominational pluralism, personalism, innovation, feminism, voluntarism) have had little impact on Israeli Judaism. Similarly, what may be some of the potentially most useful aspects of Israeli Judaism for American Jewry (for example, the emphasis on family; national interpretations of Jewish symbols and holidays; appreciation for the meaning of land; a sense of commandment; Jewish familism) are hardly even recognized in the United States.

The challenge for those concerned with maintaining and enriching the Israeli-American Jewish relationship on many levels, including the cultural and the spiritual, will be to develop mechanisms to put the divergence between these two communities to good use. How to do so is the topic for another essay, if not another analyst.

A Response

Martin J. Raffel

Predictions of future scenarios must be based on an understanding of the past and an accurate, unflinching assessment of present trends. Steven Cohen has provided us with a remarkably insightful analysis that serves this purpose well.

If the age of romanticism in the Israeli-American Jewish relationship began with the 1967 Six-Day War and the period of realism emerged in the late 1970s, then a third era may be marked by the firestorm generated over the "Who is a Jew" issue.

The extraordinary strength of the American Jewish community's response to a possible change in the Law of Return both challenges and supports Steven Cohen's thesis. The angry passion aroused by this controversy rivals in intensity the very different kinds of emotion stirred by the Six-Day and Yom Kippur Wars. No sign here of Jewish lay leaders "dis-attending" to Israeli affairs. On the other hand, Cohen's observations about the low level of mutual understanding and the gulf between these two communities in terms of their very separate and distinct forms of Jewish identity are validated most dramatically.

The immediate crisis provoked by the "Who is a Jew" controversy subsided with the formation of a National Unity Government in Israel. Since then, the American Jewish leadership has been called on to deal with elements in Israeli society pushing the country in nondemocratic directions, including the supporters of "Kahanism" and segments of the Israeli Orthodox community who seek the extension of Halakhah over ever-wider areas of public life. This development threatens both Israel and the overwhelming majority of American Jews. To counter these nondemocratic forces requires us to seek new and creative ways of participating in the shaping of Israeli society.

Moving from the period of realism largely characterized by American Jewish passivity with regard to Israel, to a time of active and full engagement will present us with enormous challenges. In addition to the elements that Cohen describes the technical, but not unimportant, aspect of geographic distance also separates our communities.

Early patterns of an active engagement have surfaced during the last 10 or 12 years: Project Renewal; Israel forum, which attempts to promote lasting friendships between Israelis and American Jews; American Jewish Committee programs to bring Israeli leaders, especially from the Sephardi community, to the United States; the American Jewish Congress summer dialogues in Jerusalem; and the opening in Israel of offices representing the Council of Jewish Federations and the San Francisco and Los Angeles Federations. The rapid expansion of the New Israel Fund, which targets specific programs in Israel for support, is worth noting. If I am correctly assessing the impact of the "Who is a Jew" issue, these developments represent the wave of the future in terms of American Jewish interaction with Israel.

What might we reasonably anticipate will appear on the agenda of the organized American Jewish community in the years ahead?

There already has been some discussion regarding the establishment of a legislative lobby in Israel primarily to respond to periodic attempts to amend the Law of Return. But the issues are too complex and far-reaching to be addressed through this vehicle alone. What is required is a well-funded, multifaceted program to promote religious pluralism in Israel—in other words, a Project Renewal for religious pluralism.

The American Jewish community will seek opportunities to work closely with Israeli officials as well as with nongovernmental organizations to develop new educational programs for Israelis that will help bridge the understanding gap.

This is not to suggest that the American Jewish community should attempt to shape Israeli society into its mirror image. This would not succeed even if it were desirable for the structural reasons Cohen points out. American Jewish pluralism exists within a particular context, as a voluntary community comprising a small fraction of the general population.

Israelis will have to evolve their own approach to pluralism emerging from Jewish sovereignty and majority status. But elements of the American Jewish experience might contribute positively to this process. These include a general tolerance of religious difference and the ability to work cooperatively on matters that affect Klal Yisrael. A coalition of modern American and Israeli Orthodox movements could contribute a great deal here.

The American Jewish establishment, like the New Israel Fund, might begin to direct greater financial and human resources to reinforcing those elements in Israel supporting democracy and for the opening up of Israeli society to a variety of Jewish religious forms.

Exchange programs between Israel and North America will be expanded. Shlichut will come to mean not just Israelis promoting aliyah and Israeli cultural activities in the United States but also American Jewish doctors, engineers, teachers, religious leaders, and others spending extended periods in Israel. Congregations will encourage their rabbis to spend sabbaticals in Israel to offer alternative religious experiences to greater numbers of Israelis.

Communications experts will examine potential uses of audiovisual materials, computers, and space-age technologies with a view to bridging the distance between Israeli and American Jews. For example, the Council of Jewish

Federations' satellite network system, which has enabled our two communities to exchange perspectives during periods of political crisis, will be used widely and routinely in the future for educational purposes.

Since most Israeli leaders welcome American Jewish involvement in this arena, all that limits us are the boundaries of our own commitment and imagination.

Another area in which American Jews will feel increasing pressure to become actively engaged is political and strategic issues related to the Arab-Israeli conflict, especially the Palestinian question. Clearly, not all Israeli leaders or even large sections of the public will welcome greater American Jewish involvement here. In contrast to the previous set of issues, certain restraints may be appropriate on this front.

I think Cohen is quite right in rejecting any demand by the Jewish establishment to toe a party line. It is incumbent upon the mainstream organizations, such as the umbrella agencies of the National Jewish Community Relations Advisory Council (NJCRAC) and the Presidents Conference at the national level, or CRCs and federations at the local level, to encourage as wide a range of political expression and debate within the community as possible.

Any individual or group who approaches these issues with the long-term security and welfare of Israel in mind should be welcomed to participate as the total Jewish community seeks to develop positions and programs that are responsive to those concerns.

At the same time, we ought to recognize certain realities. One of them is that American public support for Israel derives, at least in part, from the sense of an American Jewish community united around a number of fundamental positions. These include support for adequate foreign aid to Israel to help it shoulder an enormous defense burden, opposition to the transfer of weapons to Arab states that are still at war with Israel and that could jeopardize its security, and support for the principle that a political settlement of the Arab-Israeli conflict must be achieved through direct, face-to-face negotiations between the parties themselves, not by coercion from third parties.

Those who participate in community-wide discussions of these and other issues should have the freedom to express their personal visions and to seek widespread support for them. At the same time, they ought to accept voluntarily the responsibility of community consensus. They should not undermine the community's ability to reach agreement on certain fundamental issues and to project that agreement to American decision makers and opinion shapers and to the public as a whole.

It is the fervent hope and prayer of all of us that the Arab-Israeli conflict, which has been a central feature in the Israeli-American Jewish relationship, will be consigned to the history books by the turn of the century, if not sooner. The Palestinian uprising and the opening of a dialogue between the United States and the PLO may have set in motion a process that could lead to a resolution of the Palestinian dimension of the conflict. How the American Jewish community responds will have special importance in the period immediately ahead. One can reasonably foresee enormous pressures building for the establishment of a Palestinian state. Thus far, the United States and Israel have rejected this idea as inherently destabilizing and threatening to Israel's existence. Israel's diversity of opinion on how to deal with the Palestinian issue will be reflected in the American Jewish community. This period offers opportunities to draw closer to Israeli Jews as issues involving their physical safety will be debated and acted upon. We have a special role to play in this drama in honestly communicating our own ideas directly to the Israelis and, at the same time, continuing to support a peace process that leaves final decisions up to the parties themselves. In the end, the Israelis must be persuaded by credible Arab peace initiatives directed toward them and not by world public opinion. This view is accepted by a broad consensus in Israel and among American Jews.

The political, religious, and cultural issues that lie ahead for Israeli and American Jews are as complex and fateful as any they yet have faced. We cannot afford to confront them without a strong sense of interdependence and mutual understanding. A new period of active engagement is not just desirable—it is absolutely necessary.

7

Facing the Jewish Future

Philip M. Klutznick

The action word for this volume is *imagining*. The specific topic assigned to me, however, asks not that I imagine but that I *face* the Jewish future.

The terms *imagining* and *facing* tend to be concerned with a tomorrow. They suggest that we can make tomorrow better than what we have known in the past or are experiencing today. If so, the forward-looking aspect of the terms wears a hopeful air. Still, as Baruch Spinoza observed, "If you want the future to be different from the present, study the past." And Winston Churchill said, as if to extend the same thought, "The farther back you look, the farther forward you can see."

In facing the Jewish future, one proposition strikes me as being central to all the others. It is that our future is wrapped up in the position and fate of Israel, the first Jewish state in about 2,000 years. What happens to and in Israel, for good or for ill, will be revisited on significant aspects of Jewish life elsewhere. The Jewish community in the United States, for example, is far larger than the one in Israel or anywhere else in the world. It came into being before the State of Israel itself was born, and it possesses the means of independent survival without reference to the State of Israel. Yet if we credit the evidence of our own senses, we know that Jewish communal life in the United States since the birth of the State of Israel differs profoundly from what it was prior to that event.

I lived approximately the first half of my life during a time when no Jewish state was in existence. I have lived the second half during a time when a Jewish state has existed, albeit thousands of miles away from the United States. The first half of my life was marked—in the tradition of Jewish experience over the millennia—by hope, by imagination, and by repeated prayers that next year we would celebrate the High Holy Days in Jerusalem. In the second half, which began on May 14, 1948, I saw the unfolding of a fundamental revolution whose form and force was felt throughout the Jewish world. It was, I must quickly add, a revolution that reminded us anew that the problems of success can, ironically, be as great as the problems of failure.

During the first half of my life I was privileged to participate in youth programs and in the YMHA of Kansas City, Missouri, whose limited facilities served our needs before the more splendid structure of a comprehensive Jewish community center took its place. The local Zionist movement was only of modest size and was mainly confined to families whose origins were in Eastern Europe. Those at the forefront of Jewish leadership in Kansas City were the descendants of an earlier wave of immigrants from Western Europe. Largely non-Zionists, they rejected Herzl's philosophy and his dream of a reborn Jewish state. In fact, my only boyhood contact with political Zionism was through relationships with the young girls of Junior Hadassah.

Yet, for most of us who attended a traditional *heder* and spent the High Holy Days in the synagogue with our parents, there existed the quasi-religious, quasi-poetic hope of a "next year in Jerusalem." What is more, the periodic modest gifts we made to the Jewish National Fund, often by way of the blue and white can into which we dropped our nickels and dimes, amounted to a small, practical down payment on that hope.

As time went by, some of us helped organize the Junior B'nai B'rith, known as Aleph Zadik Aleph, which began in Omaha, Nebraska, and some of us assumed junior level responsibilities in our Jewish communities. The hope for "next year in Jerusalem" continued to grow slowly in the world of real things. Even after the Nazis won control of Germany, the gains made by political Zionism in the United States continued in the main to be the work of first-and second-generation immigrants from Eastern Europe. So things went until the unspeakable tragedy of the Holocaust, with its six million slaughtered Jews, forced into existence the State of Israel. Even then, two major national Jewish organizations withdrew from the American Jewish Conference when it concluded by a decisive vote that it should support the creation of a Jewish state. The decision to support Israel was based largely on the proposition that this would facilitate the rescue of the victims of Nazi persecution. The event reordered the priorities of life among Jewish communities the world over and has continued to reshape the commitments and the programs of Diaspora Jewry.

One illustrative detail, measurable in dollars and cents, says something about the matter. In the United States and elsewhere among Jews, we now take for granted the multimillion-dollar campaigns addressed to helping meet Israel's primary needs and those of other Jewish communities. Yet I recall as if it were yesterday what happened when the first multimillion dollar fund-raising effort for Israel was mounted in the United States.

American Jewish communities, for whom a $40,000 or $50,000 fund-raising campaign used to be big money, questioned the boldness and magnitude of what was being sought after the creation of the State of Israel. And they were full of questions when Golda Meir and Henry Montor started to sell the idea of Israel issuing its debt paper—Israel bonds, as they are called—to be sold in the Jewish world as well as in banking circles. This was a far cry from coins in a little can. I recall a chance meeting with that wonderful and determined pair in the Detroit airport when I was there on a B'nai B'rith mission. Why, I asked, were they in Detroit? They said they had come to the city to promote the sale of Israel obligation bonds. At first I thought they were pulling my leg. It seemed beyond the realm of practical reason to call on the people of the U.S. and other nations to buy the obligations of a new, struggling little state called Israel. Yet the passing years disclosed how the campaigns for gift dollars and for borrowed dollars escalated from a few million to tens of millions of dollars at a time when the value of the dollar itself had a value far in excess of its present worth. The differences over the validity of a Jewish state melted under the pressures of necessity. The Jewish communities of the U.S. and elsewhere were themselves transformed and energized.

The Jewish world has supported the State of Israel in far more than monetary and economic terms. It has done so as well when the very survival of the new Jewish state depended in no small measure on how the political and security issues it faced were met and mastered. This is not the place to detail what I saw at close range about the nature of that help. It is, however, the place to say that at each stage of Israel's growth over the last 40-plus years the Jewish state has faced different challenges among her neighbors and the world community—not least of all in her relationship with the Diaspora.

Prior to the miraculous victory of the Six-Day War, there was little time for extended introspective examination of Israel-Diaspora relationships. It was also beside the point to exchange outcries about who was at fault for the lack of peace between Israel and her neighbors. But some of the crucial problems that had existed prior to the Six-Day War appeared to be under better control afterward. That permitted questions previously raised only in whispers if at all to become the subject of public discussions. In particular, with only 25 percent of the total Jewish people living in Israel, irrepressible questions came up for debate among Jews worldwide. Did the majority, for example, have the right to disagree with Israel? To whom did the State of Israel actually belong? What authority did the State of Israel have to decide the "correct" Jewish stand worldwide on religious, sociological, and philosophical matters?

In the aftermath of the Six-Day War, it turned out that in one respect at least it was easier to be an Israeli than a Diaspora Jew. Israelis could openly agree or disagree with their government—whether through a political party or personally. Either way, their loyalty to a reborn Israel was not questioned. The whole world could hear the noise of the internal conflicts among Israelis, but the Israelis themselves did not charge their disputatious fellow citizens with an intent to destroy the unity of the Jewish people. On the other hand, any so-called "leader" in the Diaspora who openly disagreed with a particular act or policy of the Israeli government was likely to invite reproach from other Jews in the Diaspora or by officialdom centered in Jerusalem.

Yet the relationship between Israel and the Diaspora since the birth of the State has not stood still, nor can it stand in one place like a painted soldier on a battle canvas. Precisely because it is a living relationship, it *moves*. As it moves from the present to the future, I hope it will turn away from the premise that the Diaspora should be only the giver and lender, that Israel should be the decision maker and the Diaspora should be the silent follower in political and international affairs. I also hope it will turn toward accepting the proposition that this relationship can be truly fruitful only if there is mutual candor and free communication between Israelis and Israel as a sovereign state, and Jews the world over who feel a special relationship to that state, and who might thus share some portion of any success it gains or pay some part of the price for any failure.

What do mutual candor and free communication mean? Again, drawing on my personal experiences and reflections over the years, let me attempt a definition.

First, the Diaspora must grasp the distinction between the acts of Israel as a sovereign power on the one side and, on the other, the life, institutions, and behavior of Israelis as Jews. There may be gray areas where sovereignty is not supreme, but we who believe in Jewish peoplehood must recognize that a partnership between a sovereign state and Jews who are scattered all over the world cannot be a full and equal partnership. Israel, through its democratically chosen government, has a responsibility for the security of its people and its land and for the maintenance of its political viability in the world.

As a state, it may assume positions and take actions which even its own citizens resent. Their remedy is to change their government. Jews who are not citizens of Israel have the right to disagree, to debate and decry such acts of the Israeli government as they find objectionable—the same right they exercise in the democratic lands of the Diaspora. But the Diaspora cannot expect, nor should it argue for, a role in government decision making within the sphere of Israel's legitimate concerns as a sovereign state. With respect to such concerns, the decision rests with the State of Israel itself, whether on the side of what is far-sighted or blind.

Second, there are areas where the State of Israel acts but in which the Diaspora has a grave concern and where its counteractions could affect what the State itself does. This is the most difficult area for both the State and the Diaspora. To be explicit, this is the case when the interests of peoplehood get mixed up with Judaism as a religion and where its religion gets mixed up with sovereignty and politics.

I firmly believe in the desirability of a religious tone for Israel as a state and as a people—just as I believe in it for Jewish communities in the Diaspora as a whole. But what happens when established religious bodies within Israel form a kind of state-within-a-state capable of dictating the laws of the regular civil government?

The Diaspora has its agnostics and atheists, even as Israel does. Though Judaism in the Diaspora remains the basic sustaining force for Jewish survival and progress, in the Diaspora religion by free choice entails a respect for pluralism. Many Jews in the Diaspora have elected to be Reform, Conservative, Orthodox, or Reconstructionist. Each has its claim to an interpretation of Halakhah. But the disqualification by the State of Israel of all except Orthodox rabbis from the performance of religious rites authorized by the state could create a major rift between loyal Zionists and the state.

Any informed person is aware of the complex character of this issue. Many of us would live with the requirements of rabbinical marriage and divorce provided it included all properly ordained rabbis, whether Orthodox, Reconstructionist, Conservative, or Reform. But to excommunicate many recognized rabbis of the Diaspora from performing their functions within Israel could eventually poison the wells of cooperation between large parts of the Diaspora and the State of Israel. We have a duty to see that this bleak prospect for the future is averted by the intervention of those spokesmen for Orthodoxy who take to heart the last injunction of Moses—''Choose life, that both thou and thy seed shall live.''

What I have so far said about Israel-Diaspora relationships and what they portend for the future merges into the larger questions concerning whether Israel and the hostile states that are her neighbors will join in a common pursuit of such opportunities for peace as may present themselves. Over the last 40 years only one of Israel's adversaries—Egypt, which is her largest Islamic neighbor—had a leader with the vision and courage to go to Jerusalem to make peace. For one who was there—as I was—at the Knesset when the desire for peace was expressed on both sides, the thrill associated with President Sadat's visit can never be forgotten. Yet he paid for the prevailing peace with his own life.

For my part, I believe—and have said on other occasions to the dismay and criticism of some of my friends—that the only ultimate answer for Israel and her neighbors is to meet face to face and arrive at a settlement that mature and thoughtful people can accept. It is true, of course, that peace in the Middle East never depended on the resolution of the Israeli-Arab conflict alone. In years past, regional and international tensions—Soviet moves in the Horn of Africa and Afghanistan, OPEC price aggression and supply threats, revolution in Iran and the Iran-Iraq war, dangerous instabilities and hostilities within and among the Arab states, the Soviet–Arab–Third World coalition against free democratic states—all worked in their own way to derail any serious attempt to resolve that specific conflict.

Recently, however, we have begun to see some shafts of light through the overcast regional skies. The crumbling of communism, and therefore of Soviet belligerence; changes wrought by the Gulf War; and massive Soviet Jewish emigration might improve the atmosphere for general peace in the Middle East. On top of the list are the easing of tensions in Soviet-U.S. relations and the restoration of diplomatic ties between the Soviet Union and Israel. If all this helps lead to a just and supportable peace in the Middle East between Israel and her neighbors, the consequences will serve the interests of Jewish communities the world over—and thus we must now render what help we can to bring such a peace into existence.

I do not suggest that no difficult barriers remain. But there is at least a semblance of hope that these beginnings could lead to revolutionary changes for the Jewish agenda if they are nurtured by all involved.

Yet, as is so often true, there is some bitter with the sweet. In Israel itself the prospect of debate and action on the definition of ''Who is a Jew?'' threatens to create a terrible disunity which neither Israel nor the Jewish world can afford. An Israel in today's and tomorrow's world which would settle for a formula that disowns the greater part of the largest Jewish community in existence, risks unseen hazards upon which I prefer not to speculate. Aside from dividing Jewish life, the repercussions could make a viable peace between Israel and her neighbors less likely. It would challenge a great number of Jews all over the world to rethink their historic commitment to an Israel reborn. There are many minor and major threats to the unity of our numerically small people. I stop here, for I hope and pray that those who hold the power to create an unbelievable setback to the Jewish world and particularly to Israel will avoid taking such action. Believing that they will act responsibly, I turn back to a more hopeful future.

The prospects of what peace will mean to the Jewish future in terms of community, culture, and theology are mind-boggling. First, it will enable Israel to reach the level of self-sufficiency that its industrial technical competence and infrastructure justify. Knowledgeable international experts agree that Israel is a modern miracle of a small nation starting its economic development virtually from scratch. At its birth it gave little evidence of industrial and technical competence. It was desperately short of food even as late as the mid–1950s, when I made my first visit to the country as international president of B'nai B'rith. At that time, when I asked then Prime Minister Moshe Sharett what Israel needed the most, he said ''50,000 tons of grain.'' Without grain, there could be no cattle, and without cattle, no meat, no milk or dairy products. I helped to secure the 50,000 tons from the United States under a foreign assistance act. Not much later Israelis comically depicted one of the great enemies of the Israeli economy to be the ''cow,'' the source of more milk, and hence more dairy products than Israel could consume domestically.

There is little question that an Israel at peace with her neighbors could be an economic leader in all of the Middle East, Africa, and in some respects the Far East. The state would be more attractive to foreign investors—non-Jewish as well as Jewish. This attraction would be greatest for firms best able to benefit from one of Israel's chief economic advantages—an abundance of highly qualified scientific and technical manpower available at relatively low cost, backed up by first-rate research and development capabilities and duty-free access to the U.S. and the Common Market for a wide variety of products.

Secondly, a condition of peace between Israel and her neighbors would have phenomenal consequences for the culture of Jewish communities in the

Diaspora. If Jewish life in the Diaspora is to prosper, it must strengthen the instruments that help to develop, advance, and transmit ancient and current Jewish knowledge. We have made progress in modernizing our efforts in this respect—great progress, if the measuring stick is the *heder* of yesteryear. All in all, however, we operate at a deficit in terms of the Jewish cultural context from preschool, elementary school, and high school to the college level. We desperately need added resources and manpower, facilities, and students.

Saving and preserving Jewish life in its physical form is a constant priority, but a failure to preserve and advance Jewish knowledge and commitment to Jewish culture can be the Achilles' heel of our people. Yet the demands for help in meeting the physical security needs of Jews lessen the availability of resources for meeting Jewish cultural needs. If major progress is made in substantially settling the security problems of Israel and of the Jewish people, we will reap the benefits of what modern technology can do for Jewish education. If sufficient resources are available, the next generation of Jews—at home in Hebrew and abreast of modern Jewish affairs—can become the most literate in Jewish history.

I recall in this connection what happened during the period when I served as an officer of the Claims Conference. The funds provided in the claims settlement with the Federal Republic of Germany had a major positive effect on the development of Israel. Jews in Israel and elsewhere are still receiving personal reparations payments for a variety of justifiable reasons. More than 25 years ago, however, a serious debate occurred among the leaders of the Claims Conference over a recommendation made by Nahum Goldmann, then the chairman of the Conference. On the eve of what we thought might be the last payments by the Federal Republic of Germany, he proposed that some of the funds due should be set aside to strengthen and perpetuate Jewish culture as a memorial to the six million Jews who perished in the Holocaust.

The proposal encountered stiff opposition. Some members of the Conference argued that every available cent from the payment on claims should be applied to the physical needs of the survivors of the Holocaust. Others argued that the survivors, in the main, were getting the material help they needed. The Jewish people as a whole, however, through the loss of the six million had suffered an immense cultural loss.

It was Goldmann's contention that what had been lost had to be compensated for in some measure. After an extended and difficult debate, the views of those of us who sided with Goldmann prevailed, and the Memorial Foundation for Jewish Culture was established. It was my privilege to be Goldmann's successor as president of the Foundation and to serve as such until 1988. I believe it is fair to claim that the Foundation has operated with a high measure of success—and a low profile—in assisting worthy cultural and educational efforts throughout the Jewish world, not least of all in Eastern Europe, including the Soviet Union.

Today the needs of Israel for fiscal assistance from the Jewish world, plus the needs of the Diaspora for those programs that sustain and advance the cultural aspects of Jewish life, are stretching the philanthropic potentials of our people. With luck, an Israel at peace will be a prosperous nation able to contribute in many ways to the sustenance of Jewishness elsewhere. The resulting shift in the use of Jewish communal funds will be to a greater emphasis on support of Jewish cultural activity. This could result in increased aliyah to Israel as the study of Hebrew and Jewish history in the Diaspora intensifies. If we will it, imagining the Jewish future in this way does not need to be only a dream. It can mean facing a future in which community, culture, and theology will be better understood, even if marked by differences between Israel and the Diaspora and within them. Aliyah would become a more natural component of the relationship between Israel and a Diaspora in which Hebrew was freely spoken as a second language, while Israel's improved economic condition would permit a greater participation in the cultural support of Jewish life elsewhere.

I once heard my revered mentor, Mordecai Kaplan, voice his concern over the gulf between Israel and the Diaspora. He then suggested that an international group be convened at Sinai to frame the terms of a "new covenant" that would bind the world Jewish community together. No new covenant was framed, no group convened. Yet Israel and the Diaspora must at least come to a meeting of the minds on the issue of power. For 2,000 years we were a powerless people. Suddenly our generation enjoys status and power. The state of Israel by its very existence embodies power in its internal affairs and in its relationship to other states. Power, however, is a double-edged sword for individuals and for nations. From the time of the prophets, the holders of power were admonished to use it in order to express the ideas of religion. The state and power were to be the instrument for the attainment of greater ethical and religious ideals. The great danger for everyone is to make the instrument of power an end in itself.

We have not yet reached this stage, but we must be aware of the danger. As a State and as a Diaspora people, we must endeavor to uphold our ideals when using the power we now possess, as we have tried to uphold them in our powerless past. If we return to the great universal ideals of Jewish prophecy in Jewish history—if we can show the world what a people that finally has gained power can do once it has achieved peace—we can, as if by an invisible hand, secure a bright future for ourselves and indeed be a blessing to all peoples.

Section IV

Family, Community, and Morality

8

Jewish Family Ethics in a Post-halakhic Age

Martha A. Ackelsberg

My vision of the Jewish future is centered in a revitalized and inclusive Jewish community, the members of which are engaged in a continuing struggle to realize the presence of God in their midst. Such a community would value and support those characteristics we have come to associate with families: making it possible for people to achieve and sustain relationships of intimacy, solidarity, and nurturance; fostering mutual support and interdependence; and providing opportunities to express generativity. It would be a community that recognizes that people may express or experience those characteristics, needs, and potentials in a variety of contexts and constellations; a community that would not limit its members to expressing them, or having them met, only within the structures that have traditionally been defined as "family." In fact, structures that have worked in the past are no longer dominant (whether in the Jewish community or outside it) and are often no longer functioning well. If our communities are fully to meet the needs of their members, we must be open to changing forms that have traditionally addressed those needs.

From the title of this essay—presented by the editor of this volume—we can learn a great deal about the assumptions that underlie our conversations, the questions we confront, the tools and approaches we have at our disposal. First, the term *post-halakhic:* The term takes for granted that we find ourselves in, at best, a complicated relationship to Halakhah (Jewish law)—possibly even a relationship that can only be described in the past tense. It implies that what has been handed down to us is not necessarily adequate for our situation, that we are in a time of transition and redefinition. At the same time, to use the term "*post-*halakhic," rather than, say, "*non*halakhic," is to assume a continuing presence of Halakhah in our lives and communities, even while acknowledging a lack of unanimity as to its interpretation or its binding nature.

A second term calling for attention is *ethics*. To couple that term with "post-halakhic" is to presume that it is possible to develop codes of ethics and criteria for behavior even in the absence of unanimity on what constitutes the right path. To be in a state of transition is not necessarily to be without guideposts, though the guides we come to depend on may well be other than the traditional ones.

Finally, the term *family* seems to assume that there is an entity that we know and recognize as such—or, more specifically, as a Jewish family—and that we share (or at least might come to share) an agreement as to what that entity is. Further, the title treats "Jewish family" as a modifier of "ethics"; it assumes that we can develop an ethics that is specifically appropriate to Jewish families—presumably, both in their internal relations and in relations with other families, individuals, and institutions in the community and in the larger society.

I share many, but not all, of the assumptions and presuppositions reflected in this title.* I begin with Jewish tradition, but also with a recognition that tradition has changed, and must continue to change, if it is to meet the challenges of the contemporary world. My reading of Jewish history, and my understanding of the world around me, leads me to believe that there never was, nor is there now, any one entity that we can label and define as "the Jewish family." To the extent that we are part of the larger society in which we live, our family forms are necessarily affected by the world around us; they have been many, varied, and changing, and they will continue to be so. For example, in the early stages of Jewish history, the basic unit was the tribe or clan, consisting of many families as we now know them. Later, the extended family became dominant, frequently including adult siblings in the same household. Members of that family often worked closely together for business purposes and in fact may well have understood their relationships more in economic than in emotional terms. The shift away from the extended family to the nuclear family (of mother, father, and their biological children) occurred gradually with industrialization. Further, as trends in recent years indicate, the classic one-marriage nuclear family no longer reflects the experience of the majority of families. We cannot assume, then, that we all mean the same thing by "family."[1] Finally, although I do believe that ethics is possible—and necessary—I am not convinced that there is such a thing as a uniquely Jewish family ethics. Once again, as our lives and communities change, we are called upon to change with them—and not only as Jews. Yet resources for a response to these changes can be found within Jewish tradition. Furthermore, both the community as a whole and families in particular will be strengthened by the changes I advocate here.

Ours is surely a time of major transformations, within both the secular and the Jewish communities of which we are a part. As Jews in the United States, we are hardly sealed off from the changes going on about us; we confront daily the challenges posed to everyone in a society often characterized by a series of "post-" adjectives: postcapitalist, postfeminist, postindustrial, and so on. Much that we once took for granted is now open to repeated examination and questioning. Such moments of transition are trying—they evoke both fear and excitement: fear of what we have lost and might become, excitement about the possibilities of developing new, albeit preliminary, visions of the future. My own perspective is to welcome this moment, and to aim at maximizing the opportunities for growth it offers—both to us as individuals and to the Jewish community as a whole.

The changes and challenges we experience as Jewish citizens of the United States manifest themselves in specific ways when we look at families. Jews have not escaped the trends affecting the society around us: more people are marrying later, or not at all; divorce rates are high; many children are growing up in other than two-parent households (or, at least, in households headed by adults who are not necessarily their biological parents); poverty is on the increase, especially among children and in families headed by women; ever-higher percentages of women are in the work force, making the traditional nuclear family of father who works outside the home and mother who stays home with the children largely a phenomenon of the past. Debates within the Jewish community have targeted many of these changes as potentially disruptive not only to families but to the future of the community itself. Thus, although divorce rates are somewhat lower among Jews than among non-Jews, rates are higher in the Jewish community than they were 20 to 30 years ago; Jewish families tend to form later and to contain fewer children than do non-Jewish families; and an increasing proportion of Jewish young people are choosing to marry non-Jews.[2] For a community that has typically defined ''family''—in particular, the traditional nuclear family—as its central building block, these changes can be experienced as threatening, indeed. Any new Jewish family ethics must confront and address these trends.

The Communal Context of Families and Ethics

My own efforts to define a Jewish family ethics begin from the position powerfully articulated by Martin Buber 70 years ago—that it is not family, but community, which is the locus for the realization of God in the world:

> The Divine may come to life in individual man [sic], may reveal itself from within individual man; but it attains its earthly fullness only where, having awakened to an awareness of their universal being, individual beings open themselves to one another, disclose themselves to one another, help one another; where immediacy is established between one human being and another; where the sublime stronghold of the individual is unbolted, and man breaks free to meet other men. Where this takes place, where the eternal rises in the Between, the seemingly empty space: that true place of realization is community, and true community is that relationship in which the Divine comes to its realization between man and man.[3]

To understand the community, and relations within it, in this way is to recognize that contemporary Jewish concerns over the breakdown of traditional families may well be misplaced. What matters, I would argue, is not the particular form that our "intimacy constellations"[4] take, but rather whether they provide the between spaces in which we can realize and experience the divine. To the extent that traditional family structures provide such spaces—contexts in which members relate to one another with honesty and openness, mutual respect, and dignity—traditional family structures contribute to the creation and maintenance of a vital Jewish community. Similarly, to the extent that "alternative families," other intimacy constellations, provide contexts in which their members meet one another in relations of honesty and openness, mutual respect, and dignity, they too can be contexts in which we experience the divine, relationships that are essential building blocks of a revitalized Jewish community. The ethical imperative for Jewish communities, then, is to support and sustain all those family forms, regardless of their particular configurations, that provide contexts for striving toward the realization of the divine.

To put it another way, this perspective on the nature and purpose of Jewish community highlights the importance of the quality rather than the form of relationships. It highlights the value and importance of diversity, of the multiplicity of ways we may experience or meet God in our lives, and in our relations with one another. And it generates a wariness about defining any one pattern of relationship, or of family, as the uniquely acceptable one. As God is one, even as God's faces are manifold and unnameable, so if our community is one, its unity too must incorporate the diversity of its membership. Therefore, the Jewish family ethics I propose to address and develop here refers as much, if not more, to our community's relationship to families (in all their variety) as it does to the quality of relationships within those families.

Why a new Jewish family ethics now? Because, as I have suggested, family structures are changing and the traditional prescriptions no longer seem to fit. Efforts by the Jewish community to arrest change—to increase the Jewish birth rate, to stop the rising numbers of divorces and intermarriages, to increase rates of marriage—have proved largely unsuccessful. Further, to the extent that the community continues to conceive of traditional nuclear families as the best, if not the only, building blocks of a Jewish future, current trends must surely make it fearful about that future. Increasingly, of course, alternative voices are suggesting that we need not be so fearful, that we can imagine a strong and positive Jewish future constructed around much broader understandings of families and of their relationship to the community. But to do this we need to develop and articulate precepts appropriate to the new structures—precepts both for those who would participate in the structures, and for the Jewish community in relationship to them.

Families do not exist in isolation: they are products of the society and communities of which they are a part. If we are to understand recent changes and be able to respond effectively to them, we must recognize the ways in which families are social constructs.

Too much of the existing discussion and debate about changing families and Jewish communal responses has failed to take that context into account. It tends to treat family structures strictly as the products of individual, self-interested choice, and those who choose to live in alternative structures (whether they be childless couples, those living together without being married, singles, widows, roommates, divorced families, intermarrieds, gay or lesbian families) as having put their "personal" concerns above those of the "community." The community, in such formulations, presumably does not make choices; it simply exists. Many of the common prescriptions for action—for example, increasing communal incentives and/or disincentives in an effort to entice, cajole, or encourage individuals to choose so-called traditional families, or, conversely, to punish or marginalize those who do not—are based on a presumed opposition between what the individual wants and what is good for the community. As a result, such suggestions tend to reinforce an adversarial sense of the relationship between the community and its nonconforming members, and contribute to the alienation and marginalization they are presumably designed to overcome.[5] They force out of the community many who are capable of contributing both creativity and energy to the Jewish community.

This adversarial understanding of the relationship between individuals and communities is both false and misleading. As Jews living in the United States, we ought to have learned only too well that individuals are not so easily separable from their communities. Most Jews have rejected full assimilation as a goal and have come increasingly to recognize and insist that our particularist, communal ties are crucial to our individuality, and that our Jewish identities are inseparable from our American identities. A healthy society, liberal Jews have argued, requires not just tolerance for, but active welcoming of, diversity. Thus, as Jews, we have come to value true pluralism; we strive to create a society in which all of us can participate and contribute in the fullness of our identities as Jewish Americans—a society where we do not have to leave that identity behind at home or in the synagogue. In such a society, not only are Jews and other minorities more secure, the freedoms we enjoy allow us all to contribute more fully and effectively to the community at large.

However, although we have learned this lesson well in the context of American politics and culture, we have only rarely taken it back into our own community. Instead, we as a Jewish community have come to believe not only that there is just one set of norms, but also that there is only one way to meet and fulfill them. Instead of seeing individuals and communities as involved in dynamic, mutual relationships, we freeze our idea of community, define it in terms of certain acceptable patterns of behavior (in this case, family constitution), and then marginalize the individuals who do not meet those norms, while at the same time worrying about Jewish survival and a shrinking Jewish population.

There is another way. We must recognize that we live our lives, including our Jewish lives, in a context. The rugged individualism that dominates American culture is a misleading description of reality: no one "chooses" in the absence of community. Communities affect what we choose, our sense of the choices, as well as our feelings about ourselves and others. Further, communities are themselves human creations. Communities do not exist in some unchanging realm outside of history, but change as people and circumstances change. Consequently, communities are subject to some conscious human control. Those of us who understand ourselves to be living in a post-halakhic age should be particularly aware that, through our constructions, we *create* our communities and the values they incorporate at the same time that we are products of them.

The Jewish communities in which we live reflect and participate in many aspects of the larger society. While American society has not always lived up to its pluralistic democratic promise, that vision has exerted considerable influence over the institutions and practices of the Jewish community. The Jewish community has become both more permeable to the world around it and more internally democratic than it was in the past. Such changes have significant implications for the development of a new Jewish family ethics.

To be more specific, Jews in the rabbinic, medieval, and early modern periods lived in communities that were, if not isolated from the world around them, at least semiautonomous entities. They were governed internally by Jewish law and overseen by Jewish communal/legal bodies (always, of course, within constraints set out by the rulers of the surrounding non-Jewish community). It was not until Emancipation that Jews were accepted into the surrounding political communities as more or less full and equal members, subject no longer to Jewish law but to the secular law of the polity. Although the Jewish community was never hermetically sealed from the communities around it, the processes of emancipation and modernization have broken down its monolithic character. We are left with a variety of Jewish communities possessing various standards of behavior and with growing numbers of unaffiliated Jews who live their lives totally outside of any organized Jewish community. Existing Jewish communal structures have become more permeable to the influences and trends of surrounding communities and steadily less able to set standards for their membership that differ from those of the world "outside."

Related to this increased permeability of Jewish life is its growing democratization. Traditional Jewish communities were hierarchically organized and strictly controlled by Jewish communal authorities. Contemporary American Jews, as a result of the democratization that has accompanied modernization, tend to define community in increasingly open and egalitarian terms. In the traditional Jewish community, upper-class, educated (and usually wealthy) males were granted the right and the authority to set the rules and guidelines by which everyone was to live. Contemporary Jewish communities are both more diverse and, in theory at least, more inclusive and egalitarian. We insist, for example, that women as well as men be fully participating members of the community in both religious and secular contexts. In addition, we have little ability to enforce standards of ritual or moral behavior. With few exceptions, those who declare themselves Jews—regardless of whether they observe Shabbat or kashrut, and regardless of the standards of behavior they follow in their professional or personal lives—can claim membership in the Jewish community. We as a community have no sanctions to use against them; nor would many of us want to use them if we did! Moreover, many of us are striving to create a community that is egalitarian in an even broader sense, one that challenges the barriers and hierarchies associated with class as well as with gender. We want a community that values and validates the contributions of as wide a range of our membership as possible. In short we live in a world where community membership is defined more broadly than in the past.

Moreover, as community boundaries shift and we develop new understandings of who and what constitutes the community, patterns of power and authority present themselves for reexamination. In a society that takes gender and class hierarchies for granted, power and authority are "naturally" expected to reside in upper-class males (in the Jewish context, in Jewishly educated males). But that expectation leaves unasked, let alone unanswered, questions about the implications of policies that take those assumptions for granted. Let us take, for example, the case of *shelom bayit* (peace in the home), a long-standing precept expressing the belief that the whole (the family) is more than the sum of its parts (the individuals who make it up), calling on those who constitute the family to curb their desires and their differences for the sake of the family as a whole.

Shelom bayit offers the ideal of a unified and peaceful family whose members work in close cooperation toward goals about which all are in agreement. At its best, the value of *shelom bayit* promotes harmony within each family member as well as among them. Importantly, it assumes a family that is also governed by other characteristics, such as fairness and open communication. When those characteristics are absent, pressure to conform to *shelom bayit* can mask oppression.

If we look at *shelom bayit* from the point of view of those dominant in the community (and in the institution of the family), the suppression of discontent is generally a good thing. Those who are in positions of relative power and authority are by definition those who benefit from the status quo. Given the formal power relations within traditional Jewish families, men who were dissatisfied with their lot could leave and/or divorce their wives; women were left to grin and bear it, or to risk the humiliation and shame of turning to rabbinic courts for relief. But if we look at it from the point of view of the traditionally subordinate member of the community (and the family)—the wife—the admonition to suppress one's concerns in the name of *shelom bayit* takes on very different dimensions. As both Faith Solela and Marcia Cohn Spiegel have argued, even in our own day all too many battered women are sent back to their husbands and households by the rabbis and Jewish communal workers to whom they turn for support, and told to hold their peace in the name of *shelom bayit*. For those women, such advice has often meant resigning themselves to continued abuse, hardly what *shelom bayit* might mean if understood from their perspective![6]

In short, an accurate rendering of the meaning of *shelom bayit*—or of any other communal-ethical precept—must take into account real differences in power as they exist within the community. In fact, in such cases we might well adopt the perspective of liberation theologians and argue that in the face of existing power differentials, the only way to assure truly ethical and egalitarian treatment is to ally ourselves with the weak—in this case, women and children. A Jewish family ethics for an egalitarian community must develop standards and principles of conduct that empower the weak and/or dependent, even as they attempt to contribute to the continuity of the community. The supposed well-being of the family or the community cannot be given priority over the physical and spiritual health of its constituents.

How, then, does a changing community, characterized by new patterns of power, authority, and leadership, define standards of behavior? What are the parameters of acceptable and unacceptable action? What criteria may we use for judging? Where traditional rules and regulations do not serve us, we must rely on the injunction to be a holy people, to attempt to realize God's presence in our midst.

In a truly egalitarian, inclusive community, standards of behavior must be defined in terms of the concrete relations in and through which people live. To return to Buber's formulation, we realize God in our midst not simply by following abstract dictates of action, but by interacting with our fellows in ways that recognize the presence of God in each other and in the relationships we create among ourselves. We cannot draw a blueprint for a community by mapping out abstract precepts, but we can articulate as goals the ways in which we want to interact with one another. It is in this context that I believe we must attempt to develop a new Jewish family ethics.

Families: Old and New

Surely much of our communal attachment to traditional family forms—and our fears of what will happen if those forms are no longer normative—derives from a belief that families meet important human and social needs. We think of families, in fact, as the prime contexts in which people meet their needs for companionship and emotional intimacy, for mutual economic support, for generativity (child-bearing and child-rearing), and, particularly within the Jewish context, for preserving tradition and contributing to the continuity of the community. The Jewish community has tended to view "singleness" as a state of alienation and isolation to be overcome through marriage; economic interdependence as one of the core benefits of family life (rarely, if ever, achieved outside of it); traditional families as the only reasonable contexts for raising children; and bearing and raising children as the primary way of transmitting tradition and ensuring communal continuity. Such beliefs result in the fear that as traditional families change, and as more and more people live in alternative, or nontraditional, structures, individuals will become isolated, community weakened, and the Jewish future threatened.

As I have argued elsewhere, however, families cannot always meet these needs effectively, and in many cases nontraditional arrangements meet them as well or better.[7] Families exist and function within a social context that greatly influences their effectiveness. Both historical and contemporary evidence clearly show that a significant proportion of heterosexual nuclear families are unable to meet the needs of their members for emotional, physical, and economic support. Consider the existence of *hevrei kadishah* (burial societies), *hachnasat kallah* (dowry societies), and *maot hittin* (Passover food groups), for example, and the myriad of other charitable Jewish communal organizations that flourished in the shtetls of Eastern Europe and among immigrants to the United States. They serve as evidence of the Jewish community's recognition that families cannot always support their members. And they attest to the assumption of a communal responsibility to meet the needs of individual Jews.

In our own day, reports of wife battering, child abuse, homelessness, and abandonment make clear once again that families at all levels of the social and economic scale often find it difficult to create and sustain the nurturing, loving environment we have come to expect of them. Further, as feminist critics have noted, families often restrain, limit, and disempower the women and children within them, while masking the inequalities of power under the name of love. This is not to say that all families are abusive, or that people have no need for interdependent relationships. It is to suggest, however, that what is ideologically defined as a system of love and care is often lacking in true mutuality, to the particular detriment of women and children.

Treating the nuclear family as the only normative family model also fails to take into consideration how many people are excluded—singles, the divorced and widowed, "blended" families, and single parents, to name but a few. Giving the nuclear family first-class status makes everyone else second class. The truth is that only a minority of American Jews live in intact traditional nuclear families. Unless we face that fact and move beyond a myopic focus on mother, father, and their biological children as the only normal family, we will be unable to address the needs and problems of the majority of Jews.

Beyond recognizing that traditional families do not always do all they are supposed to do, it is important to realize that clinging to the ideal of the traditional family blinds us to the ways that other relationships may meet many of the same needs as effectively or better—particularly if they are given the appropriate communal recognition and support. Thus, many people find satisfying emotional relationships outside of marriage—either in unmarried heterosexual relationships, in gay or lesbian relationships, in circles of close friends, or in collective living arrangements. Friends and/or communal groups may well help to sustain such relationships economically. Many people raise children without a legal spouse, or in the context of a gay or lesbian family. And many people, both married and unmarried, have found ways other than parenting to express their commitment to raising Jewish children and to contributing to the vitality and continuity of the Jewish community—as teachers, social workers, rabbis, or community service workers, to name just a few.

In short, many of the values we associate with families can be, and have been, met in contexts other than the traditional nuclear family. If we as a community are concerned with having certain needs met in a Jewish context, then it is surely in our interest to assure that those who live in alternative family structures be included in the community, welcome to join in communal activities, and to take advantage of communally offered support services. Those who live in nontraditional ways have all too often reported feeling like pariahs—feared, perhaps, as examples of what might happen to others, or seen as threats to the supposed sanctity of the traditional families everyone finds increasingly difficult to maintain.

But those whose intimacy constellations differ from the norm need not be on the margins of organized Jewish communities. Most are eager for full inclusion as long as the price of inclusion is not the abandonment of their uniqueness. From our vantage point as a Jewish minority in American culture, we can see that the strength of the larger community depends on recognition and support for our particularity. So, too, we should recognize that, within the Jewish communal context, strength and unity depend on recognizing, welcoming, and supporting all those who would wish to contribute to our common project.

New Families, New Challenges

By including those now marginalized, we increase the size and strength of the community. In addition, I believe there are specific resources that those whose intimacy constellations differ from the norm have to offer to the community at large.

Many elderly people, for example, now live alone; their isolation makes it difficult for them to cope with illness, the death of loved ones, and the responsibilities of household management. Group living for healthy older people not only improves the quality of their lives; it reduces the demand placed on their extended families and often on community resources. Perhaps more important, many older people find this way of living more secure and satisfying. It provides opportunities for giving to others, both at home and in the broader community.

Group living arrangements of this sort might well prove more generally valuable: they could be important to single people of whatever age, providing a context for breaking down isolation and loneliness. And they might also offer an alternative for traditional families at various stages of life, who find it difficult if not impossible to sustain an independent life: there is no reason why, for example, a group living arrangement might not include one or two young families with children, some single people, and some elderly people (whether or not related to the younger ones). Such a household could offer substantial benefits to all. To date, Jewish communal organizations have given little attention to such alternatives, perhaps because they do not seem to reinforce the traditional nuclear family.

Gays and lesbians represent another group whose living arrangements have been similarly marginalized by the Jewish community. What would it mean for the community to make gay and lesbian Jews, and members of our intimacy constellations, fully equal members of the Jewish community?[8]

Gay and lesbian families come in all shapes and sizes. Some are constructed along the lines of heterosexual nuclear families—two adults in a committed relationship, and their associated children—except that the two adults are of the same sex. Some may consist of an adult parent and her/his children, without an adult lover present. In other cases, because so many lesbians and gays have been married, have had children in those marriages, and now "share" them with an ex-spouse in some form of joint custody, lesbian or gay households will sometimes have children present and sometimes not. In their variety, gay and lesbian families do not differ significantly from heterosexual families. Nevertheless, some significant differences open new possibilities for the Jewish community at the same time that they seem to challenge deeply held values and commitments.

Challenging Homophobia

Gay and lesbian families do not share in heterosexual privilege, and family members are subject to societal homophobia. On the surface, one might argue that homophobia is not of great consequence to those already in relationships: if we have our love for one another, what difference does it make if that love is validated by others? But if that were so, if we could all live without social validation and recognition, why would anyone go through the formalities of (heterosexual) marriage?

Of course, marriage confers immediate benefits that are denied to gays and lesbians, as well as to others who may be living together outside of legal marriage.[9] Many of these are fairly obvious: the inability to claim and publicly celebrate those relationships most central to one's being; denial of "family memberships," whether in a museum or a synagogue; denial of visiting privileges with a partner if he or she is hospitalized; invisibility and lack of support (or even awareness of the loss) when a relationship ends or a lover dies; fear of losing one's children in a custody battle, or of not being able to continue a relationship with the children of a lover should the lover die.

Many of the consequences of living in a society oriented around the conventional nuclear family are much less obvious. Most significant, perhaps, is that the expectations and social supports that help sustain heterosexual families through the vagaries of interpersonal conflict and familial tension are largely denied to others. In many areas of the country—and in most Jewish communities, in particular—few resources are available if a lesbian or gay couple (or even an unmarried heterosexual couple) runs into trouble and wishes to seek counseling. While most Jewish communal organizations have a clear commitment to helping families sustain themselves, that commitment has rarely been explicitly extended to gay and lesbian families. When we are victims of homophobia on the streets, at work, in school, or in the synagogue, there are, in most cases, no Jewish communal organizations to come to our aid. And when our children have to confront homophobia—whether from their peers or other adults—there are no resources in the Jewish community to which they can turn.

Taking account of that difference in the experience of different family types and fully including gay and lesbian families within the Jewish community would mean acknowledging and addressing homophobia, heterosexism, and their manifestations in the Jewish community. Homophobia and heterosexism affect heterosexuals as well as lesbians and gays, locking us all into confining sex roles and behaviors out of fear that we might be labeled "queer." Addressing those issues directly within our communities would free all of us to live in ways more expressive of our full selves. Moreover, it would mean making counseling and other support services available not only to those in gay or lesbian families, but also to others attempting to cope with new family structures (for example, as a result of divorce, widowhood, single parenthood, or childlessness), and to those struggling with issues concerning sexual orientation—thus overcoming the isolation of many individuals and families and opening the community to many who now avoid it for fear of rejection. Heterosexual families as well as gay and lesbian families would benefit from the infusion of energy that attention to such issues could entail.

Sexual Equality

One largely unresolved issue facing families is that of sexual equality and the dignity of every family member. We live in a male-dominant society, which means that even with the best of egalitarian intentions the average nuclear family must continually struggle against male dominance and conventional sex-role definitions and expectations. It is the rare heterosexual family, for example, in which the woman does not feel some greater responsibility for child-rearing or for the administration of the home.

One of the main feminist criticisms of traditional families has been the way in which they participate in, and reinforce, the societal dominance of men over women. Much of the contemporary debate over families focuses precisely on this issue of equality/inequality, and of what happens when women insist on full equality with men in all aspects of familial life. The conservative position, of course, is that families will not be able to sustain the strain, that someone must be at the head, and that given the organization of our society, it makes sense for that someone to be the male. The spate of recent books on "women who love too much" suggests even more specifically that intimacy between men and women is possible only in a context of inequality (where the man does the economic work and the woman does the emotional work).

The absence of a full commitment to women's equality in the Jewish community can be seen in its silence about wife-battering and child abuse, and the consequent lack of financial support for counseling and shelters. It can be seen in the failure of the community openly to confront sexual abuse. And it can be seen in our failure to promote models of equality in schools and communal organizations, as well as in synagogues. More thought is needed as to what it would take as a community to sustain all families on a truly egalitarian basis.

As I have suggested, Jewish feminists have criticized the presumption that Judaism is based not just on families, but on families constructed on the basis of sexual inequality. Jewish feminists have demanded of the community that it provide what is necessary to support and sustain more egalitarian family constellations—for example, communally sponsored day care, child care at synagogues, and flex-time schedules—and have challenged communal definitions of *shelom bayit,* which give primacy to maintaining the family even at the cost of the health and safety of the women and children within it. If Jewish communities begin to question and explode the myth of Jewish family, to recognize the variety of actual family types, and to meet the needs of real members of families on a broad scale, the benefits will accrue to a very wide range of people, including women of whatever familial constellation, single parents, and lesbian and gay families. Attention to these needs would, in turn, remove some of the major obstacles that have prevented women from full participation in the work force and the community.

Intergenerational Continuity

Later marriage, high divorce rates, and increasing rates of intermarriage among Jewish men have combined to produce large numbers of single Jewish women in their late thirties. They are faced with the difficult choice of never bearing children or becoming single mothers. Despite rhetoric about the need for more Jewish children, there has been little discussion of whether, or how, to support women in their decisions to bear children outside the context of a traditional nuclear family. Little has been done to provide for the special needs of single mothers, whether divorced, widowed, never married, or involved in lesbian relationships. This makes the community's message about the need for more Jewish children problematic at best. Commitment to increasing the Jewish birth rate must mean recognizing the potential for (and actuality of) childbearing for those not conventionally married.

Of course, bearing and raising children is *not* the only way to contribute to the Jewish future. Judaism has long recognized that generativity comes in many forms and guises. Susan Handelman has noted that Jewish tradition holds that one who teaches another's child is as if s/he gave birth to that child. Teachers, community leaders, those who care for the young, the old, the sick, all make their contribution to the vitality and continuity of the community. Single people, the elderly, gays and lesbians have all made major contributions to culture and religious life as teachers, social service workers, community supporters, rabbis, songwriters, poets, writers, critics. Expanding our notion of what constitutes generativity can relieve many childless Jews—whether married or unmarried, heterosexual, lesbian or gay—of the shame or guilt of childlessness while at the same time freeing them to develop and recognize the variety of ways in which they do contribute to the future of the community. Such a shift in perspective can benefit us all.

Sexual Ethics and Family Stability

These same factors of later age at marriage, high divorce rates, and the so-called sexual revolution have posed other significant challenges to traditional Jewish ethics concerning family and sexuality. Jewish attitudes toward sexuality have in some ways been enlightened: Judaism acknowledged that sexuality is an important and valued aspect of our humanity. At the same time, however, the traditional view has been that heterosexual marriage is the only appropriate context for the full expression of sexuality. That view, of course, is now much more honored in the breach than in the observance: the majority of Jews today do have sexual relations before marriage, and many also have sexual relations outside of marriage. Of course, to deny the possibility of sexual intimacy and connection to those who are not married would seem only to compound the frustrations of their existing marginalization from the community.

We are, in short, in desperate need of communal discussion about an appropriate sexual ethics for our post-halakhic age. Some such discussion has already begun.[10] I would only emphasize here the value Judaism has traditionally placed on mutuality and respect in sexual relationships. Thus, as in each of the areas I have discussed so far, what is needed is a commitment on the part of the community to retain that emphasis on mutuality and respect while at the same time recognizing that mutual and respectful sexual relationships can take place between young people before they are married, elderly people who are no longer married, and among others who are not married, whether heterosexual or homosexual. What is crucial is the quality of the relationship, rather than the legal relational status of those who constitute it.

Further, as I suggested earlier, the community must actively address the consequences of changes in family constitution (whether these result from divorce, death, or other reasons). Few synagogues or Jewish communal organizations provide counseling or other services for children or other family members struggling with issues of family dissolution or recombination. Rabbis and other communal leaders have been notably silent on the financial hardship most women and their children experience after divorce. As there is little sign that divorce rates (and rates of family reconstitution and recombination) will diminish, hand-wringing on the part of the community is insufficient. What we need—in addition to ethical standards for ending and beginning relationships—is a wide range of supports and services for people experiencing these changes.

Families, Community, and Spirituality:
Toward a New Communal Ethic

I want to end by returning, once again, to Buber, and to the vision I articulated of a Jewish community characterized by joint striving to realize the presence of God in our midst. I have argued that if we are to create such a community, it must be based on a recognition of mutual respect and dignity, and that a community cannot be built and maintained at the expense of its weaker members. I have also argued that as a community we have much to gain from the full incorporation of those whose intimacy constellations or family types now make them somewhat marginal. In our struggle to incorporate difference and diversity, our community as a whole can grow much richer.

The spiritual dimension underlying many of these arguments has been stated mostly by implication. I wish to conclude by addressing it more directly, and to argue for the recognition of an important interconnection between spiritual fulfillment and the social-political and familial context in which we live. I believe that a recognition of this connection (encapsulated in the notion of *tikkun olam* [repairing the world]) generates a further demand for the active engagement of the community in struggles to make both Jewish organizations and communities, and our society at large, places where people can live out their differences and realize the full range of their personhood.[11]

If we meet God in the Between spaces, then the institutions and relationships which define the Between are essential components of our spiritual lives. A community that strives to realize the presence of God in its midst therefore cannot limit its concerns to the narrowly "spiritual" realm (whatever that might mean). It must, instead, engage in the business of *tikkun olam*, by which I mean that it must commit itself to building, sustaining, and enriching the day-to-day relationships in which people live and work. Those relationships provide the contexts in which we experience the divine. Since relationships of intimacy and commitment are one context in which we experience the presence of God, those relationships must have the support of our communities on a variety of levels.

Most basic, of course, is economic survival. At a minimum, meeting our day-to-day physical needs and those of our loved ones is an expression of loving commitment. Provision of basic levels of physical and economic security for all families and intimacy constellations is, consequently, a spiritual, as well as a political, imperative. A contemporary Jewish family ethics must include a communal imperative to struggle for adequate physical and economic supports for all families, whatever their form.

Second, there must be a recognition of the variety of ways intimacy can be (and is) experienced, and families constituted. Traditional families are surely one context for intimacy, but many experience intimacy elsewhere—outside of formal marriage, or in relationships with people of their own sex.

If we are truly committed to everyone's spiritual growth, we must also welcome and validate (both within our own community and within the larger society) the varied contexts in which people experience that growth. Intimacy is too important, and unfortunately too rarely achieved, to limit the acceptable contexts in which people strive to achieve it. To treat married, heterosexual families as the only legitimate context for intimacy, and to deny the legitimacy (and the spiritual nature) of other intimacy constellations grounded in mutual respect, is to deny an important aspect of that humanity which our tradition should foster. Further, it prevents a range of people—unmarried heterosexual couples, singles, the divorced, widows, gays and lesbians—from experiencing foundational aspects of themselves in the context of spiritual/religious community.[12]

Finally, regardless of the form that our intimacy constellations take, our efforts to contribute to the Jewish future must be welcomed. Our community must support all its members in their decisions to raise and nurture children. Those who choose not to have children, or are unable to do so, also deserve respect and understanding. They should have opportunities to develop relationships with others' children and/or ways to contribute to the continuity of our communities and traditions.

Each of these imperatives is related to the tradition of *tikkun olam,* which recognizes a spiritual component to engagement in the world. Just as families do not exist in a vacuum, neither do our spiritual lives. They have a social and political—a communal—context. If, as members of a Jewish community, we are committed to people being able to express and fulfill themselves spiritually, then we must work to create the conditions that will make that fulfillment possible.

What this approach offers us is the image of an inclusive community. Such a community is, of course, one of the goals of our democratic political system, which we, as Jews, have adopted. Inclusiveness should also be the goal of a community committed to meeting the spiritual needs of its members, and, therefore, the essence of a Jewish family ethics for our post-halakhic age.

A Response

Esther Ticktin

Martha Ackelsberg's thesis is deceptively simple. She sees American Jews as living in a changing community characterized by greater permeability to the world around us and greater internal democracy, including more egalitarian and inclusive patterns of power and authority, than were most previous Jewish communities. It is within this changing Jewish community that individuals as well as families define themselves as Jews. This new social reality includes many more, and more varied, patterns of living than did the traditional heterosexually constructed nuclear family, which has in the past been the Jewish norm. The choice for the Jewish community then, it seems to me, is whether to accept the changing patterns of family and life-style structure as inevitable and to proceed from there, infusing whatever emerges with holy purpose, as Ackelsberg proposes, or to oppose and stand in judgment of the world around us by sanctifying the traditional family, using all our communal resources to help it function at its best and taking our stand behind it as the model building block of Jewish life.

I am going to end up in exactly the same place as Martha Ackelsberg—affirming a pluralism of life styles and family arrangements within a God-centered Jewish community—but I won't get to it as quickly as she does. I need to make a detour first, taking my time to mourn for the declining Jewish family. I grew up in such a family, and I know what it can be at its best—grounded in and surrounded by at least the memories of a cohesive Jewish community. To me *shelom bayit* means respect for every member of the family, recognition of the different needs of every member, and mutual responsibility for each other's physical and emotional well-being. In the Jewish family that I knew there was equality in the sense that all our opinions counted and no one claimed to be more important than anyone else. It was from this vantage point, in fact, that we judged the other community institutions: the rabbinate, the schools, welfare and cultural institutions, and the synagogue, in all of which, indeed, the power lay in the hands of upper-class educated males and the laws that empowered them. My own Jewish family happened to survive the destruction of all the other Jewish communal institutions; even under the humiliating conditions of living as refugees, it continued to function as the main resource for our emotional and spiritual needs and the major anchor of our Jewishness.

Of course, one can no more generalize from a single good experience than one can from a bad one. To be trapped in an abusive and exploitative family must be one of life's worst tortures—especially for women and children, whose alternatives are limited in so many ways. And yet the traditional Jewish family is attractive not only to those who have had good experiences with it. I believe that the vast majority of the new "reborns" (I resist calling them *ba'alei teshuvah*) who turn to Orthodoxy and Hasidism do so because they long for the kind of family life they find there. There is something enormously comforting, especially for a child of a broken marriage, in a stable, reliable constellation of a father, a mother, and all the children that God has given them. The comfort derives precisely from their right to be taken care of in a predictable environment independent of such unreliable factors as their parents' sexual attraction for each other or career ambitions, or any other circumstance that to a child must seem totally arbitrary. This right is simply a result of having been conceived by this couple and therefore placed by God under their care. And whatever else may be its shortcomings, a community that protects and nurtures parents and families like these appears very desirable to a fragmented, lonely, uprooted young Jew who doesn't know where he belongs or whether she belongs anywhere at all.

There are many "between spaces"—to use Buber's and Ackelsberg's phrase—in such a family where the individuals can "realize and experience the divine." I mention two such spaces because they seem to me specific to the heterosexually structured nuclear family. One is the role of the father. For obvious biological reasons, the father is more distant and removed from his offspring than the mother: there is a nine-month interval during which he can easily forget his relationship to the developing child, and after that, even in egalitarian setups, the nursing mother's responsibility for the infant is more immediate and direct. But in the traditional Jewish family a father's responsibility for his children begins even before their conception; it begins, in fact, with his marriage. I believe that this sense of responsibility for others, which is not contingent on love or preference or choice, but is experienced as a God-given imperative, is a prototype of all true responsibility and is best learned in the traditional family.

Similarly, the value of faithfulness, which can probably be fully appreciated only by those who've experienced a broken faith, whether as spouses, children or friends, is also best learned in the traditional family where it is the basis of all the relationships: between husband and wife, between parents and children, among siblings, and between children and aging parents.

So as a Jew, as a religious person, and as a psychotherapist, I do not disparage the heterosexually structured nuclear family nor do I rejoice in its decline. But that decline is evident wherever we look, and Ackelsberg gives many examples of it. The reasons for the decline are easy to find. To become established, social structure has to meet many needs of many people. The patriarchal family did not become a dominant structure only because it provided a relatively safe environment for children to grow into responsible adults, but also (and mainly) because it fit in with the economic requirements for the time and the political aspirations of those in power. As the economic and political configurations change, different needs of different people have to be met, and long-established social institutions become open to question. The previously powerless begin to realize how little the institutions have met their needs and how oppressive they have actually been. Thus, in our time women as women, gays and lesbians, unmarried or childless men and women are starting to recognize how the Jewish community's single-minded emphasis on family and children has undermined their self-esteem and interfered with their ability to create meaningful lives for themselves.

And perhaps equally important, the children who have grown up in semi-isolated, small nuclear families are beginning to realize how they have suffered under the system, not only because they have all too often had to submit to abuse in the secrecy of the self-contained family, but also because they have been deprived of other intimate relationships and early models other than their parents. With the prolonged adolescence that our economy and educational requirements are foisting on us, these children are quite numerous and quite articulate, and they are strong witnesses to the shortcomings of the nuclear family for meeting their needs.

Ackelsberg reminds us that these needs are not necessarily selfish at all. In fact, they are often anguished cries of people who want nothing more than to be useful members of the community. But now that other options are available to them, they can't go back to the institutions that deny their existence or their right to give meaning to life, and they now contribute to the community and the shape of the future in their own way. Largely as an outcome of the women's movement, gays and lesbians, divorced and other single parents, childless couples, unmarried men and women, and even intermarried Jews—recognizing how the Jewish community's emphasis on a monolithic image of family has suppressed their needs as human beings and as Jews—are now claiming their rights as equal members of the household of Israel, and the life-styles and intimacy constellations they are creating are a judgment on the inadequacy and limitedness of the traditional Jewish family.

I find Ackelsberg's call for the acceptance of a pluralism of family structures and life-styles and for an all-out effort of the Jewish community to support all sorts of alternative arrangements very compelling. And I also agree that we will all be enriched by this pluralism and that everyone, including those of us in traditional families, can learn and benefit from alternative arrangements, especially since these newer forms are arising out of a failure of the old system to meet the fundamental human needs for respect and dignity of all members.

Let me end my remarks on a midrashic note. My teacher Will Herberg held that Judaism is a declaration of permanent resistance to idolatry, implying that total and unreserved allegiance is due only to the Living God to whom all other powers, concerns, and allegiances are subject. There are many good and useful objects, concepts, and social institutions in the world that deserve our love and loyalty, but when we begin to put them in the center of our lives—in the place where only God, the creator of all, belongs—then they become idols and our worship of them will lead us astray.

One such institution was the Temple. The prophet Jeremiah, as well as other prophets, warned us not to put our trust in its saving power, not to confuse the symbol with the Living God. When the Temple was destroyed, it was a major catastrophe for the Jewish people. Nevertheless, the people survived the tragedy and created new institutions because the prophets had prepared them not to confuse God with the means through which we attempt to reach the divine; by the time we had to accept exile, we had learned to accept alternative ways to worship, which have proven to be both more transcendent and more enduring.

Many midrashim and innumerable sermons have compared the family to the Temple, and the family dining table to the altar. We are now in danger of making an idol of the traditional Jewish family just as our ancestors were tempted to with the Temple—as though our existence and our salvation depended on it. In an autobiographical essay, Philip Roth says that the fundamental article of faith in his family was: "Hear oh Israel; the family is our God; the family is one." He goes on to show how destructive a faith it was, how it kept the individual members from recognizing and expressing their needs—to the detriment of all.

From a broader perspective Ackelsberg has told us the same: The alternatives to the traditional family have arisen because the traditional family does not meet all the needs of all of its members and is, in fact, destructive for some of them. Let us not make an idol, therefore, of a particular social arrangement. Many alternative forms have possibilities of "in between" spaces where people can relate to each other with equality, mutual respect, and caring—spaces where we can be in touch with the divine. And who knows if these alternative models will not contain elements that will prove more valuable and enduring for the majority than our present image of the Jewish family—even at its best.

A Response

Elliot N. Dorff

Martha Ackelsberg's deeply human and hopeful essay is admirable for its openness, its compassion, its honesty in facing changes, its recognition of the fear change entails, and its reassurance that we can gain from changes in family structures. Its argument from American experience that pluralism is not only possible but desirable should be cogent for any American, but especially for Jewish Americans, who have gloried so much in the benefits of that pluralism. Its clear commitment to applying the Jewish tradition to our new circumstances, including its typically Jewish refusal to be satisfied with individual spirituality alone, makes this a serious engagement not only with modernity, but with Judaism. And the writer's examination of the title assigned to her so as to clarify and respond to its assumptions warms this philosopher's heart.

And yet I have some serious reservations about Ackelsberg's conception of the future. The editor instructed the respondents to suppress their impulses to respond to scholarly details. Following Ackelsberg's lead, then, I start with the assumptions of the title, for my problems begin there; I then mention a few of my objections to Ackelsberg's analysis and suggest my own vision of Jewish family life to come.

"Post-halakhic" is one word in the title that troubles me. In the sense that, since the Enlightenment, we have not been forced by agencies of the government to abide by Halakhah, we clearly are in a post-halakhic age. That which has been handed down to us may not be adequate for our situation, as Ackelsberg claims, but historically that has often been the case. The Jewish response, though, has been to apply the law in new ways, not to proclaim that we are somehow beyond it. Jews often disagreed as to what form it should take, but a lack of uniformity did not make them turn elsewhere for instruction. In the right hands, Halakhah can stretch quite far to respond to new circumstances with wisdom and sensitivity while yet retaining its moorings; but, as even contemporary Reform scholars have recognized,[13] ignoring Halakhah altogether is to give up crucial guidelines for Jewish behavior. Judaism embraces a full civilization; but given the centrality of Halakhah in defining that civilization, I have difficulty understanding how a genuinely post-halakhic movement could be identifiably Jewish.

"Jewish ethics" are the other words in the title on which I want to pause. Ethics involves not only "codes of ethics and criteria for behavior," as Ackelsberg describes it, but a set of ideals for which to strive, heroic models who achieve those ideals, and, crucially, a communal structure that supports morality through instruction, positive and negative sanctions, motivational tools such as songs and stories, and emotional sustenance.[14] For Jews, many of these elements are uniquely Jewish in character, and hence, despite Ackelsberg's reservations, the existence of a specifically Jewish family ethics. Even in the narrow sense in which Ackelsberg uses the term, Jewish ethical rules concerning sexual relations, abortion, and the obligations of parents and children to each other, for example, are markedly different from those of Christianity or the American secular ethic. And Jewish family ethics is not only Jewish; it is an ethic and as such it involves norms.

I mention these terms because what bothers me most about Ackelsberg's presentation is, first, its lack of any real attempt to make traditional Jewish family ethics live in our day and, second, its lack of norms. Even she expresses doubt as to whether there is a uniquely Jewish family ethic; I question not only whether her vision is Jewish, but whether it is, strictly, ethical. Put positively, I would want a future Jewish society whose family relations are in form more normative than Ackelsberg suggests and in content more Jewish.

Let me be specific. It is of course true that Jewish families in the past have included divorced, widowed, single, orphaned, abandoned, and adopted people, and now much greater percentages of our families are blended from one or more divorces or are headed by a single parent. It is also true that the Jewish community should be as open to and supportive of the members of these families as possible, making sure that they are welcomed in word and deed to participate fully. Such people are, after all, not only creatures of God, but Jews, and often their personal status is not a matter of their own choice. But to pretend that any of these states is ideal is to pervert the Jewish family ethic. It is also a misrepresentation of the facts, for most such people, I would guess, would prefer their situations to be otherwise.

Put another way, it is one thing to recognize and accommodate to realities of Jewish family life; it is quite another to approve, much less applaud, all forms of marital status. For all of the multiple forms of Jewish family life in the past, the ideal was a stable, heterosexual marriage in which the two partners produced and raised at least two children. It was actually more than the ideal; it was the reality in a large percentage of Jewish families. That may not be the case any longer, but I, for one, am not willing to give it up as the norm that we should teach and strive for.

It is not at all clear that alternative arrangements can as often meet the needs of both the individuals involved and the community as the traditional family can. The long-term experience of organizations like Big Brothers has demonstrated the need for both male and female role models in a household.

Grandparents, uncles and aunts, and good family friends can sometimes fill the gap, but most families do not have the benefits of an extended family nearby. Moreover, the sheer time and energy involved in raising children make it extremely difficult for a single, working adult to do it alone. Even such parents who cope cannot possibly do for their children what two parents could do. Child care, which is itself in very short supply, can at its best supplement parents' involvement with their children; it cannot substitute for it. Aside from these psychological and physical needs, Jews also expect families to bear major educational responsibility in transmitting our tradition to the next generation, and that too becomes more difficult in the absence of parents of both genders. One thing feminism has demonstrated is that in important areas of life, religion certainly included, the significant differences in the experiences of men and women derive directly from the fact of different genders.

I know that these sentiments are not popular. As Americans raised largely after World War II, we are used to having virtually everything our heart desires. We want to say that any and all family arrangements will work out fine for everyone; we want to say we can all spend hours working at fulfilling jobs and yet provide for all of our children's needs. The trouble is that increasingly we are finding that this is not the case, that reality has a nasty way of intruding on our desires. Of course, as Ackelsberg correctly points out, the traditional family structure has not always served the needs of the adults and children involved either; conversely nontraditional family arrangements sometimes work well. There are simply no guarantees in life, for better or for worse. There are probabilities, however, and we have long experience to show that children from broken homes or homes with absent fathers or mothers fare considerably worse on a percentage basis than do those from homes with two parents. The black and Mexican-American communities have illustrated this dramatically, and we have no reason to expect that Jewish families will be any different.

I hope it is clear that I am in no way supporting wife battering, child abuse, or abandonment. I am, in fact, a member of the Board of Directors of the Jewish Family Service of Los Angeles and a member of its Family Violence Committee. Some right-wing, Orthodox rabbis have unfortunately abused the concept of *shelom bayit* to condone such violence for the sake of maintaining the family, as Ackelsberg reports. But Jewish law specifically prohibits wife beating, and some authorities instruct rabbinic courts to force a man to grant his wife a divorce on that ground.[15] (I am not, by the way, in favor of "humiliation" or "shame" in divorce proceedings either; we should recognize, though, that divorce by its very nature makes for raw feelings and that behavior that the parties experience as insensitive is not unique to divorce courts operating under Jewish law.)

Shelom bayit denotes that people within a home—all people within a home, not just women—must compromise (not "suppress") some of their desires and feelings to make the family work. That, of course, is the nature of any relationship; as Locke and others remind us, you give up some rights when you leave the state of nature and enter society. You are not crazy to do so; on the contrary, you simply cannot have some of life's richest rewards unless you forgo some of your power and enter into relationships with others. This willingness to look beyond oneself is particularly important in the family, where so much rests on the mutual care and concern of all members for each other. People do this not because they are interested in a life of continual self-sacrifice, but on the contrary because they discover that they cannot fully realize themselves except in a family relationship. And yes, Ackelsberg's essay notwithstanding, I would say that the whole (the family) is more than the sum of its parts (the individuals who make it up); the benefits of family life cannot be obtained unless all members are willing to waive or modify some of their own desires and work for the good of the family. That, as Erich Fromm told us a long time ago, is the essence of love.[16]

Ackelsberg's disdain for "suppressing" one's selfish desires in the name of the family is one instance of a broader issue that divides us. The underlying values of her vision are, it seems to me, power and freedom. She wants to empower women and children, and she wants "all of us to live in ways more expressive of our full selves." But that is a skewing of Jewish values beyond recognition. American, secular ideology stresses individualism and power; Judaism emphasizes community and responsibility.

I note, for example, that Ackelsberg, in her family ethic, never speaks of an imperative to have children; one may choose, according to her, to express one's generativity that way, but other ways are just as good. But as the tractate *Sanhedrin* (19b) says, "One who teaches other people's children Torah is like one who has given birth to them"—*like* one who has given birth, not equivalent to one who has done so. Some may not be able to have children; that is a totally different matter. I personally have devoted my life to teaching Judaism; one need not remind me of the significance, the joys, and, yes, the creativity of being a Jewish teacher. But physical propagation remains an important command of our tradition.

Similarly, "full participation in the work force" is one of Ackelsberg's desiderata. Judaism certainly appreciates work; God, after all, commands, "Six days shall you labor and do all your work" (Exodus 20:9). The tradition furthermore declares that work honors the person who does it and that lack of work leads to lewdness, mental instability, and thievery.[17] Judaism recognizes, though, that work is not the ultimate goal in life, that it is a necessity, not a blessing. Work is a means to the ends of supporting and educating a family, contributing to the fixing of the world, and having the time to study Torah; it is not an autonomous virtue.[18] These values transcend that of work—a lesson that men as well as women are beginning to learn. It is American secularism that makes work the sole source of self-worth. A wiser, Jewish view is that while work is important, family, study, and social action are more so.

In my view, Ackelsberg has not only overvalued the advantages of alternative family configurations; she has also misrepresented and undervalued the traditional family. A heterosexual marriage is certainly not necessarily, and as far as I can tell not usually, an affair in which the man dominates and/or abuses his wife and children. Most of the married people I know divide the tasks of life according to who does what best, or who minds it the least. If one must talk of dominance in such relationships, it is not at all to be taken for granted that the man dominates. The stereotype, remember, is of a domineering Jewish woman and a timid man, not the reverse. That stereotype blasphemes Jewish men and Jewish women, but it would never have existed if the men always overpowered the women. More important, missing from Ackelsberg's depiction is any appreciation of the loving give and take that marks a marriage. In the best of marriages, and there are many good ones, spouses do not measure and compare their varying tasks on a quid pro quo basis; rather, they take pleasure in doing things for each other as one way of expressing their love.

All in all, I find Ackelsberg's vision of the future curiously rooted in the notions of the late 1960s and early 1970s. It was then that people thought they could have everything in life at no cost, that self-fulfillment was the chief goal. In the 1980s, people came to realize that there are real prices to be paid for emphasizing work over all other values, relegating child care to others, relying on divorce to solve marital problems, and raising children without both male and female parents. Both parents may need to work for economic reasons, but two working parents should not be elevated to an ideal. Similarly, divorce may in some instances be the right or only solution, but it nevertheless must be recognized as the failure it is—just as the parties involved inevitably feel it to be. Child care may be necessary if both parents must work to support the family, but it is never the equivalent of parental care. Work is important for everyone's self-respect; but parents surely work in maintaining a home and raising children, and the value of work outside the home must be weighed against that of devoting one's best time and energy to one's family. Life's goods are not unmitigated; they must be carefully, and realistically, balanced.

My vision of the future of family relations, then, resembles Ackelsberg's in some respects, but it is quite different in others. Like her, I expect that people will come to take a variety of family configurations for granted and will plan accordingly. Like her, I hope that synagogue, educational, and communal services will be available for families of all sorts. Especially since many who find themselves in nontraditional families do so through no desire of their own, the Jewish community must go out of its way to lend them not only physical and monetary support, but Jewish educational assistance as well.

Unlike Ackelsberg, however, I project that as we learn more and more about the implications of other arrangements, people will once again consider a two-parent, heterosexual family with children to be ideal. As people rediscover the rich meanings and rewards of life-long commitments to each other in marriage, women and men will together recognize, as they are increasingly doing now, that such a setting is the best not only for their children, but for them, together and independently. We will educate our children and adults to be understanding of other configurations and considerate of the people in them, but the Jewish ethic will be what it has been in the past—not because of its historical roots, but because of the real personal and communal needs it serves. That ethic will be, to rephrase the title, a Jewish ethic for a postsecular age.

9

The Coming Reformation in American Jewish Identity

Egon Mayer

The specter of cataclysmic change, change whose sources are uncertain, whose directions are portentous, and whose ultimate outcome is unknown, haunts the imagination of Jews concerned about continuity and survival in contemporary America. The trends of intermarriage, low birthrate, continued assimilation, and varieties of religious schism and *kulturkampf* spur a collective anxiety that impels attempts to peer into the future. We need to give shape and meaning to what remains a fragmented and hazy apparition.

Calvin Goldscheider and Alan S. Zuckerman have argued that "the power of structural factors (e.g., economic, political, and demographic shifts) over values, ideologies, and preferences" best explains patterns of long-term communal change and the level of cohesion among Jewish communities.[19] Yet we take for granted that in everyday life people make choices about conduct, life-style, and attitudes. The amorphous flow of vast structural forces is mediated through values, ideologies, preferences, feelings, and beliefs—however well or poorly informed they may be. It is through them that people make the otherwise impersonal forces of history personally meaningful. It is also through them that people come to be more than mere victims of historical flux.

I am attempting here to delineate the emerging complex of values, ideas, and preferences through which America's Jews appear to be making their way into the next century and millennium.

Who will be America's Jews a generation from now? How many Jews will there be? What will be their manner of communal and religious organization? In what ways will they express themselves as Jews? What relationships will they have to historical trends of Judaism and to each other as subgroups?

Will there be one united Jewish people, or several deeply fissured? Will there be a large, growing community, or only a small "saving remnant" left behind isolating ghetto walls—with the rest of their cousins long ago having assimilated into the mainstream of the symbiotic relationship between the Jewries of the Diaspora and Israel? Or will the partnership have long dissolved, with no more ties between American Jewry and Israel than between American Jewry and the Jewries of, say, Australia or South Africa?

These are but the most obvious questions that come to mind as one attempts to imagine the future of American Jewish identification and affiliation.

Responding as a Jewish sociologist who has been involved in the empirical observation of the demography, conduct, and public opinion of America's Jews for nearly 20 years, I project a vision partly rooted in available research and partly in a somewhat wishful interpretation of that research. Others might draw different inferences from the data that describe present-day American Jews. But I take the invitation to imagine as an invitation to wish, precisely because the realities of the moment can result in very different futures. I believe that some of those alternatives are more desirable than others, and that in forecasting social character, culture, identity, and the like, *sof ma'aseh b'machshavah techilah:* real outcomes are often the function of what was imagined in the first place.

American Jewry in the Next Generation

Demographic Revolution

The explosion of intermarriage among America's Jews since the end of the 1960s has stirred a veritable demographic revolution in the Jewish community.

At the dawn of the 20th century, American Jewry was characterized by a growing homogeneity, the result of mass migrations from Eastern Europe. Between 1880 and 1924 approximately two million Jews from the Russian Pale were rapidly resettled in the urban ghettos of New York, Chicago, Philadelphia, and Boston. This resulted in shaping the culture and structure of American Jewry in the image of Jews whose primary concerns were economic survival, social acceptance, and the perpetuation of an ethnic culture with a religious core.

The homogeneity of that culture was further guaranteed by the very low incidence of intermarriage (about three or four out of a hundred), patterns of dense Jewish settlement, and shared experiences of economic, social, and geographic mobility.

The grandchildren of that generation were raised with a high degree of security and advantage, but a rather low degree of familiarity with the social, political, cultural, and religious concerns of their forebears. They have produced a community whose basic Jewish homogeneity—with all the commonalities such homogeneity implies—can no longer be taken for granted. An example from one major Jewish community should suffice to make this point.

In 1984 the Federation of Jewish Agencies of Greater Philadelphia published a study of the Jewish population of its area, which represents the fifth-largest Jewish community in America. The study estimated that there are 256,000 persons "living in Jewish households" (households in which at least one adult was reported to be Jewish). Based on the figures provided by the study, it has been estimated that as many as 60,000 of those people (about 23 percent) are non-Jews married to born Jews, or are the children of such couples. Another 7,500 people (about 3 percent of the total) in the Philadelphia community were converts to Judaism. In other words, *more than one-quarter* of the households that could be construed in some sense as Jewish did not include two adult Jews who shared common Jewish historical memory or ancestry.

Figures from more recent studies of American Jewish communities point to the same trend, only in greater magnitude. Current projections suggest that there may be as many as 9.5 million people in the U.S. who live in a household that contains at least one Jew over the age of 18, but less than 5 million Jews who live in a household where all the people over the age of 18 are Jewish. These figures put numbers to the fact that Jews who marry non-Jews produce twice as many households as Jews who marry other Jews. Given the rapid rise of intermarriage from the low figures in the early 1900s to over 40 out of 100 marriages by the end of the 1980s, it comes as no surprise that the Jewish community, like the Jewish family, is becoming an *erev rav,* a mixed multitude.

The most vexatious question concerning this demographic trend, which has exercised the American Jewish community since the mid-1970s, is what it portends for both the quantity and quality of American Jewry.

Since the dire but discredited projections of Elihu Bergman,[20] more forecasts have been made as to the dramatic decline of American Jewry as a result of "net assimilatory loss" fueled by intermarriage.[21]

At the moment, however, the evidence is much too ambiguous for such dire predictions. It is just as possible that American Jewry stands at the threshold of a major population explosion, if the majority of its intermarrying sons and daughters opt to remain within the community and bring in their spouses and children.

Which outcome is more likely to be the reality 20 years hence depends on the choices that those individuals make about their own identification, affiliation, and child-rearing. Yet it does not depend on them alone. The outcome also depends on whether Jewish communal policies and practices will encourage or discourage the choices that would bring them into the Jewish community. It is envisioned here that by the early 2000s the mainstream American Jewish institutions—synagogue, Jewish community center, school—will be fully engaged in reaching out to the intermarried families who comprise the American Jewish population in ever-growing numbers.

Although it appears, as we shall see below, that most American Jews are in favor of encouraging "outreach" to the intermarried, American Jewish leaders are divided on the matter, and are particularly divided on just what sorts of policies and practices constitute legitimate Jewish outreach. This division among

American Jewish leaders, particularly within the rabbinate, is fueled by the politicization of the issue in Israel, in the guise of the debate over the Law of Return.

Some of the other facets of American Jewish identity that have been emerging from local and national surveys are what make the image of a burgeoning and ever more heterogeneous American Jewry the future envisioned here.

Decline in Denominationalism

One of the distinctive features of American Jewish identity is its "denominational" character. American Jews are unlike prewar Eastern European Jews, who either classified themselves along a continuum of greater or lesser religious observance or as Zionists, Communists, Hasidim, or *freie* universalists, and unlike contemporary Israelis, who continue to identify themselves along similar lines with a few additional political wrinkles. For the better part of the past century most American Jews have identified themselves with one of four major branches or denominational bodies—Orthodox, Conservative, Reform, Reconstructionist.

To be sure, both the laity and the social scientists who have studied the community acknowledge that there is nearly as much diversity within each group as there is between them. Nevertheless, the denominational labels have been the convenient identity hooks on which most American Jews have hung their sense of Jewishness.

In a 1954 report on Jewish sociology presented to the Conference on Jewish Relations, Marshall Sklare noted that in his emerging studies of American Jews in suburbia, 80 percent described their grandparents as Orthodox, but only 20 percent described their parents as Orthodox.[22]

In 1970 the authoritative National Jewish Population Study (NJPS) showed that whereas about 40 percent of American Jews identified themselves as Conservative and 30 percent as Reform, only about 10 percent identified themselves as Orthodox. The remaining 20 percent identified themselves as having no denominational preference, or having a preference other than the three most popular branches of American Judaism.

The 1990 National Jewish Population Study shows the Orthodox as having shrunk to 7 percent, and the Conservative movement to 38 percent, while Reform has grown to 42 percent, Reconstructionists 1 percent, just Jewish 5 percent, and other 7 percent. Orthodoxy is still the smallest branch of American Jewry, not counting the Reconstructionist movement, which can properly be seen as a branch only recently separated from Conservatism. Orthodoxy is certainly a far cry from becoming a major force in the life of the great majority of American Jews. Nor does it show any signs of becoming such over the next 20 years.

At the same time, the data on denominational trends also show an alarming decline in the percentage of American Jews who continue to identify themselves with the two largest branches. Comparing Cohen's 1986 figures[23] with the 1970 NJPS figures, it appears that the greatest growth has occurred among those who regard themselves as "just Jewish" and identify with no particular branch of Judaism. These figures do not suggest a general decline among American Jews' willingness to identify themselves as such. There is no evidence of such a generalized trend toward apostasy or disaffection from Jewishness. Rather, there appears to be a disenchantment among a large and growing segment of the American Jewish public with the denominational labels that have served as the identificational reference points of their parents and grandparents for the past hundred years.

In short, there appears to be a decline in associational Jewishness, as expressed in denominational identification, and a corresponding increase in what Thomas Luckmann might have called invisible Jewishness: a privatized sense of longing, belonging, and meaning that is more psychological than communal, more felt than articulated. Such invisible religion, as Luckmann called it, draws from the same wellspring of collective symbols and memories as institutionalized religion. But it refuses to be constrained by the boundaries and social controls of the formal institutions (such as synagogues, Jewish organizations, schools) that claim to specialize in the perpetuation of the particular system.[24]

Perhaps of equal importance is the apparent divergence between the official positions of Reform and Conservative Judaism and the opinions expressed by large segments of their members on key issues of Jewish identity.

In a special follow-up analysis of his 1986 survey sample, Steven Cohen looked into the opinions of American Jews on the much debated issue of patrilineal descent.[25] The position, taken by the Reform and Reconstructionist movements, maintains that the children of mixed marriages can be presumed to be Jewish even if their mothers are not Jewish and they did not undergo conversion to Judaism, as long as the father is Jewish and the child is raised as a Jew. Both the Orthodox and Conservative movements have taken very strong stances against this position.

Cohen reports that a little over 80 percent of those who identify with one of the denominational branches of Judaism have at least heard about this debate. By contrast, only about 60 percent of those who do not identify with one of the branches and only about 60 percent of those who are not members of a synagogue know about it. The percentage of people who accept the patrilineal definition of Jewish identity seems to follow denominational lines fairly closely: 12 percent of the Orthodox, 47 percent of the Conservative, and 83 percent of the Reform accept the patrilineal definition of who is a Jew. About 70 percent of those without a denominational label also accept the patrilineal definition. It is instructive to note, however, that less than half the Conservative respondents in Cohen's sample subscribed to the standard of their movement on the issue.

Moreover, when the question is phrased in terms of whether the respondent "would be upset if your child married a patrilineal Jew," the numbers change considerably. First, Cohen asked: "Would you be upset if your child married a non-Jew?" The affirmative response to this question was 85 percent for the Orthodox, 68 percent for the Conservative, 39 percent for the Reform, and 38 percent for those respondents who described themselves as "just Jewish." Of those who reported no synagogue affiliation, only 22 percent indicated that they "would be upset" by their children marrying non-Jews.

When Cohen asked the question, "Would you be upset if your child married a patrilineal Jew? the affirmative response was: 78 percent for the Orthodox (indicating a high degree of consistency), but only 33 percent for the Conservative (an even greater divergence from the standards of the movement), 11 percent for the Reform, and 11 percent for those who did not subscribe to a denominational label. Of those who reported no synagogue affiliation, only 7 percent indicated that they would be upset if their children married patrilineal Jews.

From these figures, it appears quite clear that except for the Orthodox (who are a small minority), the great majority of American Jews, including Conservative Jews, have widely accepted patrilineal descent as the basis for Jewish identity. Thus, the Conservative movement, which has taken a very strong stand against the patrilineal position, must face the reality that the majority of its members vote differently in their hearts, and that their children may vote very differently in their ultimate mating choices.

The Reform movement is in a somewhat similar situation with respect to its position on rabbis officiating at marriages between a Jew and a non-Jew. In a 1987 study of some 2,700 delegates to the Union of American Hebrew Congregations (Reform) biennial convention, Mark Winer, Sanford Seltzer, and Steven Schwager found that the respondents to their survey were evenly split on whether to agree or disagree with the statement: "A rabbi should officiate only if the prospective bride and groom are both Jewish."[26] This is in spite of the fact that the movement has gone on record advocating against rabbis officiating at mixed marriages. Upon further questioning, the research found that though the great majority of respondents were opposed to rabbis officiating at a mixed marriage if the wedding were to be held in a church (90 percent), or if the couple said that they wanted to expose their children to both religious traditions (63 percent), the majority of the respondents approved of rabbinic officiation if the couple joined the temple (53 percent), or if the couple promised to raise their children as Jews (58 percent).

In short, the popular attitudes of members of both major movements of American Judaism reveal serious departures not only from historic concepts of the meaning of Jewish identification, but also from the currently professed positions of those movements. These divergencies will exert great pressure on the major movements for change in their understanding of Jewish identification: a pressure for greater acceptance of process and syncretism in the development of Jewish identity. At the same time, they are very likely to increase disaffection from the existing patterns of denominational Jewishness over the next 20 years. Such departures pave the way for the emergence of greater schism, new movements, and counter-movements.

Affiliation and Participation

In addition to the pattern of identification with the three largest denominational bodies, most American Jews are thought to have expressed their identity by belonging to and participating in the activities of synagogues and other Jewish organizations. In fact, however, only about half of America's Jews report that they are affiliated.

Citing figures from 1953, Will Herberg noted that in a nationwide survey only about 50 percent of American Jews replied affirmatively to the question: "Do you happen at the present time to be an active member of a church or a religious group?"

The NJPS of 1970–71 found that only 47 percent of its respondents reported belonging to a synagogue. In Cohen's 1986 survey, about 51 percent of the respondents indicated that they belonged to a synagogue.

Given the apparent stability of the rate of synagogue affiliation over the past 30 years—hovering around the fifty percent mark—there is little reason to expect any significant rise or fall in that proportion. But given the significant demographic revolution currently under way, there is every reason to expect that the mixture of people who comprise synagogue-affiliated families will include ever greater numbers of intermarrieds, non-Jews, half-Jews, and patrilineal Jews.

Attendance at synagogue services, like affiliation, has also shown a certain constancy over the past 30 years. A January 1956 Gallup poll dealing with attendance at religious services asked a cross-section of Americans: "Did you happen to attend any Sunday or Sabbath services during the last twelve weeks?" While 82 percent of Catholics and 68 percent of Protestants answered the question in the affirmative, only 44 percent of Jews did so.[27]

In 1970 the NJPS report showed that only 18 percent of America's Jews attend synagogue services "regularly," while 28 percent indicated that they "never attend," another 28 percent indicated that they attend only on the High Holidays, and the remaining 26 percent indicated that they "attend occasionally."[28] The 1986 Cohen study found that about 26% of the nationwide sample of American Jews reported attending synagogue services "at least once a month."

While synagogue attendance might have been somewhat more common among America's Jews in the mid-1950s (probably owing to the postwar baby boom), it was certainly lower than the incidence of affiliation even then. It was also lower than the incidence of religious service attendance among non-Jews. The decline from 44 percent reported by Gallup in 1956 to the 26 percent figure reported by Cohen in 1986 may also be more apparent than real because of the phrasing of the questions. The Gallup question that generated the 44 percent figure inquired into religious service attendance "during the last twelve weeks." When Gallup asked the question in terms of religious service attendance "in a typical week during the last year," the pattern of response was: 74 percent for Catholics, 42 percent for Protestants, and only 27 percent for Jews—a figure that is virtually identical to Cohen's finding some 30 years later.

Taken together, the figures on synagogue affiliation and attendance show a remarkable stability over the course of the past 30 years. It is possible, of course, that the influx of former Christians into the community may increase synagogue attendance as well. But the prospect seems unlikely to affect the overall rate of synagogue attendance. The central forum for Jewish expression is likely to continue to be the Jewish home, and central acts of identification are likely to continue to be carried out within the private lives of those who consider themselves Jewish. However, as we shall see below, those acts are more likely to be acts of the heart and mind than of deeds linked to the formal mitzvah system of institutionalized Judaism.

The Sliding Practice of Jewishness

Ceremonial and routine practices comprise the daily conduct that constitutes a distinctly Jewish life-style. Over the past few decades, a succession of local and national Jewish community surveys have used several practices as indicators for total Jewish expression. On the whole, studies of Jewish practice indicate greatly diminished Jewish activity within the daily lives of most American Jews.

In his 1986 survey, Cohen found that 84 percent of his respondents had attended a Passover seder in the past year, and 82 percent reported lighting Chanukah candles. But only 20 percent use separate dishes for meat and dairy (a requirement for a kosher home). In his 1983 survey, Cohen also found that only 34 percent of respondents light Sabbath candles at home.

Hasty conclusions about the recency of any declines in the level of observance among America's Jews can be avoided by recalling some of the earlier studies of different communities around the country. For example, a 1955 study of the Orthodox community of Milwaukee found that 66 percent lit Sabbath candles and 62 percent had separate dishes for meat and dairy. But in the same sample it was found that 66 percent ate meat in nonkosher restaurants, and 88 percent would handle money on the Sabbath. Moreover, only about 2 percent indicated that their married sons were as observant as they were.[29]

In their 1963 survey of the Providence, Rhode Island, Jewish community, Sidney Goldstein and Calvin Goldscheider also found a steady slippage of observance from one generation to the next. For instance, with respect to the weekly lighting of Sabbath candles, they found a wide disparity between the immigrant (first) generation (61 percent), their second-generation children (37 percent), and their third-generation grandchildren (25 percent). They reported similar disparities with respect to having separate dishes for meat and dairy (53 percent among the first generation, 25 percent among the second generation, and 16 percent among the third generation), as well as with respect to bringing only kosher meat into the home (62 percent among the first generation, 34 percent among the second generation, and 19 percent among the third generation).[30]

Interestingly, attendance at the Passover seder and lighting of Chanukah candles seems to have been fairly impervious to change—at least in terms of the frequency with which Jews reported those observances.

One Jewish activity that seems to have increased appreciably over the last 20 or so years is travel to Israel. According to the NJPS of 1970, about 16 percent of America's Jews had visited Israel at least once. According to Cohen's 1986 survey, the number was about 33 percent. Though various crises in Israel and the Middle East have in the past cut into the travel of American Jews to Israel, there is reason to expect that over the next 20 years ever larger proportions of American Jews will visit there at least once. The declining significance of Eastern Europe as the reference point of Jewish ethnicity can only help to bolster the ethnic magnetism of Israel.

These fragmentary glimpses of the life styles of America's Jews provide little reason to differ with the assessment offered by Marshall Sklare in the mid-1950s. The practices that continue to have the widest appeal are those that are joyous, do not require rigorous devotion or daily attention, do not require a high degree of separation from one's non-Jewish neighbors, and are in some way connected to life-cycle transitions. There is little reason to expect any change in this pattern in the next 20 years for the masses of American Jews.

Change is most likely to occur in the specific observances that may yet emerge in conformity with Sklare's general principles. Some of these observances, which have not yet surfaced in the data of Jewish community surveys, include such ceremonies as baby-naming (for daughters especially), conversion, and adult bat and bar mitzvah (particularly for women who came of age at a time when bat mitzvah ceremonies were not yet popular).

Another area of change not yet documented by community surveys is that of consumption habits aimed specifically at expressing and enhancing their identificational impulses of American Jews. The erstwhile preference for kosher-style foods and Yiddish humor has been augmented, if not replaced, by the acquisition of Judaica (largely from Israel), the frequenting of restaurants run by Israeli and Russian immigrants, political activism on behalf of Israel, travel to sites of once-thriving Jewish communities in the Old as well as the New World, and the watching of films, plays, and television productions of Jewish cultural relevance.

These forms of Jewish self-expression are consistent with Sklare's general guidelines, but they also build upon the consumerist tendencies of a highly gentrified Jewry. This Jewry seeks to express its commitments not merely with a bow toward tradition, but also with the élan of educated good taste. This tendency to express Jewishness with the good taste of a sophisticate is of particular relevance to a population whose majority within the next 20 years will benefit from high levels of postsecondary education, high levels of discretionary income, and a relatively low birthrate—making investment in quality of life a key personal and familial value.

Looking Beyond the Numbers

Up to this point the futurology in this presentation has closely followed available data concerning patterns of Jewish identification. Yet such a cautious approach to the future is severely limited. Therefore, the remainder of this essay looks at some wider social forces, both structural and cultural, in terms of their possible/probable impact on Jewish identification in the next 20 years.

The Role of Women

Probably no social force has had a greater impact on our understanding of human identity than the growing equalization of the roles of men and women. With the large-scale entry of the postwar baby-boom generation of women into higher education and then into the labor force, Americans as well as people the world over need to adjust their gender-based role expectations. Given the high mobility aspirations of Jewish women in particular, this aspect of the sexual revolution has resulted in an influx of women into the rabbinate to the point where some can now envision the large-scale feminization of that profession much as education and social work became feminized several decades earlier.

But of course the number of women seeking to enter the rabbinate is minuscule compared to the number of their sisters who have sought careers in the other major professions, such as medicine, law, accounting, and business management. While these trends have produced considerable stress within both the American Jewish family and the American synagogue, it is quite possible that over the next 20 years they may, in fact, have a salutary effect upon American Jewish identity.

The large-scale entry of Jewish women into the labor force over the past 20 years has meant that many more Jewish children are exposed to a greater amount of Jewish fathering, since as a result Jewish fathers have been compelled to take a greater share in child rearing. Whatever small advantage in Jewish education Jewish fathers have had over Jewish mothers (and there is evidence of some), it can be expected that children's greater exposure to their fathers may have a positive effect on their Jewishness 20 years hence.

The large-scale entry of Jewish women into the labor force has also compelled modern Jewish families to make greater use of early child-care services, as well as the services of available Jewish grandparents. To the extent that they have made use of child-care services under Jewish auspices or made use of Jewish grandparents, there is every reason to expect a favorable impact upon the Jewish identification of their children over the course of the next generation.

The equalization of the role of women in the synagogue, culminating in the elevation of women into the pulpit, has resulted in increased opportunity and interest in serious Jewish learning and self-expression on the part of the female half of the Jewish population. At the very least, that trend has increased by 100 percent the number of Jews who might seriously engage in the social production of Jewish identification from the pulpit and from other venues.

Increased Market Demand on Leisure Time

The increased education and economic well-being of American Jews has made them an ever-growing target of merchants of leisure-time use. From health clubs to unique cultural programs to exotic vacations, Jews, as an elite market segment, are more susceptible than ever to the general purveyors of leisure-time products and services. As an increasingly aging community with a great deal of disposable income, they are also much sought after by those who market to the retirement population. The value of the Jewish community as a market segment is bound to present a serious challenge to the traditional Jewish institutions (centers, synagogues, clubs, fraternal organizations, and the like), which must now compete for the time, money, and loyalty of their constituents. Such competition will inevitably produce Jewish products, services, and experiences that will serve to enhance the character of Jewish identification, even as they expand the range of choices in the manner of Jewish self-expression.

The Growth of the Electronic Frontier

Jewish institutions and the patterns of Jewish identification in 20th century America have developed largely out of the encounter between the traditions of an ancient religious system garbed in the ethnic cloak of premodern Eastern Europe, and the challenges and opportunities of modernity, urbanization and sub-urbanization, economic advancement, and education. Each of these encounters represented a frontier for Jews as individuals and as a community; each was a locale and milieu where we had not been before. In each, Jews sought to integrate their desire to retain some of the valued aspects of their heritage with the opportunities that the wider society had to offer. Indeed, the shape and form of contemporary American Jewish identity is the mark of how well Jews have mastered these frontiers.

However, most of the challenges faced by American Jews have been personal, posed by a non-Jewish world to Jews as individuals. Whether educational opportunity, career opportunity, or residential opportunity, Jews approached each frontier as a challenge uniquely addressed to them. Yet getting into the best school or the best firm or the best neighborhood was seen by each individual, and indeed by the Jewish community as a whole, as not merely a wonderful personal achievement, but as a collective Jewish achievement. Having successfully

met the personal challenges, many thought that the collective well-being of
Jewry was also secured. For the better part of the past 40 years, that equation
has held fast.

The tremendous diffusion of television, VCR, computers, and other forms
of electronic technology provide a profound challenge to Jewish identity. This
challenge complicates the encounters between tradition and modernity, science
and religion, ethnicity and mobility—all important encounters playing themselves out within the lives and psyches of individual Jews and shaping Jewish
identity patterns for much of the 20th century. The challenge in the coming decades will be a collective one. It no longer involves integrating the Jew into various new frontiers. Now it is integrating the information flow necessary to
perpetuate Jewishness into the massive flows of information to which all modern Jews now have access.

Most Jews are inundated with a flow of symbols, images, and ideas of every imaginable kind in their professional, personal, and recreational lives. Their
identity, like all human identity, is shaped by the interplay of individual psychic
economy with those information systems. The successful reproduction, perhaps
even reconstruction, of Jewish identity in the coming generation will depend
very heavily on the capacity of the Jewish community to transmit information to
its members within the varied informational facilities that individual Jews now
have at their fingertips.

Uncertainty and Hope

Even as one attempts to develop answers to the questions about the Jewish
future, several caveats loom large on the intellectual horizon. First, there are the
chastening words of Rabbi Yochanan of the Talmud, *Bava Kama* (12b): "From
the time that the Temple was destroyed, the gift of prophecy was taken away
from the prophets and given over to fools and children." There is a certain element of childishness in believing that just because one would like desperately
to envision the future one has, in fact, done so.

Then there are the caveats of history. Most of us, attempting in 1938 to
imagine the Judaism and Jewries of 1948, or 1958, or 1988, would have made
very poor visionaries. There is little reason to expect that we will be any better
at envisioning just how we will look in 2008. Fifty years ago neither my parents
nor my grandparents imagined that their lives as Jews would be radically altered
in a matter of just a few short years, first by the Holocaust (they were deported
from Budapest in the spring of 1944), then by the birth of the State of Israel
(where my grandparents settled in 1948).

Self-fulfilling or self-negating prophecies, catastrophes, and unanticipated
consequences are among the familiar pitfalls that plague the would-be futurologists among us. The concepts of self-fulfillment and self-negation caution us that
we may bring about historically unnecessary outcomes by imagining they will

naturally flow from existing trends. Alternatively, we may waste our energies attempting to thwart some historical inevitability because we find it highly undesirable.

Unanticipated (and unintended) consequences are the often undesired, unexpected, and highly inconvenient results of some of our most well-intentioned activities. In helping to bring about a highly desired condition, or in working toward avoiding some highly undesirable one, we fail to notice what sociologists have called the *latent functions* of our purposeful activities. We can readily point to a number of hotly pursued Jewish activities that have had unanticipated and unintended consequences in the last 50 years.

For example, the intense focus on fighting anti-Semitism; or the "edifice complex" of the 1950s, which led Jewish communities throughout the United States to invest hundreds of millions of dollars in buildings; or the headlong emphasis on the integration of Jews into the mainstream of American society; and even the focus on the centrality of Israel and the commemoration of the Holocaust, have had such "downside" consequences for contemporary Jewish culture as religious illiteracy and massive indifference on the part of young adults.

There is also the caveat of conceptualization, which cautions us to notice that the terms contained in our questions do not remain static over time. We would like to think that the meaning of words like religion, community, and identity remain more or less the same over long periods of time. In fact, we know they do not. Thus, at least a part of our difficulty in imagining the future of Jewish identification and affiliation stems from the fact that we cannot envision just what these terms might mean to our grandchildren 20 years from now.

The Caveat of History

Marshall Sklare recalls that as progressive a Jewish leader as Isaac M. Wise—who believed that the future of liberal Judaism lay in the New World and not in the Old—was appalled to discover upon his arrival in New York City in 1846 that "there was not one leader who could read unpunctuated Hebrew or had the least knowledge of Judaism, its history and literature . . . ignorance swayed the scepter and darkness ruled."[31] For that reason, the famed Rabbi of Slutsk, Jacob David Wilowsky, visiting New York in 1900, declared to his listeners that any Jew who migrated to the New World was a sinner. Judaism had no chance of survival in the New World. In much the same spirit, the famed Chatam Sofer decried modernity some two generations earlier: "All that is new is forbidden by the Torah."

Had more of Eastern European Jewry followed the visions of the Slutsker or the Chatam Sofer, many more would have perished in the ashes of the Holocaust, and Israel might never have been reborn.

The visions of the radical reformers of the late 19th and early 20th centuries have fared no better: witness the stands taken by the Reform movement on such

matters as Zionism, the use of Hebrew, the bar mitzvah, and the role of spirituality and ritual in Jewish life.

The purpose of these reflections obviously is not to cast aspersions on the
limitations of the religious leaders and Jewish visionaries of yesteryear. Rather,
it is to remind us of the perils of trying to predict how Jews will fare in the future, and what courses of collective and private action are most efficacious in
advancing the cause of Jewish survival and creativity. The ruptures of modern
Jewish history, and the suddenness with which they can occur, have made even
short-term predictions appear foolish. On the other hand, some of the unanticipated consequences of certain long-term communal strategies have yielded surprising results.

For example, the emphasis on the bar mitzvah as the primary object of Jewish education may well have been a key factor in prompting adolescents to drop
out of Jewish education as soon as they achieve that rite of passage. On the other
hand, the ethnic and civil rights ferment on the college campuses in the 1960s
and early 1970s, coupled with the decline of secularism, has been clearly associated with the flowering of Judaic studies programs in American universities.
Thus the assertions of ethnicity in general American society and the breakdown
of the traditional liberal arts curriculum paved the way for the rebirth of Jewish
education in a new and unexpected locale—a locale that until the late 1960s had
been regarded as the setting par excellence for Jewish assimilation.

The Caveat of Conceptualization

Since Alexis de Tocqueville surveyed the cultural landscape of America in
the mid-nineteenth century, observers have concurred that this land is populated
by a nation of joiners. Membership in a church or synagogue, club, fraternal
organization, political party, recreational fellowship, and so forth is essential to
most Americans' sense of social placement. Will Herberg was perhaps the first
to describe in detail how the dispersal of Jews to suburbia in the postwar baby-
boom era combined with the American penchant for "associationalism" in his
brilliant social commentary, *Protestant-Catholic-Jew* (1955). That combination
produced a community whose identity and commitment was embodied in formal
organizations and expressed primarily through formal affiliation. Later case
studies of suburban life, such as John Seeley's *Crestwood Heights* (1956), Herbert Gans's *The Levittowners* (1967), and Marshall Sklare's "Lakeville Studies"
(1968), all confirmed the salient points first noted by Herberg:

1. The move to suburbia, coinciding as it had with the coming of age of the
    third generation of American Jews, was accompanied by a high degree of
    anomie, secularism, and root-seeking.
2. Because this condition affected all Americans regardless of religious or eth-
    nic background, it became more acceptable for Jews to "reconnect" with
    their own heritage instead of seeking to blend into a culturally amorphous
    America.

3. The move to suburbia also coincided with the growing affluence of American Jews, as well as the break-up of the traditional family (in its extended and nuclear variations). The building, staffing, and organizing of ever-larger and more multiservice synagogues and community centers became a principal component of Jewish collective activity throughout the 1950s and 1960s. For the individual, affiliation became the primary act of religio-ethnic affirmation.

The trend toward an associational expression of one's sense of religious and ethnic belonging mirrored both the sectarianism that characterized America's predominantly Protestant majority, and also the consumerist attitude with which Americans had come to view all their wants and needs, including their religious preference. To identify entailed buying into particular institutions.

This trend toward associationalism also altered the way in which both the typical Jew and students of Jewry had come to view the nature of Jewish identity. In sum, the nature of Jewish identity has been transformed from an ascribed status that adheres to the person by virtue of birth to an achieved status that one must attain through voluntary effort.

For the masses of Eastern European immigrants, who comprise about three-quarters of the ancestors of modern American Jewry, Jewish identity was an inexorable existential fact to which they were heir by virtue of being born. While its particular religious, educational, political, or aesthetic contours might vary, one's Jewishness was neither optional nor a matter of degree on some hypothetical continuum. For the vast majority of immigrant Jews, as well as for most of their children, residential concentration in urban ghettos; occupational concentration in such industries as clothing, jewelry, real estate, or retailing; shared fears of anti-Semitism and shared liberal political responses to that fear all served to reinforce the givenness or tacit existential necessity of Jewish identity.

For their suburbanized children, and even more so for their grandchildren, joining and participating in the formal activities of synagogues or of Jewish philanthropic and cultural organizations became the acts of faith par excellence by which they affirmed their Jewish identity. In the absence of those formal ties, Jewishness becomes vague, amorphous, and tenuous, not only in the eyes of others, but in their own eyes as well.

But even as associational and denominational ties have weakened, there is reason to believe that an appetite for the symbolic universe of Judaism and *yiddishkeit* remains. This appetite is reflected in the conversations of Jews who flock to Woody Allen movies or films like *Crossing Delancey,* or to the wildly popular one-man show of Jackie Mason. We see it reflected in the conversations of Jews who marry non-Jews and then enter "self-help" workshops to understand why it is that they feel so much stress as to how they will raise their children.

Significantly, the social science that has grown up in the past 30 years seeking to describe and explain the nature of contemporary American Jewish identity has been largely, if not exclusively, the product of American Jewish social scientists who have come of age concurrently with the transformation of the community. Even as they (we) grew into adulthood and acquired professional identities, most were trained in a discipline that sought to operationalize modes of consciousness, feelings, sensibilities, and dispositions by means of objective measures of conduct. Thus, the associationalism that had come to characterize modern Jewish identity in the experience of the typical American Jew of the postwar era found its social scientific adumbration in Jewish community surveys that have come to measure "Jewishness" by means of behavior and attitude scales and other social yardsticks pegging identity to belonging. We have been far less adept at picking up the quiet signals of the invisible Judaism that continues to animate Jewish identity alongside or independently of formal affiliations or the public and private acts that are generally considered the appropriate operational expression of one's Jewishness.

Consequently, any attempt to peer into the future, whether 20 or 50 years hence, to imagine the shape and nature of Jewish identification, must grapple with both the factual implications of the current measures of Jewishness and the question of what those measures may have missed hitherto in conceiving of Jewish identity.

A Response

Richard J. Israel

Looking into the Jewish future is generally assumed to be a good way to do orderly planning in the present. If we are going to get from here to there, it is best to do it thoughtfully. If we do our homework well, we will not be overwhelmed by surprises and may even gain some control over the process.

We all have a powerful need to know what is in store for us. This need has kept fortune tellers in business for all of recorded history and probably a lot earlier than recorded history as well. Nevertheless, our tradition has some doubts about the enterprise: "There shall not be found among you any one who is a consulter with familiar spirits or a wizard. . . . For all that do these things are an abomination unto the Lord . . . '' (Deut 18:10–12).

One who asks questions of ghosts may in some measure traffic in the past, and therefore need not concern us here, but the interdicted trafficker in spirits, one who knows things, sounds to me suspiciously like a long-range planner.

Why are they prohibited? Because, as Rambam says, "It is all nothing but the activity of the imagination." That is certainly not what we would like the Rambam to say about a volume dedicated to imagining the Jewish future.

But whether they were aware of Rambam's view or not, most of the contributors to this volume, including Egon Mayer, have noted the precariousness of their speculations before tiptoeing gently into the future, and have been quite explicit about their nervousness concerning the nature of their assignments.

The writers were told to avoid niggling over details, to be bold about the future. But being bold may be the one thing you cannot be about the future. These paragraphs by Gerald Bubis are worth quoting:

> When I look back at the nearly four decades that I've been involved in Jewish life in America, I can note the major events which have informed and really by their nature, forecast the shape and the nature of today's Jewry. To name some: 1) the Holocaust, 2) the birth of the State of Israel, 3) the Six Day War, 4) the war in Vietnam, 5) the drug culture, 6) the Yom Kippur War, 7) the Jew's penetration into the economic, political, academic, literary, artistic and military elite circles, 8) the Lebanese war, 9) the resurgence of Orthodoxy, 10) the

growth of cults, and 11) the rise of homophiles. None of them was forecastable; none of them was affected in any significant way by the American Jewish community's strategic planning before the fact.

"Further, when one identifies the success stories of Jewish life in America, 1) the growth of higher Jewish learning, 2) the growth of day schools, 3) the establishment and/or expansion of Jewish museums, 4) the growth of the seminaries, schools and programs of Jewish communal service, 6) Jewish scholarship, 7) the association of Jewish scholars, 8) the proliferation of artists working on and in Jewish themes, 9) the havurah "movement," 10) CAJE, 11) CLAL, 12) Brandeis Bardin Institute, 13) Jewish Archives—*none of them* was a result of long-range strategic planning. If anything, all of these phenomena, organizations, or institutions were at one time or another stymied, ignored, or otherwise discouraged by the so-called organized Jewish community.[32]

These rather global comments led me to think personally and concretely about some specific factors relevant to the formation of my own Jewish identity. What could have been predicted about them?

As I was growing up, educated in the 1940s in a classical Reform synagogue, Israel had absolutely nothing to do with my Jewish identity. I did not even see a Blue Box until I went to college. For the past 30 years, and until the last year or two, if any one had asked me, I would have said without the slightest hesitation that the state of Israel will be a permanently important segment of our Jewish identities, that you cannot be a Jew today, or at least are very unlikely to be one for long, if somewhere in your soul there is not a significant Israel corner.

At the present moment, seeing the many dilemmas Israel creates for today's college students—the extent to which pro-Israel students feel themselves a beleaguered minority on campus—I am no longer sure about what Israel's place in Jewish identity is going to be. If there is peace, will Israel finally become a true light unto the nations and a center for Jewish cultural and religious life, contributing to our identities in immensely important ways, or will an Israel without enemies cease to engage us? Maybe our North American Diaspora communities will get bored with an Israel that is not under siege and come to view Israeli Jewry as they currently do Australian Jewry, with benign indifference.

If Israel's hard line is maintained in the face of all international pressure, and that position does not yield peace, will our young people continue to defend Israel no matter what and become prouder Jews than ever, or will they want to disassociate themselves from it? The drop in young people's tourism to Israel is not a good sign, but it is far from hard evidence. On the basis of what I know about the past and the present, it remains absolutely impossible to imagine what the future role of Israel will be in the Jewish identity of our young.

To take another dimension of the question of the role of Israel in future Jewish identity: Unless Israel makes an immense oil or gold strike and becomes very rich, there is every reason to assume that migration from Israel to North America will continue to grow, as will intermarriage between Americans and Israelis. Does this mean that Israel will become a new-old country for us, a Jewish resource of the sort that Eastern Europe once was, or will the Israelis become Americans rather than Jews? Without knowing any of these outcomes, making useful assumptions about the future role of Israel in the formation of Jewish identity would be completely unjustified.

I thus find myself in agreement with the observation that has been attributed to the economist Paul Samuelson, that predicting things is difficult, especially if they are in the future. In commenting on Egon Mayer's splendid essay, in which he delineates the confusing nature of the problem without ever being confusing, I wish to distinguish between my enthusiasm for his comments on the Jewish present and my nervousness about his speculations concerning the Jewish future.

Regarding the Jewish present, I find his observations shrewd and on-target. His remark that the new Jewishness is more psychological than communal sounds correct and important. His most powerful point is in asking us to reflect on the meaning of what he refers to as invisible Jews. At one time we called them ''cardiac Jews,'' those who were Jewish at heart. We simply do not know whether to take them seriously. Having been alerted to the issue by Egon Mayer's comments, I was surprised to find the same point being made in the 1965 Boston CJP demographic study, which was written in 1967 after the Six-Day War. At that time we were trying to understand the sudden appearance of Jews out of nowhere who had not previously been heard from—Mayer's ''invisible Jews.''

My private theory is that God's promise to Abraham—the promise that one day we would be like the stars in the sky (Genesis 15:5)—refers to them. It does not mean that we will become great in number, as the verse is usually understood, but rather that, like the stars, most of us will come out only at night, when things are tough. We are challenged to bring such people from the periphery into the center, but as Egon Mayer reminds us, the greater challenge is to determine to what degree that pattern of invisible Jewish life can be transmitted from generation to generation and whether these invisible Jews will continue to come out even at night.

His observation that denominational members and leaders often do not believe the same things is important. This is hardly a new phenomenon, for denominational labels have probably always represented more what the rabbis believed than what most Jews themselves thought. But it is clearly an issue that must be considered, particularly in the ''Who is a Jew'' controversy.

Mayer's treatment of the magnitude of the future influence of Orthodoxy is a bit too casual. In my suburban Boston neighborhood, in the Conservative and Reform synagogues, the average young family has two children. In the Orthodox synagogues only a few blocks away, whose families are from the same socioeconomic group, the comparable families have four children. This is not only happening in Boston. At this point, considerably more than 2 percent of the Orthodox children in Milwaukee (the figure Mayer cites from 1955) would be as observant as their parents. Orthodoxy may outstrip the other denominations demographically. It should also be noted that unless there is a radical change, Orthodox Jews will not continue to fund the same institutions to which non-Orthodox Jews have become accustomed.

In regard to Mayer's imaginings concerning the immense potential energy to be brought into the synagogue by an influx of women, we should reflect upon the SAJ (the first Reconstructionist synagogue), which integrated women in 1922. To the casual, unsophisticated observer, the SAJ would look like a rather average liberal Conservative synagogue, not energized by anything more or less special than any other Conservative synagogue that has recently integrated women.

It is true that in new two-career families fathers may spend more time with their children than they used to, and that is indeed happening in a few specialized circles, but from what I see around me, two-career family fathers are more likely to make special efforts to generate extra income so that additional professional child care can be purchased. Neither do I know many grandparents who are near enough or willing enough to entertain, much less actually help raise, their two-career children's children.

Though I generally find myself in the camp of optimistic Jewish observers, I do not believe there is any information at all that suggests that the majority of the intermarried will choose to remain within the community, and there are more than a few indications that they will not. The intermarried are the only Jews who still have Christmas trees in significant numbers. That is surely not a good omen.

If Mayer is merely imagining the future as he would like it to be, I can only say I am not convinced that Mayer's proposed directions are likely to become reality. If we were to imagine a Jewish identity for the future, I suspect that most American Jews would want the same sorts of things. We would want to see Jews whose Jewishness requires that they be kind, that they care about one another and the world in which they live, that they be Jewishly literate, that they live according to the rhythms of the Jewish year and the sancta of our tradition, that they be engaged in and pass on our rich heritage and be enthusiasts of good Jewish art, music, and literature. Is hoping our only recourse for creating such an identity? I think not.

If we look at the original Bubis list of success stories, we see that no group was able to change the Jewish world, but that each one that succeeded was able to create its own institutions better to serve its own needs affecting the Jewish world in the process. CAJE was clearly a self-started operation, a creation ex-nihilo. A group of Jewish educators felt they needed more support than they were getting from the educational establishment and created an organization to provide it. Jewish education, while not having arrived at a messianic future, is better off because of CAJE.

As long as we do not engage in grabbing more than we can manage, and instead choose limited, specific goals, working with institutions over which we have some control, we can make a difference. For example, it is not possible to get Jews to marry earlier and have more Jewish children. It is possible to establish Jewish dating services that may raise the odds that Jews will marry other Jews. It is not possible to create fleets of warm, loving Jewish educators or Jewish grandparents who live near, but not too near, their grandchildren. It is possible to create more early childhood Jewish education centers of quality.

We will not solve the problem of enhancing Jewish identity with gimmicks or comprehensive field theories or any sort of quick fix. Our future will be determined by committed people doing hard work, endlessly and selflessly, in many areas over a long time. It will be determined by people devoting themselves to specific projects in which they have deep personal investments. By acting like thieves in a hotel, trying every door in the hope of finding one that will open, with a little luck and a lot of persistence a few of our well-chosen efforts will yield good results.

None of the innovations Bubis describes will survive without such support. Nor will any of the new directions considered in this volume. The real hope for the growth of Reconstructionism came when it began seriously to address this very issue.

Amidst ostensible visionaries, I am a tinkerer; I like to tighten a bolt in the system here, change the oil there. I presume that I am in the midst of many who want to change the energy source altogether. If forced to choose between a pure and noble vision and small incremental change, I will go for the incremental change every time because, as the French say, God is to be found in the details.

The following story was told to me by David Schimmel, a professor of education at the University of Massachusetts, Amherst. When David was a Yale Law School student in 1958, he and a classmate devised the concept of and made preliminary drafts of legislation for the establishment of the Peace Corps and urged Senator Hubert Humphrey to propose it, which he did. When Humphrey gave up his presidential campaign after the West Virginia primary, Jack Kennedy picked up the idea, won the campaign and established the Peace Corps.

A few years later, David applied for an administrative position in the Peace Corps. When he was interviewed, he was asked why the Peace Corps should be interested in having him on staff. "Why should you be interested in me? he asked. "Because I am one of the people who invented the Peace Corps." He then went on to explain his contribution. The interviewer responded, "You did not invent the Peace Corps. You only invented the idea of the Peace Corps, and ideas are a dime a dozen. What is great about the Kennedys is that they know how to implement ideas, how to turn them into reality."

So a poor young man seeking his fortune goes to the king and asks for the hand of the princess in marriage. As the parable has it, the king replies; "She is yours." But if, as is more likely, he were to say, "My daughter? No, you cannot have my daughter, but there is someone else I would like you to meet," even if she is not as dazzling as the princess we should consider the offer very seriously.

A Response

Deborah Dash Moore

Egon Mayer's carefully constructed essay leaves little room for comment in the traditional sense. He manages not only to suggest future trends but to reflect upon his suggestions and to indicate some of the pitfalls of soothsaying. The essay is at once theme and response, elegantly knit together. I will try to be "bold" as urged by the editor and use Mayer's paper as a departure point for some additional reflections rather than response in the strict sense.

Mayer begins, quite properly, with demography. Who are American Jews today, and who will be American Jews tomorrow? These questions quite naturally make me think of my own sons, for they are in fact the future Jewish adults of America. Though it is rash for any parent to predict what her children will do, I can at least say with confidence that they have been given the tools—the family life, the knowledge, the connections with a larger Jewish community—to live as Jews. When I compare their Jewish upbringing to my own (I was raised as a Reconstructionist) the largest single difference I can see is the importance of Israel in their lives as compared to mine. For a child growing up in the 1950s, Israel was a dreamland, a place of wonderful fantasies. For my children, Israel is a very real country, a land of cities and farms, buses and movies, schools and stores. It is a country they know from their own experience and about which they have few fantasies. The matter-of-factness of Israel—or potential matter-of-factness—is an issue I will return to. But thinking of my children also prompted me to contemplate my friends' children—or rather the absence of my friends' children. Most of these children are growing up in environments substantially different from that of their parents—in small towns rather than in large cities; in day schools and private schools rather than in public schools; as non-Jews rather than as Jews; as upper-class rather than as lower-middle-class; as nuclear families rather than as extended families. The changing character of American Jewry is astounding, and the rate of intermarriage Mayer mentions is in many ways only the most visible sign of change.

Let me suggest two additional demographic features to consider in imagining future patterns of affiliation for American Jews. The first derives from migration patterns of Jews and the second stems directly from immigration. As Jews have grown to resemble other Americans socially and culturally, they have picked up the American penchant for moving. The United States is an extraordinarily mobile society, with one out of five persons moving every five years. Jews now also move around the country in impressive numbers, and their migrations have encouraged the reemergence of a communal pattern of affiliation initially associated with immigrants to the United States. This type of affiliation draws upon the peer group and emphasizes common values and shared experiences. Unlike the intergenerational model of family-based affiliation, the peer group model unites Jews of roughly the same age and social situation. The growth of *havurot* reflects the popularity of peer group association, which offers an alternative to family and neighborhood. This pattern can accompany the inviolable Jewishness Mayer describes because it assumes the individualistic and portable character of Jewish identity. I think that the future of the American Jewish community is going to see the intergenerational and the peer-group patterns of associations coexisting in virtually every settlement large enough to have more than one Jewish institution. If I am correct, then Jewish organizations will have to learn how to speak simultaneously to these very different types of affiliation.

Mayer mentions the unpredictability of the future and cites his own family's situation 50 years ago. I would extend his observations by venturing to predict that immigration will reappear as a significant aspect of American Jewish life. I expect that the future will bring more Jewish immigrants to the U.S.—from the countries of Latin America, from South Africa, from the Soviet Union, from Israel—and that these immigrants will leave their mark upon American Jewry much as did the survivors, especially the Orthodox and Hasidic refugees, of the World War II era. When one combines the estimated 500,000 recent Jewish immigrants to the U.S. with the numbers of intermarried, the conclusion is that over a third of American Jewry will be new to the majority experiences of three and four generations of American Jews of Eastern European background. I was struck one November day a few years ago by a small aspect of this change as I left YIVO Institute in New York. I walked out of the building with one immigrant from Canada, one immigrant from Israel, one immigrant from Poland, and the son of survivors. Of the five of us, I was the only one planning to celebrate Thanksgiving. The rest looked at the day as at best a holiday on Thursday or at worst an anti-Judaism holiday. One of the few genuinely American holidays that can be celebrated by individuals of all faiths and backgrounds meant nothing to these American Jews. They are not alone. A quick, unscientific check among my son's Asian friends indicated that few, if any, celebrated Thanksgiving. The character of Americanization has clearly changed in the last 40 years, and we would do well to reexamine what it means to be a Jewish immigrant to the United States of the 1980s. The future of at least a tenth of our current population is intimately linked to that experience. Perhaps it is time to rethink the *Faith of America*—not just the concept but also the volume of ritual by that name devised by Kaplan, Kohn, and Williams in the late 1940s.

The consensus that American Jews once shared on religio-political issues is quietly crumbling. What is the prevailing point of view on public schools and their relationship to democratic and Jewish education? Do parents who send their children to parochial or private schools disavow the once nearly universal Jewish support for public education? What is the prevailing view on separation of church and state? Do the large public menorahs, often sponsored by the Lubavitch, indicate that a new Jewish consensus is emerging? These issues, like the more explosive question of patrilineal descent, require consideration for anyone who wishes to image the future. They are often the bread and butter of many of our national secular American Jewish organizations.

I can only second Mayer's observations about women. Enormous changes will spring from their Jewish enfranchisement. Not only will there be innovations in ritual, but the issues animating the leadership of American Jewry will change as that leadership includes more women. The different methods of rearing Jewish daughters as compared to sons will affect the public sphere. We know too little about how Jewish daughters are brought up to be able to predict what the impact will be. However, I suspect that less competition and more cooperation are encouraged among daughters than among sons. I would urge that cooperative activities come to greater prominence in Jewish communal endeavors—in synagogues and in secular organizations—and that the system of acquiring *koved* through competition be replaced by cooperation. To get some idea of how women might shape the future, we can look at how one of the most successful American Jewish women's organizations, Hadassah, is coping with the new Jewish women, whom they are recruiting successfully into membership. Though Hadassah does not carry much weight with either Jewish intellectuals or religious leaders, it does represent an authentic voice and organization of American Jewish women and as such deserves more thoughtful scrutiny than it has so far received.

I promised to return to the subject of Israel with a programmatic statement. Israel, as I have urged privately for some time, needs to become more of a lived reality for American Jews. The recognition of Israel's importance for American Jewish religious leaders, expressed in the year of residency and training required there, should be extended not only to secular leaders but to all American Jews. It would be valuable for all to live in Israel for a minimum of six months; an entire year would be even better.

A year in Israel should be a part of all American Jews' education, one of the things that is accepted as "normal," like going to college. It should not be tied, as the Israelis would prefer, to aliyah, but should be linked to a sense of informed Jewish citizenship. It is dangerous for Israel to exist only as fantasy, or not to exist at all, in the minds of American Jews. By contrast, it is vital for Israel to exist as matter-of-fact reality, to be assimilated into the invisible Jewishness Mayer describes, consciously chosen by each American Jew when defining a Jewish identity. This means that we must develop new modes of relating to Israel and to Israelis.

Israel cannot just represent "homeland" for American Jews. It must be part of their world, a place peopled with friends and relatives, a society that is understood, a language spoken and a culture shared. Although this proposal may seem utopian, American Jews now have the resources to do it. Furthermore, the distance separating American Jews and Israelis is not so great that it cannot be overcome, especially if the value in overcoming the distance is made clear. Israel represents a genuinely Jewish civilization, and Jews—especially American Jews, who have become exceptionally adept at living in two civilizations— should welcome the opportunity to live in a Jewish civilization for at least some sustained period of their lives.

This brings me to my final comment: We must remain aware of what the future holds for America because our fate as American Jews is now intimately linked to the United States. These reflections on the future are taking place after several decades of what has been dubbed "the American century." The position of the United States in the world and the situation of American society will impinge upon any future we can imagine. If the United States is becoming a more conservative society, if it is inclining toward a revival of fundamentalism, if it is a less racist and more permissive society, if it is becoming more egalitarian— then American Jews will be swept along in these changes. We must consider two questions: What is the American condition? And where is America going? Is the gloomy assessment of the condition of community in America made by Robert Bellah in his *Habits of the Heart* an accurate one? Is this a society where individualism rules, untempered by the constraints of conformity or the impulse to join others in volunteer activities? Jews rarely swim against the tide in America, though they may often be found riding the first waves into shore. The enormous impact of the women's movement on American Jews should remind us of the significance of American civilization for our own American Jewish synthesis. And here, I confess, I have a great difficulty imagining where America will be 20 or 30 years hence, in part because the literature on American character is so contradictory that it is difficult to know where to place one's bets. However, to expect continuities seems reasonable, and this means certainly the continued dominance of individualism in public and private life and probably the continuation of its corollaries of conformism and voluntarism.

10

Social Justice: Reenvisioning Our Vision

Arthur Waskow

As a science fiction fan and a long-ago lover of Edward Bellamy's problematic utopia in *Looking Backward*, rather than writing *about* the future, I take my stance for this essay *in* the future.

I chose the year 2015 in the Western calendar (5776 in the Jewish calendar) because it is a year of *Hakhel*. According to a little-known ancient tradition, this moment comes once every seven years. During the harvest festival of Sukkot, the whole Jewish people is to assemble to hear some key passages of Torah read, to review in the light of these passages its behavior as a people for the previous seven years, and to reassess what its path for the next seven years should be. *Hakhel* is thus a kind of collective, long-range Yom Kippur. It was supposed to come just after the completion of a *shemitah* or sabbatical year, when the land would have been allowed to rest from all cultivation, and when all debts would have been annulled so as to restore a greater balance between the rich and poor.

The socioreligious analysis that underlies my 25-year leap into the future is this: Among North American Jews in the last 25 or 30 years, there has emerged a large group of people with considerable affluence and political clout who have continued to hold "progressive" values of social justice that are usually associated with the poor and powerless. Some basic elements of Jewish practice and identity—especially the collective memory of and reidentification with being a band of runaway slaves—have helped to shape and preserve these values. Even more surprising than the resilience of progressive values among large numbers of North American Jews has been the resurgence of their sense of religious and spiritual connection with some aspects of Jewish tradition—as understood by such teachers as Martin Buber, Abraham Joshua Heschel, and Mordecai Kaplan; as influenced by feminism; and as practiced in *havurot* and other networks of Jewish renewal.

In some kind of fusion of hope, prediction, and imagination, I am therefore suggesting that these people—creatively religious and politically progressive

Jews—might turn to the Torah's call for a cycle of social reconstitution in the sabbatical year/Jubilee year cycle, as a framework for addressing issues of social justice. I am also suggesting that they might bring their affluence into greater consonance with their progressive values through concerted efforts at socially responsible investment and the deliberate use of such invested funds to support social change in America.

Now we leap to 2015 C.E., 5776 A.M....

First, I want to thank the Philadelphia Kehillah for the honor of being asked, in this year of the Fourth Hakhel, to be one of those who review the changes we have made in Jewish life these last 21 years.

For this year (2015 C.E., 5776 A.M.), all seven of us *kohelot*—assemblers—have been asked to take as our reviewing point that extraordinary moment back in 1994 when we renewed the Torah's ancient command to do Hakhel, to come together in a great assembly to review the previous seven years and look ahead seven years more.

I can still remember the excitement during Sukkot of 5755 as we came together to recreate Hakhel, not in a frozen, automatic replay of the ancient scene but in our own way as postmodern Jews. And of course I remember the excitement, the trepidation, the fear, the hope, with which in the fall of 1994 we looked back on that incredible previous year and the Treaty of Cairo.

It was a *shemitah* year, though of course the negotiators in Cairo were paying no attention to that. And not just an ordinary *shemitah*, an ordinary sabbatical seventh year when the land is supposed to rest and debts to be annulled. No!—it was the seventh seventh year. The seventh *shemitah* since Israel's independence, the super-*shemitah* in which the Torah commands that we prepare the Jubilee, that we prepare to restore social peace and justice by giving every family its fair share of the land.

And in that year of all years, at last our family and the family of our cousins, the children of Hagar and Ishmael, chose to give each other a share of the land. So hard! There had been many years when we were ready but they were not, and then the years when they were ready to be ready, and we were not. But at last, within us both we found the courage to see how frightened the other family was.

What a gift when the moment came, that it should be in that very year, the seventh *shemitah*. For that has let us take a moment of painful prudence and ordinary *Realpolitik,* a moment when at last our internal politics and the internal politics of the Palestinians meshed—take that moment and forever make it part of our holy history, make it the moment when we rose to the challenge of the Jubilee and taught the nations that if we could share the Land of Israel, they could share the earth.

Where has it led us, and where does it continue to lead us? Not along a simple path. For every step taken in courage, two in doubt; for every sigh of relief, two of regret; for every month of peace, a week of pain. No feast of joy without its taste of anger.

I will return to that moment. But first I want to say something about Hakhel itself, that strange appendix to the Torah (Deut. 31:10–13) and the Mishnah (Sotah 7:8). It called for the king and the high priest to read some biting passages of Deuteronomy before the assembled people: "Do not pile up cavalry or silver, do not send the people back into an 'Egypt' of slavery." And this assembly had to come during Sukkot after every seventh year, the *shemitah* year.

In 1987 there were the barest hints that Hakhel was stirring in the Jewish consciousness. P'nai Or, which in those days was still the most marginal vanguard group of Jewish renewal, published a piece calling for its renewal in *Moment* magazine. The Lubavitcher Rebbe mentioned it. And the President of Israel actually went to the Western Wall to read the Torah passages, although many shouted that he was no king and should go home.

These glimmers had just enough romance to them, just enough flavor of the archaic turned contemporary—like the 28-year cycle of the Blessing of the Sun—that a few people here and there got excited. We started imagining some wonderful scenes: a thousand Jews, five thousand Jews, wrapped in *tallitot*, gathering outdoors in Jerusalem's Independence Park at dawn, dividing into separate groups to hear the reading of the Torah passages, the way the Hasidim cluster in small congregations near each other on Shabbos evening at the Western Wall, so that the many small clusters make a rainbow congregation, one large variegated congregation. . . .

And we started imagining some wonderful modern aspects of that scene: women as well as men wearing the tallit, reading Torah; unrolling dozens of Torah scrolls, one for each cluster, unrolling the entire scroll to reach the crucial passages in Deuteronomy, and having dozens of people hold the open scrolls aloft to read from; between each passage dancing an Eastern European dance, a Yemenite dance, an Israeli dance, a dance of our own. And on Sukkot, waving the lulav toward earth and heaven and the four winds. And a chance to talk, to talk about where we had been and where we were going. A chance to talk across all the usual barricades.

The oddity, the romance, the power of that picture captured enough people to make something happen. During the late 1980s the idea spread, at first by word of mouth. It was the Philadelphia Jewish Community Relations Council that first made the commitment to make Hakhel happen. By 1992 plans were under way in a dozen large communities and in hundreds of congregations in smaller towns to do Hakhel in the fall of 1994. In that first year perhaps two thousand Jews came together in Philadelphia. I remember watching the "spiritual feminists" of Mt. Airy tense up when they sat down with the "heavy hitters" of the United Jewish Appeal, and how nervous both of them became when the Lubavitchers walked into the park and came over to join in. Miracle of miracles, they hardly blinked as they saw the orange, purple, green *tallitot* on hundreds of women.

It was totally different from Deuteronomy. No monarchical reading by the king, or the president, or the chief rabbi, or any other "the." That day and ever since, *we ourselves* have been doing the reading and the arguing.

By 2001 the numbers were ten times as high and the word had spread everywhere. There was hardly a community in America that was not doing Hakhel; it had spread to Brazil and the republics of the Soviet Union.

By then the custom had arisen that for two months before Hakhel people met in their own communities to study the traditional Hakhel texts and to examine how they were doing in building a Judaism full of life. And then for Sukkot they came together to share what they had learned, to listen to seven speakers on the seven days of Sukkot, and after each speaker to break up into new-made groups of 49 where no more than seven could come from any single previous community.

Fifty thousand of us here today to share our different insights, to listen to each other as much as we speak to each other. So, *Shema, Yisrael!* And when I have done, I also will listen.

It will not surprise you that of the seven of us, I most want to examine how we have been dealing with issues of social justice. The great change has been that now when we struggle with these issues, we wrestle with the Torah. Not that we always do what the letters in the black fire of Torah seem to say; but we learn from them, we dance with the flame and fire in them, and when we are able to see the letters forming in the white fire between the lines, that *is* what we do.

Not that we ignore Jefferson or Gandhi, Medvedev or King, Day or Shariati—or for that matter Jews like Luxemburg and Goldman and Rukeyser and Michnik. But the people we have taken to our hearts have been Buber and Heschel, Broner and Piercy—those who have learned to draw on Torah to shape their thoughts and acts of social justice.

And Hakhel itself—this very meeting—I want to say, is a triumph of our wrestle with the Torah. It is a crucial part of our work for social justice that we meet this way, every seven years, to examine ourselves with clear-eyed, loving care. To examine the next step, not just celebrate the past.

And to celebrate the very cycle of our celebration. It is hard, nowadays, to remember how little we cared, just 35 years ago, about the cycles of the week, the month, the year, the *shemitah*, the Jubilee. Perhaps the most important act of social justice and *tikkun olam* that we have brought the world in this last generation has been the renewal of the cycles of life.

Our theologians used to say that celebration of the cycles was the priestly function of religion; the quest for social justice was the prophetic path. Now we see that in a world where the powerful were destroying the cycles themselves—destroying the cycles of work and celebration, of doing and being; destroying the cycles of normal hot and cold, and in so doing pulling down upon the world the danger of lethal heat and cold, the smothering heat of the greenhouse effect and the obliterating cold of nuclear winter—that in such a world, acting to sustain the cycles was itself an act of social justice, an act of fusing the priest with the prophet, of renewing the great spiral of life. Just as our Torah grows not in circles of unending repetition nor in straight lines of unending progress, but in the spirals of returning to the ancient in order to go forward to the unknown Torah—just so we live in the Shabbos that comes every week and the Shabbos that comes once a year, in the Shabbos-month of Tishri, and the Shabbos of the *shemitah* and the Jubilee.

If we had not taught the world to make the Shabbos of our techno-*shmitah*, I believe we would by now have had our nuclear Flood of Fire, we would have burned the earth empty of humans and perhaps of life. If we had not given a mighty push to the recycling of wealth through the Jubilee Reinvestment Funds that we helped to create, I think by now America would have suffered a Great Depression and a class-race war, the burning of a dozen major cities. Not just a few neighborhoods full of desperate people, but whole cities burned from the ground, bombed and strafed from the air.

Perhaps these are the most important things we have done these 21 years. So let me spend a little more time examining them.

The Jubilee Funds. Somewhere around 1990 it became clear that many thousands of American Jews had a lot of money in their pockets, and a set of Jewish values in their heads. To many of them this seemed, at first, anomalous. The values had been shaped in poverty 3,000 years ago, when we had been a nation of runaway slaves and had shaped a culture that struggled to abolish slavery. Our *zaydes* and *bubbes* had taught us how to share with our neighbors, when we hardly had what to share. But now? Rich folks do not share. If you're affluent, you cannot really be Jewish.

And then the whole idea of the kosher use of money, the idea that we in the Jewish community could create an actual kashrut of money, a communal understanding of how best to spend and invest a share of our money—this idea came to their rescue. Their cultural, spiritual, political, and financial rescue. (Imagine how it would have been if their money had been in conventional banks instead of the Jubilee Funds, when the World Crash came in 2002!)

The impetus came from the New Tzedakah Five, from the conference they called in 1990 precisely to prepare for the first Hakhel of 1994. Let us give them their due, name by name: Mazon, the Jewish Fund for Justice, the New Israel Fund, the American Jewish World Service, and The Shefa Fund. They affirmed the growing movement for socially responsible investment, they showed how Jewish tradition and Jewish institutions could enrich that movement—in both senses—and they got the Jubilee Funds started.

What they urged was that the Jewish community work to channel investment money from both individuals and institutions to worker-controlled and consumer-coop enterprises, especially but not only in the black and Hispanic communities. From the beginning, the idea was to be sure the money did not get thrown away. It would be lent (along with expert advice) only to groups of serious workers and entrepreneurs so that they could build viable enterprises. The Jubilee Funds intended to get the loans repaid so that the money could then be recycled into newer firms. "Not a fish, but a fishing pole," the original statement said; "the Rambam's eighth level of tzedakah."

As we know now, it worked—politically, financially, and religiously. The Jubilee movement grew rapidly after the New Tzedakah Five issued their call at the first Hakhel. Thousands of Jews not only began to invest their own money in the Jubilee Funds, but also demanded that Jewish institutions do so.

There were some tense moments. I remember the spring of 1995, when at five different rabbinical seminaries students and faculty were picketing their schools: "Is This Money Treyf?" "We Demand Kosher Investments." It took almost a month of television coverage before their boards were willing to see the Jubilee Funds as good investments for endowment money.

It turned out to be lucky, or providential, that the rabbinical seminary boards were stubborn. The national publicity carried the idea to congregations all across the country. Rabbis led the way. Soon no Jewish institution could invest less than 50 percent of its endowment in the Jubilee Funds without facing the charge of *treyf*, and the rest had to be invested with a strong concern for social responsibility. No investments in making first-strike nuclear weapons, or producing acid rain.

Very few Jubilee loans defaulted. People made money. Not as much as they might have in the regular business world in the short run. But then, in the World Crash, it turned out that the coop economy held up much better than the corporate banking system. Politically, the new contacts with the black and Hispanic communities made a great difference. And the religious payoff was, of course, enormous: tens of thousands of newly committed Jews who came to see a real connection between the study of Torah, the spiritual yearnings of their hearts, and the doings of their hands.

And now, if I look seven years ahead, toward 2022, I think—since we have proved the case that coops and worker control are economically effective, and since we have built such a strong network of them—that we are politically ready to take the next step. That is a nationwide campaign to recycle the investment money that still remains under the control of the remaining giant corporations, not into state ownership, but into decentralized worker/consumer-controlled businesses. Just as the Jubilee calls for the land to be redivided once each generation, so we need to recycle investment capital.

Let me turn now to our techno-*shemitah*. Beginning in the 1980s American Jews got more and more concerned with protecting the life of this planet for future generations, and with bringing a Jewish sense of the covenant between the generations to bear on this task. This energy began with the creation of the Shalom Center in the early 1980s, focusing on the danger posed by the H-bomb to the future of all life on earth, and then broadened in the ecological crises of the early 1990s.

Sukkot, the festival of fruitfulness and the fragile house of harvest, became Sukkat Shalom, a time to affirm the fragile earth, all her fragile peoples, and her fruitfulness, against the dangers of nuclear holocaust and chemical destruction.

The Tu B'shevat Seder became an affirmation of the earth and air and water and fire that make it possible for the Tree of Life to grow.

Yom Hakeshet—the Day of the Rainbow Sign—became a time for all the peoples, at Jewish invitation, to gather and join in the covenant to protect all life on earth.

And then came our great breakthrough into a more profound way of protecting the earth—our remembering of Shabbos, our retranslation of the *shemitah* year and its sabbatical pause from mastery.

The great change came when we realized that it was not just a problem here, a problem there, that we were facing—the H-bomb, acid rain, genetic recombination, the greenhouse effect, too much ozone on the ground and not enough in the stratosphere—but something more basic. When we realized that all these problems were rooted in a technology that had started out decently but had forgotten how to pause, to meditate, to celebrate, to reevaluate. When we realized that the modern world was like a cancer cell, a healthy cell that has forgotten to make Shabbos, forgotten *shavat vayinafash,* "to pause and catch a breath."

No. That's not fair. We knew all along, in some uneasy way, that beneath the specific problems there was a pervasive worldview, an aspect of modernity that had gone sour. We even knew, in some philosophical sense, that what was missing was Shabbos. What was new was that we realized there was something we could do about it, and even more that there was something *we Jews* could do about it—that there was something Jewish to do about it.

The great moment came in 2001, at the gathering of the second Hakhel. In New York the organizers of Hakhel had invited Carl Sagan and Elie Wiesel to talk about "Technology and Torah." The two great sages did something extraordinary. Instead of each giving a talk, each out of his own special life experience, they met together ahead of time and worked out a joint proposal. Together they put their prestige behind it.

People who were in New York said it electrified the crowd—such a technological metaphor! What did they propose? That the world begin to make a technological *shemitah*. First they reminded us what *shemitah* was. They reminded us about the almost forgotten *shemitah* year, when in ancient days the land lay fallow, resting. One year of every seven, the land itself got to rest, Adamah as if it were Adam. The very humus got to catch its breath as if it were a human being, to make Shabbos for the One Who Breathes All Life.

And then they said this did not have to be nostalgia only. They called upon the world to set aside one year in every seven when all technological research and development would pause. When the engineers would get a real sabbatical. Time to sing, to read, to talk with each other and with others about the goals, the intentions, and the pathways of their work.

Most important, time for all of us, not as individuals but as a society, as the human community, to pause from our technological race into Hell. Time to ask ourselves what missteps we were making, what technology ought to be.

To have Sagan and Wiesel do this together! To have the Nobel laureate for peace and the organizer of the great Soviet-American Mars Expedition of the 1990s do this together! To have the great scientist speak so powerfully not for demeaning science but for integrating it into the greater human drama in this way, to make a kind of science that could reach into itself in order to reach beyond itself! To have the great storyteller tell such an ancient story with such a modern moral!

The Sagan-Wiesel proposal was forefax news everywhere that evening. And the next day, the next week, churches and engineering schools and mosques and MIT and Buddhist temples and the National Institutes of Health began to debate the idea. And the chairman of the board of Matsushita denounced it, and the workers of St. Petersburg endorsed it.

The argument raged. And then, late in 2002, came the World Crash. Most of the economy came to a screeching halt. Talk about a year off! *Everyone* had a year off. With the *shemitah* proposal already on everyone's lips, it seemed almost obvious that this disaster was a pause, the kind of pause, the kind of Shabbos, that was bound to come through hammer-blows upon us, if we refused to choose such a pause freely, lovingly.

Wiesel went on world television to say that if we did not pause for renewal, then God, or History, or Reality, or the Kondratieff Curve, would make sure that we paused anyway—and it would be the pause of a great depression.

So the techno-*shemitah* became a public demand. Even the word, that peculiar, perfect marriage of Greek with Hebrew, of Hellenism and science with Torah, entered a dozen modern languages.

And in 2007, with the support of a dozen governments, several large corporations, and UNESCO, there was a spotty observance of the first techno-*shemitah*. This past year, as you know, the estimate is that 60 percent of the world's R & D came to a temporary halt. Right now, as we meet, many of the R & D centers are beginning to reopen. Many of them have announced that they are ready to change their research agendas in accord with the discussion their engineers and scientists have had this past year.

At last the human race is learning to make Shabbos.

I think these have been our most profound accomplishments. Of course there have been others:

I am proud that, when Pope Pius XIII issued his ferocious encyclical *De Amor Humanitatis* attacking anyone who acted upon or approved the sexual expression of love between men or between women, it was the Jewish community that stood up to say that his language echoed the Church's long history of dehumanizing Jews, a history that had come to its climax in the Nazi Holocaust.

I am proud that our protest helped to spark a deep debate within the Catholic Church. I am proud that we followed up by going public with spiritually heartening covenant ceremonies for gay men and lesbians, and by encouraging other religious communities to hallow such relationships if they were conducted in a holy way.

I think that our doing all of this helped to prevent what might have been terrible attacks on gay communities everywhere. And I think it saved millions of gay people from feeling that their own spiritual communities had abandoned them. Instead, the gay communities felt encouraged to affirm new kinds of families (instead of negating all forms of family life, as the Pope had assumed in attacking them) and to enrich all religious life with new ways of approaching God.

I am proud that the Eco-Kashrut symbol that we introduced now appears on thousands of products—the E inside an oval that says, "This product was made with economic and ecological respect—for the earth and the workers of the earth." And that millions of people check for the symbol before they buy food, or clothes, or music-makers.

I am proud that our own Rabbi Alex Schindler was the first mainstream religious leader to call for a determined effort to eliminate all nuclear weapons from the earth. At the time, we thought it was *meshugeh* to say it could be done by the year 2000, but as you know, we fell short by only five years.

Many of our actions helped to bring this about:

Our Shalom Seders in the desert at the H-bomb testing site in Nevada, year after year after year; Elie Wiesel's pilgrimages to Hiroshima, and his call on the leaders of the U.S. and the U.S.S.R. to join him there in 1993; the Sukkat Shalom that Soviet Jews actually had the chutzpah to erect in Red Square; the famous legal case in which for the first time a Soviet court ruled that the Glasnost Constitution protected public assembly, speech, and worship against a police order to tear that Sukkah down. All these were Jewish contributions to the Hiroshima Treaty of 2005.

Part of the task I was given for this Hakhel was not only to review the changes we have made since the first Hakhel in 1994, but also to share my own thoughts about what all these changes mean in the Jewish path of life, and where we may and should be journeying.

First of all, I think these changes mean we are well on the way to reintegrating three aspects of the path that during the modern age we had allowed to degenerate into separate parts of life. Those three are ritual and liturgy, the daily ethical practice of a person or a family, and social action to change governmental policy. We had grown used to the idea that only the third brought social justice.

Now we know that when we build a Sukkat Shalom in the heart of a slum, and work with the poor people who live there to make a Sukkot celebration, it is an act of social justice, as well as liturgy. And that when we choose where to invest our money or what voicewriter to buy, that is both an act of kashrut and an act of social justice.

Not only have we reintegrated our own inner lives as Jews, we are carrying Torah into public space by acting in these ways. This is something new for us— new at least since the destruction of the Temple—and we are still, I think, in the early stages of inventing this activist, assertive Judaism. As I look toward the Fifth Hakhel in 2022, this is what I hope we will be consciously creating.

To do this means to take up in a new way one of the most ancient tasks of the Children of Israel—the task of shattering idols, of overthrowing pharaohs, of transforming the life of Canaan.

In our history as it was encoded in the Tanakh, we thought that we could do this only through military power. We felt ourselves commanded to conquer and destroy the idolatrous cultures of Canaan, although it seems we rarely acted with hands as bloody as the words demanded. It was as if there were no alternative, no other way of acting if our holy path were to ground itself upon a piece of earth and be enacted. Questions about whether the holiness of the path canceled itself in this way—what benefit in wiping out child sacrifice if one had to kill children to do it—did not arise.

This vision collapsed, partly through the attractions of the partial truths of Hellenistic civilization, partly through the military power of the Hellenists. When Rome broke our power, destroyed the Temple, shattered our people, the rabbis concluded that the most we could do was to make *ourselves* a holy, decent people.

At minimum, a holy ghetto, living in the nooks and crannies of the Mediterranean world, suffering oppression and pogroms, but continuing to be within ourselves what God demanded. At absolute maximum, a model from which others could learn. We had no stronger means of transforming other peoples or the world.

But this vision also broke down. Pogroms are one thing, Holocaust another. The Holocaust showed that there was no place to hide: not even a ghetto, not even assimilation. We learned that nowhere was there safety, so long as idolatry held power on earth. So even for the sake of mere survival, we had to reexamine our mission in the world. Even for the sake of mere survival, we might have to return to smashing idols. But the collapse of the rabbinic model does not mean the restoration of the biblical model. We live in a world in which military power as a way of smashing idols has come to a dead end.

What we have begun to create, what we must continue to create, is an authentically Jewish way of transforming the world without military power. It is a kind of nonviolence that is not passive, and does not utterly forgo the possible use of violence in self-defense, but that focuses on how to change the world in decent directions so that the ultimate defense, through violence, never becomes necessary.

How do we do this? By celebrating our ancient holidays in ways that deliberately, assertively, challenge a wider public. By observing a kind of kashrut in ways that deliberately, assertively, challenge a wider public. By taking social action to demand social justice in ways that bring to the broader world the holy rhythms of sacred time and the holy practice of a daily path. By reunifying the three aspects of the Jewish path.

There is more I want to say, there are more questions I want to ask: What part have our new experiences of God, our new images of God, our new forms of prayer and celebration, played in making possible our new forms of social action? What part has the entrance of women into full sharing in the making of Judaism—women bearing the full truth of their own special life-experience—had in shaping our new forms of action toward social justice? What effect has the arena we call "sexuality," "eros," the arena of the Song of Songs, had upon the arena we call "social justice"? Are they really utterly separate, or has the search for love been at the heart of the search for community, and the search for community at the heart of the search for justice?

But these are questions I can only barely ask—for now. The time has come, the rhythm has come, for me to catch my breath, to make a Shabbos in my own work here, today. I always find this hard. Perhaps the reason I so often have preached the rhythm of work and rest, the need for pausing, is that I myself find it so hard to do. Nevertheless, I shall do it.

But not without sharing one last thought.

Only now, looking back on all the richness that we have created in this past generation, do I really understand how it was possible for the rabbis to create the great rich sea of the Talmud. Only now, feeling how new is what we have done and how deeply ancient it is, do I really understand how the rabbis felt when they discovered, uncovered, new Torah—and realized with laughter and delight that it was old.

That it had been waiting, all those hundreds and thousands of years, in the veils and beneath the veils that both *were* Torah and *hid* Torah.

Let us look forward and backward together to the delights of unveiling Torah in the next Hakhel.[33]

A Response

David A. Wortman

The task before me is to respond to the essay by Arthur Waskow. How does one evaluate words that so clearly emanate from the soul and derive from the very essence of the author? To know Arthur Waskow, as I have had the privilege to do for many years, is to hear his voice on every page of his manuscript. I will not judge his vision, but will place before you a few of my own thoughts on the future.

The link to the past that passes through me to the future is to be found in the tiniest of fragments of bone. In 1984, on a cold winter's day, I stood next to the ruined crematoria at Birkenau. Our guide knelt to the ground and retrieved a small white substance from the frozen earth. It was bone. For here stood the spot upon which the ashes of our people had been unceremoniously dumped. But they do not remain buried. They continually rise to the surface to bear silent witness to what was and what could have been.

As I stood transfixed by that bone, a chill entered my soul, and I was transported back in time—to a time of spiritual and physical exile. "The hand of God was upon me, and God carried me out in a spirit, and set me down in the midst of a valley, and it was full of bones . . . " (Ez. 37:1). With Ezekiel, I cried out to God. And with Ezekiel I heard God respond: "I will cause breath to enter into you, and you shall live." (Ez. 37:5).

Once again, my soul soared through time. Transcending the past and the present, I arrived at an era yet unseen in a place unknown beyond the world of drama. There beside me was Ezekiel with the prophets of all time, watching as the ancient dry bones mixed with the bones of Birkenau and the righteous of every generation. Then, indeed, transformation occurred. "Lo, there were sinews upon them, and flesh came up, and skin covered them above." (Ez: 37:8). After which, in the cacophony of a thousand generations of anguish and pain, in an act of ultimate redemption, God breathed into them the breath of life. At that moment, the world was filled with light. Justice prevailed. Mercy tempered. Life was renewed.

When I returned from this spiritual journey, no time had passed. I was still at Birkenau. Our guide still held the fragment of bone. Yet my life had changed.

I had experienced the past and glimpsed the future. Only this could give a new meaning to the present.

Will we, 50 years hence, be any closer to redemption? With Amos I echo: "I am neither a prophet, nor son of a prophet." (Amos 7:14). Would that Arthur Waskow's vision be fulfilled—in concept, if not in detail. The details are of little consequence. Whether new structures are created, old ones revised, or current ones expanded, in the final analysis what is of consequence is that commitment to social justice will have transformed the world and brought us closer to redemption.

The model for social justice is already embedded in our tradition. The Torah itself has taught us to choose life. The Talmud teaches that we may break all but three mitzvot in order to save a life. This suggests that the Deuteronomic dictum applies not only to choosing life for ourselves, but for others as well. The primacy of life defines our identity as Jews.

This translates into a social justice paradigm in a variety of ways. First is the obligation to deal with the instrumentalities of death. How can we fulfill the mitzvah of choosing life if we continue to devise mechanisms for its destruction? A prerequisite to a just future vision is action to end life-destructive forces. But an end to the nuclear threat is not sufficient in and of itself. It is merely a first step, meaningless unless it is followed by a further commitment to reshape the mindset that leads to war.

At Auschwitz we experienced the ultimate expression of evil, the individuation of the technology of death. At Hiroshima we witnessed the extension of this evil from the personal to the impersonal. But even the most sophisticated weapons of destruction are idle in the hands of the righteous. Then what is the more appropriate goal—the end of weaponry or the pursuit of righteousness? The obvious answer is, of course, both. I would suggest, however, that new weaponry in an unrighteous world will eventually lead to the creation of new modes of destruction.

I would further posit that when we focus on cessation of the production of life-destructive forces, nuclear and chemical warfare are merely the most graphic. Surrounding us are other, potentially equally destructive, forces. These include value-free education of our youth, the dehumanizing impersonal nature of a computer-centered society, and a pervasive cultural and ethnic particularism that exacerbates tensions between peoples.

The destructiveness of these forces is found in their feeding the voracious appetite of the *yetzer harah*, "the evil inclination." In my vision of the future, I can see progress only when we have found a way to reinfuse values into the education of our children. Their loss comes from a slavish adherence to a misinterpretation of the message of our American founding forebears. That misinterpretation nurtures an amoral educational environment capable of rationalizing the release of the forces that bring an end to our universe.

Value-free education creates a disjuncture between the messages of the formal structures of American society and our Jewish traditional orientation. This conflict forces us to choose between acceptance into the mainstream of our society and the isolation of Jewishness.

The fundamental laws of our ethnic system that govern behavior between human beings transcend the theological differences between Judaism, Christianity, and Islam. Those laws give shape to a universalism that precludes evil. To deny public affirmation of these principles in our educational system is destructive.

To act humanly, one needs to feel human. To care about life, one must feel alive. For life to be chosen, it must be worthy of choice. Consequently, the current trend toward dehumanization through computers is a potential step toward self-destruction. We have become numbers in an endless binary numeric string. In homes and in offices around the world we have learned to relate to cathode-ray tubes in place of people. Where once we would talk to people, we now read a screen. Where once we would feel the joy and the pain of human meeting, we now depress keys on a pad. How can we hope to validate life when we have succumbed to a new kind of "terminal" illness? How do we learn compassion when universal holocaust may be endangered by entering an appropriate code on a computer terminal, thus destroying unseen lives in the midst of unheard cries?

Not all technology is evil. And here I depart from Arthur Waskow's tantalizing vision of a techno-*shemitah*. To take one year in seven to reassess the values underlying our research and development is laudable. It will keep us on track. But even a moment's hesitation in the research and development of means to cure disease, to end pain, to end pollution of the air, water, and soil, to bring us to an efficient use of energy—a moment's hesitation is dangerous. If one life is lost because of our hesitation, what will we have wrought? If, as we are taught, to save one life is tantamount to saving the entire world, then what is equivalent to destroying one life?

That brings me to what I have called cultural and ethnic particularism. We live in an age when particularism dominates. This is evidenced in the myriad nationalist movements, in the self-orientation of pop psychology, and in the insistence on strongly hierarchical human structures. Unfortunately, while particularism ensures survival of particularistic group identity, in its absolute form it denies the universalism dictated by our tradition. It delegitimates our concern for the homeless and the hungry. The Jewish struggle is to balance the particular with the universal.

For many years, the Jewish liberal has been concerned with universalism and all that it encompasses. This universalism derives from early Jewish dicta. We are told in the Torah that we must be concerned with the "stranger that is within thy gates." In the Talmud, we are instructed that in most nonritual situations, *dinah demalchutah dinah*—"the law of the land is law."

Perhaps the most poignant source of our universalist tendencies is to be found in the Passover Haggadah. There we are commanded that in each generation we are to consider ourselves as if we had been slaves in Egypt. This simple adjuration not only recreates in us the mentality of enslavement so that we can fully appreciate freedom: it also allows us to empathize with those of our brothers and sisters who remain spiritually or physically enslaved.

To these examples could be added innumerable citations from biblical, rabbinic, and modern sources that would elucidate the foundations of the Jewish commitment to universalism.

The other side of the conflict has directed our attention to more narrowly defined Jewish subjects. The textual basis for this orientation is found in the first clause of Hillel's famous teaching, "If I am not for myself, who will be for me?" Although Hillel adds, "Yet, if I am for myself alone, what am I," particularists would suggest that this is an ideal state that can be reached only after all of our own needs have been addressed.

The inward focus of the particular has often provided the substance of survival. By creating institutions within our community designed to provide for "our own," we have ensured that a vibrant Jewish people is sustained. In medieval Europe, it was not uncommon for Jewish communities to create specialized societies that cared for the sick, tended to the ritual needs of the dead, comforted mourners, provided vocational education and training, and established yeshivot and synagogues.

In modern times, particularism engendered spiritual resistance during the darkest days of our history. It also fueled the Zionist fire that created a state and that still burns fiercely within our collective soul. Great modern leaders from both sides of the political spectrum have expressed primary concern for Jewish self-awareness and self-fulfillment.

The Jewish struggle continues to rest on that cusp. Neither posture taken alone or in its extreme reflects the true essence of our value system, which is at once as old as Sinai and as new as our last breath. The challenge is to maintain balance. A social justice reenvisioned for the twenty-first century would capture the middle.

Thus far I have focused upon the mitzvah of "Choose life!" Yet choosing life is not enough. Life without quality or dignity is not worthy of choice. It is the mitzvah of *tzedek tzedek tirdof*, "Justice, justice shalt thou pursue" (Deut. 16:20) that binds the quality of life to the choice of life.

By quality of life, I do not mean to imply material gain. Rather, quality of life is inherent in the word "dignity." When we infuse dignity into a person's life, we have enhanced the quality and the attraction of choice.

For instance, in Philadelphia the Committee for Dignity and Fairness was established by the homeless and formerly homeless. It is a place where those who have been subjected to the economic and political hardships of homelessness have banded together to provide dignity for each other and for others. The group acquires and refurbishes homes, then makes them available as low-income housing. A roof over one's head that one can call one's own provides dignity.

Other special concerns that occupy the front pages of our periodicals, such as minimum wage, equality in the workplace, and the inculcation of mutual respect among disparate groups, add to the sum and substance of the dignity given to life.

In our quest for dignity and social justice, we have been engaged in strengthening the relations between blacks and Jews, Jews and non-Jews, and Israelis and Palestinians. We have tried to foster a sense of mutual respect among disparate groups around the globe. This is not new. We have been doing this since the days of Abraham and Sarah. What is new is that we want to expand their conceptual purview and to make these paradigms the foundation of our future.

My vision of the future is that it is socially just only if we strive to resolve these issues. The operative word in the dictum *"Tzedek tzedek tirdof"* is not *tzedek* (justice) but *tirdof* (pursue). The pursuit of righteousness is what makes us righteous. Seeds of solution and hope have always existed among our people. Isaiah, in a moment of optimism, named his son Sheoryashuv, "a remnant shall return" (Is. 7:3). By that very act, he suggested that even in the eighth century B.C.E. there was cause for hope in a world that in his eyes looked as gloomy as our world looks to us.

That remnant, those seeds of solution, need nurturing, need water, need our help to grow. That is the *tzedek* that we must pursue.

All this would not be a rabbinic presentation if it did not remind me of a story:

Reb Moishe went to a small town in Eastern Europe noted for having deviated from the Halakhah and from the true essence of Judaism in order to teach them the Truth, to teach them Torah. And when he came, he said he would stay for a day and meet with as many people as he could. He went from door to door, attended a few meetings. At the end of the day he said to himself, "I have not accomplished my goal. I am going to stay a week."

At the end of the week, after having gone to more houses, attended more meetings, and visited more synagogues, he said to himself, "Moishe, I am not getting anywhere. I had better stay a month."

At the end of the month, after teaching classes and gathering students about him, he made an assessment. He said to himself, "This is not working. I need to stay a year."

He stayed a year. He stayed five years. He stayed twenty years. He stayed to the year of the fourth Hakhel. At which time the mayor of the community came to him and said, "Reb Moishe, I understood when you came to stay a day, you came to change us. I understood when you said you would stay a week that you came to change us. I understood that when the week became a month and the month became a year that you still held as your goal to change us. But when one year became five, and five became ten, and ten became twenty, had you not yet learned that you cannot change us?''

Reb Moishe turned to the mayor and said, ''When I first came, I came to change you. Now I stay so that I do not change.''

That is the message of *''Tzedek tzedek tirdof''*—''Justice shall you pursue.''

Many of the sparks of vision embedded in Arthur Waskow's Hakhel can be subsumed under the general heading of *rodef tzedek,* the pursuit of righteousness. His suggested rituals become the mechanisms of pursuit. He implies that traditional instrumentalities have failed us. I would suggest, rather, that it is we who have failed them. Our challenge is not only in the creation of new instrumentalities, but in recapturing the essence of the old.

Those of us who work in Jewish communal institutions and organizations need to take the word *Jewish* seriously. When we speak of a Jewish Community Relations Council, a Jewish Family Service, or a Federation of Jewish Agencies, the primary emphasis in these titles must be relocated to the word *Jewish.* We must learn and teach the values of our tradition, that our work might be imbued by them. Further, the synagogue itself has been part of the process of straying. If we take our challenge seriously, then we must bring the synagogue back to the path as well.

In the final analysis, I suggest that we have lost sight of the essence of the tradition. It has been lost in the exclusive rather than in the inclusive *siyag* (fence) that we have built around the Torah. Our search today must be to find the key to the gate of this fence so as to create a socially just future.

Spirituality, to which Waskow alludes, is the fundamental basis for a socially just world. Social justice, the pursuit of *tzedek,* the choice of life, evolves naturally from the spiritual meeting between us and God.

We are told that when God went to create the universe, God looked for a place to locate it. Being everywhere, God could not find a place in the universe where God was not present. If God made the world part of God, for what would the world strive? And so God performed *tzimtzum,* contraction, creating an empty place in the universe into which the world was placed. We have the obligation to enter into meeting with God. Since God is external to us, we come to that meeting to form a relationship. When we do so, we accomplish the creation of the spiritual whole. Social justice is the natural evolvement.

There are impediments to this spirituality in the world in which we live, the greatest of which is rationalism. The rational legacy of Kant and Hegel suggests to us that to think of God, to think of the spiritual, is to think of that which is not rational. This is even true of rabbis! In a sermon seminar at the Board of Rabbis of Philadelphia a few years ago, none of the four High Holy Days presentations mentioned God.

To me, this defines our problem. How can we enter into a meeting with a Being about whose existence we do not speak? The beginning of work toward a socially just world starts with the development of the spiritual within—setting the model and the paradigm, out of which social justice will evolve.

This brings me to Shabbat. Waskow suggests an interesting interpretation of Shabbat with which I would agree. But I also agree with what he did not say—that Shabbat in all of its aspects is but a microcosm of the world to come. If we are to accept that the world to come is the most just world we can envision, then the process of bringing a real Shabbat to us once a week, and a Shabbat of years once in seven years, is to bring a piece of the world to come into our present reality. This allows us to touch a small piece of that far distant future that will ultimately define the universe.

The challenge, therefore, is to become spiritual islands in a sea of rationalism, creating ever more spiritual bridges until the land and the sea, as at Creation, come into healthy symbiosis.

When God created the world, light was created on the first day. If on the fourth day God created the sun, the moon, and the stars, what was the light of the first day? It was the Light that emanated from God. This Light was withdrawn from the world and planted for the righteous; as we read in Psalms, "Light is sown for the righteous" (Ps. 97:11). Each righteous individual, each person who pursues righteousness, each one who takes the mitzvah of *tikkun olam*, repairing the world, seriously, brings one piece of that Light back into the world. When all of us have worked for that righteousness, have endeavored to bring that Light back to the world, that Light will once again shine.

I am not so presumptuous as to suggest that I am righteous. Rather, I suggest that our challenge today in creating a socially just world, whether that depicted in Arthur Waskow's vision or in any other way our imaginations can divine, is to continue our pursuit of the Light of God and ultimately to bring it into the universe.

11

The Synagogue and Caring Community

Lawrence Kushner

In 20 years synagogues will still be around. Many of us will not. Those two certainties are intimately related. Synagogues will be around because their main function in life is to be around from one generation to the next. In this they resemble all institutions, from the local PTA to the World Series, from birthday parties to the public library. They are, by definition, self-perpetuating—in business to keep the next generation doing what this generation thinks important. What synagogues are selling are the very occasions during which one generation hands itself over to the next. Many of us, on the other hand, will not be around because the span of our years will fall far short of *ad meah v'esrim*, 120. Realizing this, we turn to our parents and our children and an institution that we hope will give our mortality some sweetness.

We cannot do anything about the *shalshelet hadorot*, the great braid of generations. We are simply in it, held in relationship to one another, carried along, with or without our consent, like ornaments on some great invisible tapestry. Every now and then we are given permission to realize our place in this ancient fabric and stand reverent. The very existence of other generations means that we have been born and that we will die. We realize that as we hope, God willing, to outlive our parents, we pray our children will outlive us.

This realization is so universal, so commonplace, so primary to even the most simple forms of religious awareness that we are prone to ignore it. Yet this reverence before the generations past and future may be the root experience of the holy. We meet God in the faces of our parents and our children. The poets, philosophers, and artists can find the sacred in more unlikely places. But all of us, no matter how unimaginative, prosaic, or irreligious, encounter the sacred in the faces of our parents and the faces of our children, for in them we behold our own birth and death. This realization is also the mother lode of synagogue life.

I would like to offer here some stories and observations about the great passages of life, consider their implications for a healthy synagogue community, and attempt to mollify an old biblical story.

Jewish Latency

For my generation, at least, what I call "Jewish latency" lasted from high school graduation until one's first child was ready to enter kindergarten. It was not uncommon (with the exception of extreme parental duress during the first 10 days of *Tishri*) for someone never to set foot in a synagogue during Jewish latency. And then, as if an internal, prerecorded, first-child's-sixth-birthday-triggered alarm goes off, the parents walk into the nearest congregation's office and plunk down their membership dues. I have watched a parent stand in front of the receptionist's desk after Labor Day, juggling an infant in one hand, the other gently resting on the shoulder of the almost-six-year-old, and asking, "How does someone join this place?" Often they have not attended services or even met the rabbi. They have heard from a neighbor that it was a decent shul, or maybe they have just driven by on their way to the market. They are good folks. Many will grow into fine leaders of the Jewish community.

"See how nice it is here?" the mother whispers to her child, as if to reassure herself that this place could in no way recapitulate the intolerable boredom of her own religious school education. And the wide-eyed little one, forehead level with the desk, from a safe distance cautiously surveys the office copying machine. Of course there are many who join right out of college and others who find Judaism much later in life, but even in these better times of increased religious awareness, most of our members sign up because, in the words of one father, "I realized I wanted our little boy to know what it meant to be a Jew, and I wasn't sure how to do that by myself." I cite all this not for the sociological trends it may or may not augur. I mention it to evoke the strange and sacred experience of handing things down from one generation to another and the theology that necessarily nurtures such a gesture.

Abraham and the First Trial

The first, and arguably the most powerful, generational transmission in Western religious tradition occurred on Mount Moriah when Abraham bound Isaac on an altar. The midrash routinely confuses Mount Moriah and the site of the Temple. In other words, the synagogue is built where the older generation tries to convince the younger about the meaning of life. Naturally, the attempt is doomed from the start but mysteriously, in the failing, both generations learn about God.

According to rabbinic legend, Abraham's test that he sacrifice his son was the last of 10 trials. The first occurred back in his own Babylonian boyhood when God told him to leave his father's house. The key to decoding the *Akedah* is concealed back in the strange relationship Abraham, our father, had with Terakh, his father. I am chastened to learn over and over that patterns in a family recur from one generation to the next. Abraham violently separates from his father, almost murders his son. So it goes.

In his poem, "God of Abraham, God of Isaac," Joel Rosenberg has Isaac say after the *Akedah:* "(His voice now changed into a man's): 'But tell me, Abba, you have left your father's house. And will I do the same, and will my child?' " Perhaps one generation's yielding to another requires children to smash their parents' idols, and parents to nearly kill their progeny. Perhaps this is what the midrash means when it speaks of these events as the first and the last of 10 trials.

Grandparents, Grandchildren

It is *Shemini Atzeret, zeman simchateynu,* the season of our joy. We are gathered in the sanctuary for the annual *Chanukat banim,* the consecration of those entering kindergarten and first grade in our religious school. There are about two dozen children. Those who are the oldest children in their families have joined the congregation within the past month. Brothers and sisters, mothers and fathers, and what I guess to be many, many grandparents are also present. Since most of our congregants are not native to the area, many of the grandparents have come from far away. The room is filled with commotion and kvelling. Another rite of passage.

One by one, the five- and six-year-olds come up on the *bimah* to get something like a blessing from this rabbi who, in order to meet them at eye level, has to get down on one knee. Then the principal presents each child with a very small *tallit.* One child asks, "Could I really take it home and keep it all for myself?" "Yes, it's yours to keep and wear whenever you pray." I have decided that as they come to me this year, I will ask the little ones to point to their parents and grandparents in the congregation. And one by one they identify "the stock from whence they have come." The parents crane their necks, hold one another, reach out to their own parents. A few sneak a photo even though it's forbidden. Who could be angry? Then I ask the little one to look up at the *Sifrei Torah* in the open ark. "Do you know why your mommy and daddy and grandma and grandpa are so proud?" I ask. "Because of where you are standing and what you will learn. I hope you like this place very much and have a good time whenever you come here."

What is happening here is root-level synagogue life. The ceremony is so spiritually primary that no matter how disorganized (two dozen six-year-olds can get very disorganized), no matter how apparently irrelevant the liturgy or boring the speeches, there is no way to diminish its immense personal and religious power. All anyone will remember is this "sacred" moment in front of the scrolls, which means, "Now the little one is a student of Torah." The parents look to their parents. The words, "See, Mom, see, Dad, I brought them here" are never spoken.

In seven or eight years, God willing, on a Shabbat morning we will celebrate the *b'nai mitzvah.* We will invite the parents and grandparents up on the *bimah.* This time I take the scroll from the ark and hand it to the oldest generation. They are uneasy: the grandmothers often look like they are about to get scolded for touching the Torah. The grandfathers are trying to look stronger than they are. Then they take a few steps forward and hand the scroll to their children, who in turn give the scroll to the *b'nai mitzvah.* There is no liturgy, no music. We don't even rehearse. The whole thing probably takes less than two minutes. The almost-adult now stands in the center, flanked by the generations that gave birth to him. The grandparents look to their children with eyes that say, "You did good. We're proud. Thank you." The parents look to their parents with eyes that say, "May we all dance at the wedding." We go on with the service. Everything else—even the reading of the Torah—is almost trivial by comparison.

What is so powerful about great life passages that they evoke such emotional and religious intensity? After two decades of trying to help Jews find meaning in the great events of their lives and build institutions where that can happen gracefully, I am convinced that the answer lies in the dynamics of family. First comes family, then comes religion.

The Polar Ice Pack

With or without our consent, we are all determined by our placement in extended families. As systems theory and family therapy have demonstrated, we are more like elements in a living organism than autonomous individuals. Edwin Friedman has observed that our psyches are shaped, stifled, nurtured, and formed by the relationships of the other members of the system to one another.[34] One pushes, another pulls; too much pressure here, an explosion there; the balance is maintained.

In other words, while relationships can take forms ranging from intimacy to distance, from admiration to disgust, the amount of energy in the system remains fairly constant; stability is preserved. We may rechannel the energy toward another member of the family, but, as in any closed system seeking to maintain a homeostatic balance, we may not spend it somewhere else. Families, like all systems, are governed in Friedman's words by "the tendency of any set of relationships to strive perpetually, in self-corrective ways, to preserve the organizing principles of its existence."[35]

A good example of how this works can be found in what family therapists call the "identified patient" (I.P.) phenomenon. In this arrangement, one person in the family system—usually through no fault of the I.P.—becomes the target for everyone's sympathy. The I.P.'s name begins with the never uttered but always evoked modifier, "poor." Indeed, often the I.P. is made physically ill. Nevertheless, while everyone genuinely wishes poor whoever it is better health and fortune, they want even more that I.P. not get better, for they correctly intuit that once the I.P. gets well, they could be next. Obviously in a healthy family (of which there are absolutely none), relationships and their definitions are in a constant state of flux, responding to the exigencies of each new day. But for most organisms, most of the time, novelty, even when it promises renewed health, is nevertheless an anxiety-provoking nuisance. For this reason, by secret, unspoken, often unconscious mutual consent, the members of extended family systems usually work very hard to keep things pretty much the way they are. As one of my congregants once wryly observed, "Rabbi, the relationships in my family resemble the polar ice pack."

I said earlier that a family is a closed system. There is one exception. From time to time, life demands that every family organism rearrange its infrastructure. This occurs whenever there is a rite of passage, whenever the system gains, loses, or redefines one of its members. On such occasions, the relationships within the family become fluid. Or, to continue the arctic metaphor, life passages mean the possibility of a thaw. For just a while, for several months on either side of the great event, the ice melts, cracks, buckles, shifts, and rearranges itself. New relationships can be imagined. Healing is possible. And I believe this is the real reason why the great events of life occasion such anxiety, terror, and exaltation. Even in the healthiest of families, for the most joyous of events, people get a little crazy. As everyone knows, sometimes they get a lot crazy.

The father of the bride may be sincere when he says at the wedding, "I'm not losing a daughter; I'm gaining a son," but he also knows that this wedding might also profoundly affect his relationship with his own wife. The parents of a bar or bat mitzvah may be accurate when they voice their pride, but their heart also secretly trembles, for they know something else. Now their son is publicly able to impregnate a woman. (When the rabbis indexed the age for adulthood with the appearance of pubic hair, it wasn't religious maturity they had in mind either.) And, while a funeral is usually anything but joyous, here more than in any other passage lies the possibility for dramatic rearrangement of the family system. As Friedman has observed, " 'rites of passage' were the first human efforts to deal with modern psychotherapy's major areas of concern: change and separation."[36] These emotionally powerful events are religious precisely because they touch us at our core, whether or not we ourselves are religious.

For this reason, the creation of ceremonies that lend spiritual form and meaning to the great passages of life are universally entrusted to religious institutions. The generations gather to reassure us that, just as our parents and their parents before them survived birth, bar mitzvah, marriage, even death, so too can we. Indeed, whenever the generations gather, we are coaxed to transcend ourselves. Even more religious than the liturgy is the presence of the generations. Indeed, in the next decades, as the geographic dispersion of extended families becomes the norm, great life passages may be the only time that the generations will predictably and "religiously" gather. And in an almost primal sense, even the most irreligious Jews persist in their desire to gather in the synagogue.

Iconoclast

As you will recall, in the midrash Terakh ran an idol boutique in Glencoe of the Chaldees. One day, it seems the old man had to go out of town on a business trip and asked his son to mind the store. When Abraham was alone, he took a hatchet and, in what can only be called a fit of iconoclastic rage, smashed all his father's gods, except the biggest one—into whose hands he placed the hatchet. When Terakh returned he cried, "What happened?"

"I cooked a delicious dinner for them," replied his son, "but they all fought for the food. Then that big one over there took the hatchet and smashed the others. See, it's still in his hands!"

His father was furious. "Why they're just dumb statues of wood and stone! I made them all myself!"

"So why do you pray to them, you moron?" Abe grabbed the hatchet, shattered the last idol, and fled.

What I wonder is, did they ever speak after that? How did Terakh feel about it? Did he pick up the hatchet and shout, "You'd better run, or I'll use this on you!" Or did he just sit on his heap of smashed idols and cry? Did they ever talk to one another again? Maybe once a year after the *Akedah* was read on Rosh Hashanah, a three-minute phone call. If they didn't, did Abe ever think about his father and his mother, back there in the old house? Did Abe return home to visit his father in the hospital? Where they ever reconciled? And I wonder if Jewish neurosis down to this day might not be the result of the violent way in which Abraham seems to have separated from his father and all his gods or if, on the other hand, it is the source of whatever clever insight we possess into the human condition. From one generation to another, for all these centuries. Who can tell?

Family versus Congregation

A typical American bar mitzvah celebration includes over 100 invited guests. Distant friends and relatives often see one another for the first time since the last bar mitzvah. Many of them have traveled for several hours and at significant expense. Since etiquette demands much more than a light kiddush before sending them back on their long way home, the celebration routinely lasts for most of the weekend. Furthermore, since couples now have their children five and ten years later than previous generations, they are also much wealthier. Their own parents are also much older—and, alas, presumably less likely to be able to dance at the wedding. Taken all together these elements effectively have transformed contemporary *b'nai mitzvah* into weddings. Virtually every social, financial, and familial obligation once reserved for weddings now applies to *b'nai mitzvah*.

Ordinarily, this should create a happy circumstance for synagogue life, but since *b'nai mitzvah* are by invitation only and very dressy social affairs, the members of the congregation have become underdressed, expensive, and unwelcome intruders. Those brave enough to come find "their" congregation taken over by a host of strangers with their own unique agenda, which rarely includes communal prayer. As a result, in most liberal congregations, *b'nai mitzvah* have effectively destroyed any sense of ongoing Shabbat morning worship.

We must remember nevertheless that even though *b'nai mitzvah* (and weddings) presently seem at odds with the formation of an authentic synagogue community, they are potentially very religious. Synagogues in the coming decades will "go and see what the Jews are doing," and help them translate that holy energy into a revitalized institution. We cannot manufacture whole ceremonies, but we can shape them. The great task of the next generation's synagogue will be to redirect the religious power of the family in a way that nurtures the congregation. We must convince families that it is in their best interest also to invite the members of the congregation. We must extend the life passage ceremony to include the year before and the year following the event. Synagogues should become the scenes of multisession seminars, classes, and groups designed to help make families make religious and psychological sense of the great passages of life and the concomitant transformations of family. The prototypes of such programs are already visible.

Naming Babies

As is already the case in many communities, the synagogue is not only the locus of *brit milah* and *simchat bat* ceremonies, it offers programs for both expectant and recent parents. For the past few years, two of my rabbinic colleagues and I have run seasonal birth and naming seminars. They are open to the community. Several dozen couples come—many of them unaffiliated—from just the few contiguous towns we represent. We take turns giving short spiels on customs and ceremonies surrounding the birth and naming of a Jewish child; we hand out materials and sell books. The prospective parents ask all sorts of questions. Beyond the obvious technical ones, every session invariably gets around to how to satisfy the grandparents while remaining autonomous. These young couples are very eager to learn. Most of them will enroll in Lamaze and natural childbirth classes, and if a nearby synagogue offered quality instruction on how to begin raising a Jewish child—as some now do—most would enroll there also.

In my own congregation, we usually observe a *simchat bat*, the naming of a daughter, during services. The parents and their child are invited up on the *bimah*. We open the ark and after a few prepared words from the mother and father and some ancient ones from the rabbi, we invite anyone in the congregation to add a blessing. We never know what the congregation will come up with. Sometimes people cry; sometimes they laugh; but no matter what they say, it is always appropriate. Here the congregation and family are gracefully blended. Last month, the family got the instructions mixed up and, in addition to the parents and their children, both sets of grandparents came up too. At first, I thought to ask them to return to their seats, but then I realized that they knew better. They stood there, on either side of their children, their granddaughter, and the scrolls and filled the room with light.

Talmud Torah

The synagogue should not only celebrate a child's entrance into religious education, it should teach parents of young children about Jewish parenting and how to deepen and gladden the Judaism in their home. Programs for family enrichment, such as the experimental one sponsored by Boston's Combined Jewish Philanthropies and our congregation's school, in which parents actually attend classes with their children, hold high promise. In addition to regular religious school and adult education, children in the primary grades are invited to attend a series of monthly Sunday mornings with their parents. The day begins with brunch and singing and includes classes where adults and children learn both separately and together. In addition, parents attend an additional monthly evening seminar. The response has been so strong that even with a hefty tuition fee and modest advertising, we will have to create two learning tracks. Most families in which both parents work naturally resent weekend religious school, but when the synagogue becomes the locus for a meaningful family experience, they are enthusiastic participants.

B'nai Mitzvah

The synagogue should also run parallel-learning midlife groups for parents. All too often parental involvement is wasted in the commotion of social and financial trivia. We forget that *b'nai mitzvah* are even more religiously and emotionally powerful for parents than for children. After all, it is parents who must now publicly stand and acknowledge the midpoint of their lives. (Professor Norman Mirsky has wryly observed that they also have probably reached their maximum earning plateau.)

Dimly sensing this, several years ago I began to offer a class on Sunday mornings for children who are about to celebrate their *b'nai mitzvah*. In order to participate, each child must be accompanied by one or both parents. In other words, it is rated ''R.'' Each session begins with a light breakfast and runs for two hours. The curriculum draws life issues relevant to adolescents and their parents from the weekly *parashah*. During the semester the entire class goes away to a nearby camp or retreat center for a weekend *kallah*. In the opening class I tell parents and children that in a few years they will probably have forgotten most of what I tried to teach, but for the rest of their lives they will remember that each week for several months they came to the synagogue to learn Torah together.

Siyyum

The *kallah* weekend itself has become a mainstay of our congregation. During the months before any great life passage event, families are especially open to religious growth. Spending a Shabbat together with their rabbi and other families undergoing the same anxieties and joys puts the bar or bat mitzvah in a larger perspective and gives families a sense of religious empowerment in congregational life. Their mutual presence also seems to give parents the confidence necessary to make a commitment to one another that their children continue through the congregation's high school. Deprived of the example of even one other kid who "doesn't have to go to religious school," they all attend. Indeed, I am now convinced that the only reliable inducement to get teen-agers to attend anything is the presence of all the other members of the peer group. Every Monday evening we serve them pizza and two classes. It is far from ideal, but after almost a decade, the number of students who continue through high school graduation, or what we call *siyyum,* is 95 percent.

The advanced age of grandparents and the distance of the wedding now make high school graduation a major rite of passage. The measure here as elsewhere is that grandparents get on airplanes to attend. Our congregation requires each graduate to submit a 10-page paper describing and defining his or her beliefs about some aspect of Jewish thought. Selections from these are then read as part of the *siyyum* ceremony. Each graduate is presented with a shofar and invited back to sound it on *Yontif* for what we call "the big band sound of Beth El." But even more important than the ceremony is the presence of family and congregation.

Dowering the Bride

We're under the *chuppah.* The bride and groom have just arrived. They are terrified and radiant. On either side stand their parents, who now, despite their joy, look old. And in the front row sits a very old woman with a large corsage. A strapping young nephew sits beside her, a cane leans against the chair. In just a moment, after we have blessed the wine and offered some to the couple and their parents, I will walk out from under the canopy and extend the goblet to the grandmother. More than bringing her into the honor and joy of the ceremony, her presence will grace the celebration with another dimension of meaning.

Of all life's passages, marriage is not only the most joyous, it is the most expensive and the hardest to integrate into congregational life. Of course the ceremony and *seudah* are commonly held in synagogues, but engaged couples, often residing in cities far from the rabbis and congregations of their youth, wind up choosing a rabbi to perform the ceremony rather than the rabbi's congregation. Most rabbis meet with couples a few times before the wedding but, lacking a large enough group of other engaged couples, little learning, meeting, or congregational bonding occurs. In the next decades synagogues will revive the ancient mitzvah of *hachnasat kallah,* dowering the bride—not as charity for the poor bride, but as a way for congregants to help young couples negotiate marriage and to welcome them into the congregation.

Accompanying the Dead to the Grave

If families overwhelm congregations at weddings, then at funerals when they are under great duress, the congregation can overwhelm them with compassion. Our congregation, like a growing number of others, has established a *chevra kaddishah.* Its responsibilities include the supervision of all aspects of death, burial and mourning within the congregation. Seminars on caring for aged parents, Jewish funeral practices, execution of an ethical will, as well as support groups for the bereaved, bind congregations and families. Congregants should also help one another in the construction of coffins, serve as *shomrim,* or guardians of the deceased prior to the funeral, and, ultimately, participate in the actual bathing and purification of bodies.

When my father, *alav hashalom,* died last year, I cried a great deal. My children were of enormous comfort. I remember vividly the way my daughter held me and the way my oldest son took a shovel at the graveside and helped my brother and me cover the coffin with earth. And, on the morning of the funeral, my then 11-year-old son came and sat in my lap to console me. We hugged, and we cried, and we whispered, and we wept some more. Then, in a moment of great insight, the little one burst out crying again and through the tears said, "The hardest part, Daddy, is knowing that someday I'll have to do this for you."

The great life-cycle events—the births, the *b'nai mitzvah,* the weddings, the funerals—are religious because they compel the generations to gather. Even the old ones who have died long ago return for the meal. Their loving, invisible presence is palpable. And when the generations come together, time collapses. For a moment or two, all circles are closed, ages erased, the future can learn from the past.

Isaac and the Last Trial

Rabbinic authorities disagree over how old Isaac was at the time of the *Akedah.* The story evokes an adolescent: strong enough to carry the wood, yet young enough to want to please his father. But others have suggested that Isaac was much older—a full-grown man, 37 years old (*Genesis Rabba* 56.8), on the other side of a mid-life crisis, who knew all along what was going on and how to play his part in the drama. According to *Midrash Wayosha,* "While Abraham was building the altar, Isaac kept handing him the wood and the stones. Abraham was like a man who builds the wedding house for his son, and Isaac was like a man getting ready for the wedding feast, which he does with joy."

One curious feature of the *Akedah* is a frequently noted omission. In a tale that has obviously been crafted with great precision, how odd that on two separate occasions, on their way to the mountain, we are told of Abraham and Isaac that "they went along, both of them together" (22:6, 8), yet after whatever it was that really happened up there, we read only, "and Abraham returned to his servants" (22:19). What did they talk about as they went along, both of them together? "Tell me about Grandpa Terakh again, Dad, and how you used to work in his shop when you were a kid. Did you really smash all of his statues?"

You Are My Mother

In "You Are My Mother," a video drama of astonishing power and subtlety written, directed, and acted by Joop Admiral, a middle-aged man has a half dozen conversations, first in a nursing home and then in a hospital, with his aged mother. They talk about their love and struggles, about life and death. The mother and the son are played by the same actor, who is literally playing himself and his mother. That is clever but not profound. The emotional power arises from the fact that the camera never moves. The actor, wearing a hat and glasses denoting no particular age and without missing so much as a breath, first speaks as one, then with only a slight change of voice, the other—both with the same face, out of the same mouth.

I realize that this sounds anti-Buberian, even autistic, but what we realize by the drama's conclusion is that we are all our parents. "Mother," the man who is also playing his mother says to his mother and himself, "this play we are speaking is about you; you have helped me script the lines." "You," she says to her son, "are my mother."

At any one of life's nodal events like a wedding or a birth, the costumes, the years, the cultural conventions separating one generation from another are brushed away, and we stand before the generations that bore us and that we bear, blessed in our likeness. In the secret silence of the bedroom mirror, when no one else is around, the 40-year-old son realizes he is made of the same stuff as his father, the daughter, the same genetic material as her mother. Another circle closed. And in the synagogue it is reenacted year after year.

Life's great, unending, psychospiritual task is separating from one's parents. Be they near or far, loved or hated, living or long dead, it is never finished. It goes all the way back to Abraham and Isaac, even back to Terakh and Abraham. Paradoxically, we come the closest to freeing ourselves from our parents when we realize that even despite our most ingenious attempts to the contrary, we have become them. We have closed the great circle, humbly taking our place in the long line of generations. The child playing with a grandfather's *tsitsit* to pass the time during services is the same as the old man shushing his grandson for fidgeting too much. I suspect such a circle may have also been closed on Mount Moriah. But how could that be? Terakh was an idolater, and Abraham was not.

Terakh and the Last Trial

Perhaps it is time to reconsider the ram. As Nahum Sarna observes, "The depiction of a god in the form of a bull was widespread throughout the entire ancient Near East. That animal was a symbol of lordship, strength, vital energy, and fertility, and was either deified and made an object of worship or, on account of these sovereign attributes, was employed in representation of deity."[37] We remember also that the Baal idol was a bull, the sin of the Northern Kingdom was the worship of a cow, and indeed the paradigm idol in Jewish tradition is a golden calf. Perhaps it was no accident that it was a ram that was slaughtered. Perhaps it was not Abraham who killed the ram after all. Perhaps it was Isaac. Is it possible that Isaac did so because he realized that after all those years even Abraham's God had begun to harden into a graven and predictable image? No longer the unrepresentable fire of Being but now the culturally convenient image of a ram. "This is my God, O Isaac, who brought me out of Ur of the Chaldees . . . " Who can say? Only the two of them were up there together, and Isaac did not return.

From *Midrash Eliyahu Rabba* comes what may be the missing piece. Apparently, Abraham's father did not die of a broken heart, never to be heard from again. We read that "for many years Terakh continued to be a witness to his son's glory, God accepted his repentance, and when he died he was admitted into paradise. Indeed, one tradition teaches that he did not die until Isaac was thirty-five years old." As we have already noted, this may have been about the same time that Abraham and Isaac went up on Mount Moriah. The old man is waiting for his son, Abraham, when he comes down the mountain alone. He looks into Abraham's eyes freshly washed with tears and sees that they are now clear and bright.

"Dad? Is that you? What are you doing here? I thought you were dead. How did you get here? Isaac, my son is gone. I'm so confused. Is Mom still alive? God told me to take Isaac up there and kill him on an altar. Isaac even carried the wood himself. Then I don't know what happened. I tried to show Isaac how this ram we found was a beautiful way to imagine God but he only said I was blind. He said that my god had stopped moving years ago. He called me a moron. We fought. There was screaming and blood, then Isaac hacked off the ram's head. Look, I have one of its horns. Then I remembered what I had done to you. But when I turned around, Isaac was gone. Dad, I'm sorry. I didn't mean to destroy your idols. Did you really believe in them? Were they covered by the insurance? I mean I didn't mean to hurt you; I just wanted to show you what I couldn't seem to tell you. Then I ran away, and I was too ashamed to go back. All these years. And now my Isaac is gone. I don't know where he is. I swear I didn't kill him. See, I have this horn of the ram he killed instead. Oh Daddy, I love you. Forgive me. Now I understand."

Self-Transcendence

When we look into the eyes of our children and our grandchildren, or when we look into the eyes of our parents and our grandparents either in life or in the photographs that evoke their memories, we realize there is something beyond us. We are humbled and graced. We are reminded of our birth and of our death. We take our place in the long line. That is the root experience of religion. And that is why there are synagogues.

Terakh was silent. He just reached out his arms and held Abraham, his little boy. "*Vayelkhu shneihem yachdav*—and they went along, both of them together." Just another bar mitzvah.

A Response

Burt Jacobson

One of Lawrence Kushner's great gifts is his ability to look deeply into the ordinary realities of human living and recognize the sacred dimension embedded in them. In his essay, Kushner has done just that for the Jewish family.

The family is one of the foundations of Jewish life. The home is the locus around which revolves much of Jewish ritual. But it was somewhat of a surprise to me to see the Jewish family through Kushner's eyes, examining the sacred dimension of family itself.

What surprised me, I think, has something to do with my experience of my own family while growing up. My nuclear and extended families were the major formative influences on my life. Although nurturing my existence, my family burdened me with emotional issues that I would carry and contend with through much of my adulthood.

There were no Jewish holidays celebrated in my home during my early years, no rites of passage until my bar mitzvah. My bar mitzvah mentor, Milton Bendiner, *alav hashalom,* became a kind of spiritual father to me, and because of his influence my bar mitzvah became the beginning of my adolescent rebellion against my parents, and my attachment to Judaism.

Years of therapy and spiritual growth have helped me establish a loving relationship with my family. But looking back, it seems to me that had Judaism, with its many holy times and rites of passage, played a real role in my family, my growing up might have been far different—more whole, more in touch with the love my parents had for me but found so difficult to express. The rituals might have provided us with occasions for the expression of love, closeness, and belonging.

So I am grateful to Kushner for having challenged me to consider the importance of the Jewish family from a spiritual perspective. The synagogue does indeed have a great deal to contribute by teaching families how Jewish ritual can help unite the generations.

I must say, however, that my own reflection on the question of the future of the American synagogue has taken me in a somewhat different direction. Perhaps it is because I have had far less experience as a congregational rabbi. Or perhaps it is because I live in California. Without wanting to oversimplify matters, it seems to me that there is a difference between East Coast and West Coast

Jews. I am most familiar with Jews in Berkeley, so my essay is based on my experiences with them.[38]

Let's start with some statistics. One hundred twenty thousand people live in Berkeley. One out of every five of these individuals is Jewish. Only a relatively small number of these Jews are affiliated with religious institutions or the Jewish community center.

Few of the adult Jews I meet in Berkeley were born in California. Many seem to have been drawn to the West Coast by the lure of the "California dream." This dream has several components, among them California's special climate and its spectacular scenery. There is also the lure of professional and economic opportunity. But it is my impression that many of the Jews who migrated to Berkeley are here because they wanted, consciously or unconsciously, to make a clean break with their pasts, with their families of origin, and often with their Judaism and their Jewishness. They wished to be individuals, and felt that they could not develop their individuality to its fullest as long as they lived in physical and emotional proximity to their families.

Many Berkeley Jews seem to retain a sense of ambivalence toward their families and their Jewishness. This may account for the extremely high incidence of intermarriage—one out of every two in our area.

Though Berkeley may represent an extreme, there are, of course, many ways in which it is like cities throughout the nation. Individualism is part of the very fiber of American life. Intermarriage is common all over. Divorce is rampant. Professional and economic considerations have made mobility almost a way of life in the United States. Americans have little compunction about moving away from their families, if only to find better jobs. Families may fly to distant cities to come together for a holiday reunion or rite of passage, but in the United States the power of family is simply not strong enough to keep it anchored in a single geographical location.

Rites of passage have become so important to families precisely because of the attenuated nature of the American family. Families attempt to compensate for the lack of geographical proximity and ongoing connectedness through reunions that draw on the well of memory and nostalgia.

The need for sharing and closeness had something to do with my own religious and professional path. Some four years ago I started what I call a "community-synagogue" in Berkeley. I made my appeal to Jews who disliked the existing congregations: individuals and families who were searching for more warmth, for more informality, for services with real spiritual depth, for a sense of community. I tried especially to reach Jews with a politically activist bent, concerned with global as well as Jewish issues. From the very first, Kehilla welcomed feminists, intermarried couples, single parents, gays, lesbians, and non-Jews.

By the end of the second year, the time had come for members of the steering committee to meet and discuss their feelings about our enterprise. How was it affecting their lives? What did they appreciate about one another's contributions? What were their hopes for the future of the congregation? One of the individuals present was a man who had put an enormous amount of time into the synagogue. Jerry was married to a non-Jewish woman, who was peripherally involved in Kehilla. They had two children. When it came time for him to speak, Jerry told us how much this two-year experience had meant to him. He ended by stating that his greatest hope at this moment was that when he died, all of us would be there to bury him.

I was profoundly moved by his words. While reading Kushner's paper, my thoughts went back to that incident. Why did he think of *us* participating in his most momentous rite of passage? Why people he had known for only two years, and not his family back in Brooklyn?

An intentional community can never fully replace the family. Blood ties, the patterning of character in the family constellation—these will always remain a deep part of the individual's psyche. Despite this, for many people intentional community must replace the original family, because their families have become so dysfunctional, remote, or scattered. These individuals really do need something that is rare in the United States: authentic community.

Many of the values that we Jews have made our own in America are values that I cherish. Individual liberty and autonomy are important to me. I would not want to return to the parochial character of premodern Jewish life. Yet we have lost something significant in America as well. The synagogue has taken on some of the character of the liberal Protestant church. As important as pluralism and volunteerism are, the insidious ethos of individualism has penetrated to the core of the liberal Jewish life, destroying the fabric of community that once characterized Jewish society. Just as authentic Jewish life cannot survive without the family, so it cannot survive without community.

Our congregations are primarily goal-oriented organizations, rather than communities. The synagogue does retain some aspects of community. Basic to the synagogue is a shared desire for the survival of Judaism and Jewishness. The congregation provides a locus for communal worship and celebration, and it offers educational programs to pass down our heritage to young and old. Through the work of committees, individuals work together on common projects that benefit the synagogue as a whole. Sometimes these various activities engender friendships among individuals and even among families. But friendship, intimacy, and caring are not really high on the list of synagogue priorities. What seems to be missing, as far as I can see, is a larger sense of connnectedness among the members of the congregation, a recognition that the individuals and families that make up the synagogue are part of a larger organism. There is no sustained sense of serious mutual obligation among members of our congregations.

In 1969 the photographer Anders Homquist produced a lovely book of photographs called *The Free People,* which depicted life on West Coast communes.

The introduction to this book was written by Peter Marin, who is now an associate editor of *Harper's Magazine*. In his essay, Marin described what the communards were attempting to create, speaking eloquently of their successes and failures. As I was writing this essay, one passage of Marin's introduction came to mind, a paragraph in which he describes what family and community meant to him:

> A lovely warmth moves me now as I write—my wife and children asleep next door. It is, at bottom, the presence in me of all those I love, and it is that net of connections, that cradle of affection that seems to me at the heart of my own pleasure. Not long ago when I visited a college, a student said to me: "You seem to know just where you are; how do you do it?" I thought for a long time before answering, and I realized then for the first time that I was protected as if by a charm by the presence within me of my family and comrades. "The bird a nest, the spider a web, man friendship," writes Blake, and that is my sense of it.[39]

Like a family, members of a community carry the other members of their community within them. This inner identity with others is the basis of the two quintessential virtues of family and community: caring and commitment. Sometimes this kind of connectedness exists in congregations where individuals and families have gone out of their way to form friendships, but it does not seem to be a core phenomenon in our synagogues.

We have attempted to engender a greater sense of intimacy and community through *havurot,* and our congregational *havurot* have some major accomplishments to their credit. They have personalized large institutions and allowed groups of individuals to do more Jewish things together. But it is my impression that they have not really effected fundamental changes among individuals and families.

When I try to imagine the synagogue of the future, the basic question that comes to mind is how we might make the synagogue into an authentic caring community, where people from diverse backgrounds can share in one another's lives. Is it possible to develop a sense of deep bonding between our congregants, to create not merely the sense of community, but authentic community, where individuals in the congregation would not think twice about inviting the whole congregation to their simchas, because the congregation itself has become an extended family? Can we cultivate a sense of caring, so that in painful times of divorce and sickness and death, people will reach out to one another in genuine compassion? Can we develop a sense of reciprocal responsibility and commitment among our congregants?

Our social action committees extend themselves to Soviet Jewry, to the homeless of our own country, to refugees from Central America. All this is essential. But we also need to extend ourselves to those who suffer in our own congregations. When you are part of an authentic community, the social action that people do together takes on a different dimension. The commitment to *tikkun olam* has a greater staying power because the people engaged in it have real ongoing relationships with one another.

I believe that the kind of community I have been speaking of still exists in some traditional Jewish enclaves. In *An Orphan in History,* Paul Cowan describes such a community among the Hasidim he visited in the Lower East Side of New York. It also exists in fundamentalist Christian churches in this country. Unfortunately, in both cases, caring community is accompanied by a rigid belief system, by parochialism, and by xenophobia. It is as if all the love of the community is turned inward toward its own.

The question that remains is whether such a caring community can really come to exist in the liberal synagogue. Perhaps the kind of community I envision is a romantic fantasy. Perhaps we are so wedded to individualism and privatism that the traditional Jewish notions of community and caring are gone forever.

But if all this is true, it makes me wonder: What are our synagogues really about in the end? What are we dedicating our lives to as rabbis and teachers? When we preach about community, compassion, and commitment, are these mere platitudes resting on a nostalgia for the past? Will we become primarily a consumer-oriented enterprise, fitting into the privatism and self-preoccupation that characterizes so much of American life?

Several years ago I became acquainted with a woman named Diane. Diane had been a professional Jewish educator, working for one of the Bureaus of Jewish Education in the Bay Area. She had lived in Israel, she spoke fluent Hebrew, and was for a time teaching some of our bar mitzvah kids to speak modern Hebrew. Then Diane left the Jewish community, and Judaism, and became a disciple of Rajheesh. Sometime later I asked Diane why she had joined the Rajheesh movement. Her answer: "I did not find any real love and caring in the Jewish community."

There are reasons other than the need for community that drive people to join cults and espouse fundamentalist forms of religion. Some people seem to require a kind of religious certainty that liberal religion cannot offer. Others seek a spiritual and emotional depth in worship that is missing from the liberal synagogue. And yet there is no doubt in my mind that a lack of true community in the liberal synagogue is also a major cause of the loss of so many Jews to the alternative religions. Despite all the difficulties, we must begin to reenvision our synagogues, transforming them into communities that foster caring, intimacy, interpersonal involvement, and commitment.

Such a community would be doing a real service to those lonely, alienated individuals who, in their great despair, turn to cults, to Hasidic fundamentalism, or to drugs and other addictions. We could become a supportive community for singles, for single parents, for gays and lesbians. We could also reach out to our

Jewish elders, who become so marginalized in our society. And related to Kushner's point about the importance of synagogue for families, we could bolster the Jewish family by providing support systems that would bring families out of the isolation that so often breeds dissension and divorce. If the sacred can be found in authentic I-Thou relations, then the synagogue could become a community in which this dimension of the sacred might be cultivated.

In his book *Israel: Its Life and Institutions,* the Danish scholar Johannes Pederson defines the notion of community in the biblical world:

> When we look at the soul, we always see a community rising behind it. What it is, it is by virtue of others. It has sprung up from a family which has filled it with its contents, and from which it can never grow away. The family forms the narrowest community in which it lives. But wherever [the soul] works, it must live in community, because it is its nature to communicate itself to others, to share blessing with them. Loneliness, the lack of community, the Old Testament only knows as something unnatural, an expression that life is failing.[40]

Much of the anger of the prophets arose out of the breakdown of community in the urban centers of Israel and Judah. The prophets saw individuals who cared only for themselves. *Chesed* and *rachamim,* compassion, kindness, tenderness, and love were missing from human relations. Our rabbis and sages attempted to build communities of caring. *Gemilut chasadim,* acts of loving kindness, were central to their notion of community. One rabbinic saying defines a Jew as someone who is a *rachaman ben rachamanim,* a compassionate person, the child of compassionate parents.

I have asked some serious questions. I have no specific programs to recommend, but I believe the questions are so important as to warrant the sustained attention of liberal Judaism. I would like to see the Reconstructionist and Reform movements, together with the movement for Jewish renewal, create a think tank on issues related to family and community. Perhaps the Institute for the Jewish Future, which the Reconstructionist Rabbinical College is planning to launch, would be an appropriate vehicle for such a think tank. But I would want lay people and synagogue leaders as well as rabbis included in such a project. And I would certainly wish to involve many women in such a think tank. Family has traditionally been the province of women, and I know they will have a great deal to teach us regarding nurturing and caring on the communal level as well.

I would like to conclude my remarks with a Hasidic tale. Reb Moshe Leib of Sossov once confided that he had learned the true meaning of love of fellow human beings from a simple village peasant. The gentile sat in a tavern with several friends; when he was a bit tipsy, he asked his pal:

''Do you like me, or don't you like me?''

''Sure I like you,'' replied his friend.

"You say you like me," the peasant continued, "but you don't even know what I need. If you really like someone, you know what he needs and what he's missing."

And Reb Moshe Leib ended his story by saying: "It was only then that I first understood that loving people means sensing their needs, linking oneself with their pains, and feeling their troubles.[41]

A Response

Lee Friedlander

The first bar mitzvah of "the spring season," a sun-drenched morning the week immediately following Pesach, Shabbat Shemini . . . The bar mitzvah has worked hard and will conduct the Torah service, chant the Torah portion and a lengthy *haftarah,* and present an original treatise to those assembled entitled "The Ancient Ark of the Covenant in Leviticus, in II Samuel, and in Steven Spielberg's *Raiders of the Lost Ark.*" In addition to being a good student, the bar mitzvah is a good kid, the potential mensch.

The boy sits next to me on the *bimah* during *shacharit* (the morning service), in contrast to his friends, the *b'nai mitzvah* of "the fall season," all of whom sat more or less with their parents until the conclusion of the *Amidah* (silent prayer). He twitches perceptibly around the eyes this morning, as he has for the past several months, in anticipation of this day. His parents sit before us on opposite sides of the aisle in the front row, his mother with her parents, his father with his new wife and sixteen-month-old daughter. The bar mitzvah's brother is with his paternal grandmother toward the back of the room.

That is, I hope, the final scene in a family nightmare. Just two weeks before, the father of the bar mitzvah stormed out of my office threatening not to enter the synagogue if his devout Catholic wife and new child could not share his *aliyah;* this new demand followed the required five-session orientation for bar and bat mitzvah parents and several telephone conversations with him alone. Only after the Catholic wife took the initiative to call and discuss the congregation's policy with me (the only prohibition regarding liturgical participation by non-Jews in our synagogue) did I have the sense that there was a listening ear, perhaps because she was the only one who was not Jewishly involved, or perhaps because she was the only one for whom religion and religious tradition had meaning apart from this family, or perhaps because she alone could hear my voice as a voice of authority within our democratically structured Jewish community.

For the mother of the bar mitzvah, my congregant, the tradition had become a weapon to use against her former husband and against her observant parents. For the bar mitzvah's father, the tradition had become a symbol of the familial disenfranchisement of his new wife and child. As for the bar mitzvah himself, affirming Lawrence Kushner's premise that "first comes family, then comes religion," the tradition had become a source of pain, a reminder of his fractured existence, graphically represented by the aisle separating his parents from one another, an aisle that to him must have seemed a mile wide. No bonding between generations took place as a result of this sacred ceremony, unless it was on some abstract level, a bonding for the bar mitzvah with my wife and me, the rabbis of the congregation, and his surrogate parents for the occasion.

Although this case is extreme, the elements are familiar. Several of this bar mitzvah's classmates had divorced parents not separated by an aisle the day of the service, but by the body of the bar or bat mitzvah, a thin wall between two raging seas. And for every two couples surrounded by loving, beaming parents on the day of their wedding, I'll show you another one where parents turn the celebration of a new marriage into an occasion for doubt, even despair, and a forum for revenge. Often the deliberations concerning who walks down the aisle with whom and when are as complex and delicate as those between warring countries negotiating a temporary cease-fire.

For these people and for others outside the frame of the Jewish nuclear family—a growing population in our communities—synagogues do not function to link family members one to the other. Though many of us do "meet God in the faces of our parents and our children," there are others who have a hard time being in the same room with them. Our synagogues, which so honor the institution of the family reflected in our tradition, must find a way to include these people, too, on their own terms.

Is it possible for synagogues to become extended or surrogate families for all those who need them? Should, or can, the synagogue provide substitute fathers, mothers, sons, daughters, brothers, and sisters for those who are bereft of them? Are we really prepared as individuals in voluntary communities to adopt, embrace, and care for another lonely Aunt Esther or crazy Cousin Phil outside of our biological families? Can the synagogue realistically expect to provide for the senior who is alone, or for the one-parent family the link with the generations that is so easily transmitted in traditional families? Are we willing to adjust familiar rituals or create new ones or provide alternatives to meet the needs of broken families and broken people?

Even if all these questions could be answered affirmatively, it would not be enough. The synagogue must be more than a personal link to the generations for all of us, intact or fractured. Nowhere is the bar/bat mitzvah service more family oriented than at the Reconstructionist Synagogue of the North Shore, my congregation of almost 200 membership units on New York State's Long Island. An important component in the bar/bat mitzvah orientation is educating families about the service and helping them compose a supplement of readings to highlight and complement the service themes. Parents and siblings are also encouraged to address the bar or bat mitzvah that morning along with the rabbis and an officer of the congregation. People take these tasks so seriously that we have had to limit the number of readings at any given service and the number of wellwishers who feel entitled to address the new adult.

Families are elated by this experience. In contrast to most of the people who come to our meetings for prospective members, who give testimony to the traumatic process of becoming a bar or bat mitzvah that has kept them outside the synagogue well into "the latency period," our youngsters, inspired and positively identified, sail onward into our Upper School Program until they graduate from high school. But we pay a price for such personalization. As in Kushner's synagogue, congregants are absent from these services. Even those people invested with responsibilities who have had some association with the families often feel as though they are intruding on a private affair. More often than not I feel as though the young man or woman is being inducted into a cousins' club rather than being welcomed into the Jewish community.

More questions come to mind. In the context of the family search, will we do damage to the integrity of the synagogue? Although rites of passage such as baby namings, *b'nai mitzvah* services, and weddings do strengthen families (at least those families intact enough to be strengthened), how will we connect these families to the larger synagogue community and to the Jewish community outside of the synagogue? Will congregant members ever feel obligated to attend the life-cycle events of others if they are not invited, just because they are a part of the celebrant's larger community?

The challenge for the synagogue of the future is to open a door into that closed system that is a family and to create links between people connected to families and people disconnected from families, within the context of the synagogue community. I believe this to be the foremost challenge because I believe that we need one another so very much. The goal is to provide opportunities for people to touch each other's families and to feel so deeply connected to one another that every adult will see each child standing on the *bimah* in front of the *Sifrei Torah* at the annual consecration ceremony as his or her own child, and more: that the glow in the eyes of the assembled, both children and adults, will be for the learning about to begin, for Torah, not only for each other.

Can we provide opportunities, sacred occasions, to touch and connect with one another independent of family groupings but intergenerationally within the congregational community? I offer three programmatic suggestions that have provided people in my congregation with such opportunities. I have chosen to speak about modest programs or events, each of which is related to the liturgical cycle, to a minor holiday, or to Shabbat—times when people are not usually with members of their extended families, and therefore when they are unhampered by personal loyalties or feelings of obligation to those outside the synagogue community. Each of these programs is also intended to point the participant to a Jewish value regardless of family connection.

Mishloach Manot

Every year our elementary school children bake cookies and cakes and make baskets for the Jewish residents of a local nursing home at Purim. Last year, with a surging school population and a dramatic increase in family programming, many perceived the beginning of a division between those members with school-age children and those without. To bring our new children into the homes of our older members, we expanded our *mishloach manot* program to include everyone in the congregation who was not part of the school community.

Every part of the preparation and delivery of these baskets was touched by human hands, our children's hands. All the bakers, basket designers, and packers signed their names to cards and together hand-delivered each package to the particular recipient. The children were unabashed in their enthusiasm and were greeted unabashedly by surprised and till-then-unknown community members with cider and cookies and hugs and kisses and promises to keep in touch. The success of this program was evidenced by the number of members without children who attended the next school program kvelling with the children's parents and grandparents at the sight of *their* delivery boys and girls.

The Beginners' Service

This year we initiated a monthly, hour-long service ostensibly to reinforce prayer skills taught to youngsters in our Middle School. But because the service was billed simply as a service for beginners, several newer members of various ages and weak Jewish backgrounds began to attend. This is in stark contrast to our monthly Friday night family services, where it is difficult to find anyone over 40 unattached to a child under 12.

At first groups of similar ages kept to themselves, but soon the children realized that these adults knew no more Hebrew than they did and needed just as much guidance in following the service. The adults, in turn, saw that the children were but a step or two in front of or behind them. It took no more than a single service for walls to disappear between the generations in this nurturing environment where no questions are stupid and where all who attend are ageless students.

"How's your *sin* and *shin* coming along, Mrs. W?" one of our eight-year-olds shouted to a woman across the room at the kiddush table two weeks ago. "I hope as well as your *dalet* and *resh*," she responded to the boy unknown to her just a few months before. "Don't worry, you'll catch up," he reassured her.

The Maccabiyah

For years our congregation celebrated Chanukah with a covered dish dinner and dessert-to-share with a dozen. Fifteen minutes after the *motsi,* my wife and I would lead the children to the *bimah,* where we told stories, played hot potato and dispensed prizes for the longest-spinning draydl. Meanwhile the adults sat at their tables talking with their friends, glad to be relieved of their children and other people's children for half an hour before candle lighting and songs. The room was always divided according to who had children at home and who didn't. All, except the children and staff, were contentedly passive.

We were determined that things would be different this year. After a brief service we divided those in attendance into two teams, children and adults together. Except for a few specialists and three judges, no one was exempt from participating. Each team had three tasks to accomplish: (1) to dress Judah the Maccabee and his wife using live models from the respective teams, (2) for the children on each team to learn and perform a Yiddish Chanukah song and for the adults on each team to write and perform an original Chanukah song, and (3) to find or otherwise produce eight items on a list that included, among other things, a lock of Judah's hair, a new latke recipe, and since it was Chanukah, a miracle.

The response was enthusiastic. There was an immediate rush of activity in which blue-team adults and children and white-team adults and children became just blue-team members and white-team members, each doing what he/she was supposed to do or what he/she could do best. Only a 14-year-old could have imagined a computer virus folded into an aluminum foil sheath, which Judah could use to confound the military forces of Antiochus, anachronisms be damned! And it took a decorator to turn the lyric, "In the window, a Pella window, the candles burn so bright, in a kitchen, formica kitchen, the candles blue and white," to the tune of Pete Seeger's "Weemoway." Then the finale, the presentation of the treasure hunt loot. Candles, chocolate gelt, draydls, clipped six-year-olds holding large locks of "Judah's" hair, recipes for zucchini and cheddar latkes and some with chocolate chips, were presented by each team captain to the judges. And then the climax, the miracle. The captain of the blue team, last year's latke man, asks the white children to stand, and then the children of the blue team. He doesn't even have to say it. Hearts melt. Tears well and flow. The realization: My God, these really are all *our* children.

Most synagogue programs have, or ought to have, two goals. The immediate goal is for people to enjoy the program, to find it meaningful, helpful, worthwhile, somehow related to their lives and what they care about. But the program should also point to something beyond itself, to something more lasting. In trying to create sacred moments, we hope to advance Judaism into the future, to instill a deep sense of commitment to Jewish values in our members, so that when practiced well those values can be used to change the world for the good. Through these programs we hope to enable people to reach out of themselves, out of their families, to realize that all children are God's children, and that all adults are God's children, and must be cared for as such.

We can accomplish the immediate goal by "meeting the people where they are"—at least some of the people in some of the places some of the time. But to accomplish the long-term goal, synagogues will have to help people connect to the tradition as individuals, or we will lose them, and they us, whenever their lives fail to fit neatly into the standard definition of family. And for those integrated into the most stable and nurturing family systems, we need to help them to connect firmly and loyally to others in our communities, for even the most loving and secure of families cannot meet every need of every family member. Meeting the needs of people where they are might make us look successful, but we will only *be* successful if we look beyond ourselves and our families to join with generations past, present, and future in search for the divine by working for the repair of the world.

Section V

An Integrated Vision

12

Theology and Community

Arnold Eisen

Jews have never been big on futurology—perhaps because we have always, as believers in *mashiach,* taken the potential for future transformation so very seriously. We are much better as creative rememberers of the past and as perceptive critics of the present. That perceptiveness has repeatedly (though not always) helped us to survive and adapt, keeping us one step ahead of changes that might otherwise have overpowered us. Remembrance has no less helped us to survive, particularly in the modern period. It has done so by keeping us several steps behind—behind the urge to novelty that threatens to render our traditional commitments innocuous, behind the compulsion of reality, which silently challenges our view of things with the awesome force of "the facts." Our futurology, then, has been of a very limited sort. It has generally been more prescriptive than predictive, and has usually been constrained by our need to place one foot forward as far as it can safely reach, while at the same time keeping the other foot anchored firmly in our immensely usable past. I will play that sort of hopscotch here as well, jumping cautiously when I jump at all, and landing, I hope, at a place where we can all stand comfortably.

The past that I will try to make usable is of course textual, in this case two sections from a work we tend to underappreciate both because we know it so well and because it cloaks its own depth under a veil of cliché: Pirke Avot. I will be aided in jumping forward by a recent spate of efforts by American political theorists to imagine an ideal future other than the one given us by the best of 20th century liberalism, personified in this recent literature by John Rawls. Before I turn to these theorists and to Pirke Avot, however, I want to set forth several working assumptions that shape my approach to the relation between Jewish theology and Jewish community in the American future.

The first is that we are to a large extent not our own masters. That is meant to sound like a Zionist declaration, and to be one. We live in a culture not of our making, even if we continue to exert enormous influence upon it. No less important, we live in a political, economic, and social matrix far beyond our control, even if, again, our influence is out of proportion to our tiny (and shrinking) percentage of the population. Any attempt to imagine the Jewish future presumes the stability of certain taken-for-granted facts of life that we perhaps have no right to take for granted, and in any event can do little to affect.

Take for example the economic stability of this country. A serious depression would hit several Jewish economic niches with particular severity and would probably lead to a massive increase in anti-Semitism. Even barring such a depression, we face the massive and possibly unmanageable task of cleaning up our environment—the air we breathe, the water we drink, the land we farm—at a cost that will demand significant sacrifices in our standard of living, if we can marshal the political will to tackle the problem at all. I am not sanguine. Other problems too loom on the horizon. Thirty years from now I will find myself (God willing) among a cohort of baby-boomer retirees that may well overwhelm existing health and pension systems. In the interim, we will probably see further change in the balance of public versus private provision of basic services. Already our Jewish federations are reeling from governmental retrenchment in areas where 50 years ago Jews provided for their own, then ceased doing so when government moved in, and where private initiatives now seem required once more. Passage of tuition voucher legislation would, I expect, have a major impact on the economics of Jewish education, and not necessarily a positive one. Finally, there are increasing signs of social dislocation that threaten the continuity of the Jewish community as we know it. The fact that the divorce rate stands at 40 percent and is rising steadily, that already more than one in four youngsters is raised by a single parent, that teenage suicide now accounts for more deaths among that age group than all major diseases combined—these are facts of life over which we have only minimal control, and by which we are already greatly affected. Jews may find advantage in the growing seriousness of ethnic divisions in this country, or they may not; either way, we will have little influence over the course of that development.

Israelis, for all their lack of control over their destiny, have a measure of legislative power that American Jews lack, even if they too are threatened most by dangers to our atmosphere, our oceans, and our fossil fuel resources that only humankind as a whole can address. My assumption is that our planning can at best be tentative, even as we seek to affect to whatever extent possible the course of events outside our community that will so decisively affect us. The old Jewish adage, retaught by Mordecai Kaplan in our century, bears perpetual relearning. If we are to save the Jewish community, we will have to work on our country, and indeed on our world, as well. If we are only for ourselves, we are lost. There will be no problem in filling our growing hours of leisure time.

Second, there may well be a problem in finding Jews to join in such efforts. I refer here not only to our shrinking numbers, a function of low birthrate and assimilation, but to the question of whether current patterns of commitment will prove replicable in the decades to come. Proximity to the Holocaust and to the founding of the State of Israel has stimulated Jewish energies for more than

40 years. There are already signs that the influence of these forces is on the wane. Moreover, Jewish culture and community in our day rest on a financial base supplied largely by a generation of Jewish businessmen who may well be replaced by professionals less able to give as well as less willing. Donations to federations are already shrinking, once we adjust dollar amounts for inflation. Our ability to supply our own needs, then, like our ability to wield political influence, may well be at its peak right now, if not over it.

Third, the constraints within which we can imagine Jewish futures are cultural as much as economic or societal. The lesson which I carried back from graduate school immersion in social theory was that Jewish commitment, however defined, is threatened by a culture that suspects rather than reveres authority, that regards tradition as something nice to have around the house rather than as the very home in which we are all we are, and that uses the word "community" at every opportunity (as in "the business community") in part because it has little interest in any serious mutual obligation. Such a culture is not good for the Jews, because it is not good for Judaism—even though at the same time it promotes openness and opportunities so very good for the Jews, and for Judaism, that I would be loathe to trade life as a late-20th century American Jew for any in the human past I can name. It has therefore been comforting to me to find, of late, that voices in our culture other than the fundamentalists are disturbed by the sort of attitudes that threaten me. Many social and political theorists—such as Robert Bellah in *Habits of the Heart,* Alasdair MacIntyre in *After Virtue,* Michael Walzer in *Spheres of Justice*—have been attempting to alter America's notions of community and culture. Our theology can turn outward to such literature with profit, in a way it could not when social theory was dominated by radical individualism and pervasive atheism. And it must turn outward—to issues like the self, the environment, the definition of pluralism—because the alternative is mere irrelevance. The continuing encounter of the Jewish community and Jewish thought with feminism is evidence for the strength that accrues to our community and our tradition when we engage issues of great concern to contemporary Jews and find ourselves altered in the process.

My fourth assumption concerns the limits of Jewish theology as such in our time. I have come to a certain modesty here as well. The communities we build will be limited in scope by realities and ideas prevalent on the "outside" and internalized within. The theologies we construct will likewise offer more a language than a system, more a way of living and reflecting than a clearly defined regimen of practice or belief. We can know precious little of God in any time or place. In this time, without the authority of communal and personal experience enjoyed even by recent thinkers such as Heschel or Soloveitchik, bereft of the integral communities that nourished their creative remembrance, our hope for coherence is small.

I expect the principal sources of our thought to be twofold: the ancient rabbis' attempt, so like our own, to construct community and think about transcendence in a time of violated boundaries and cultural chaos; and the kabbalistic-Hasidic attempt to reach beyond reason for metaphors and analogies that will take us where we need desperately to go. Unlike either of these, however, we will be avowed pluralists: living fully in Jewish and non-Jewish worlds, admitting the legitimacy of more than one Jewish way, rejoicing in difference of gender and culture and experience. We have not the comfort of their walls, nor, for better or for worse, the limitations imposed by those walls. Like them, however, we will probably learn most from our Jewish ancestors, addressed collectively with questions that arise from conversation with our non-Jewish contemporaries.

That is meant to sound like the declaration of a *galut* (Diaspora) Jew, and to be one. My final presumption is that vital Jewish life *is* possible in this Diaspora, for the few if not for the many, if we can create living communities of Jews engaged in serious dialogue with their tradition, their God, their non-Jewish contemporaries, and each other. Vital Jewish life is possible despite the obstacles I have enumerated because, as Kaplan recognized, it offers Jews what they cannot easily find elsewhere: meaning and community. Energy can and will be summoned for those purposes. Commitments will be made and renewed. Israelis who invoke standard "negation of the Diaspora" arguments to deny the Jewish future in America have simply not recognized the uniqueness of this Diaspora, even if we tend to overidealize our prospects and deny what I have tried to emphasize above: namely, that we too are prey to the larger societal forces that have beset every modern Jewish community. The American Jewish community we imagine for ourselves should not measure itself by standards of public Jewish life achievable in the past but not in the present, nor by models achievable today only in a Jewish state. Nor can it rest, as it has so often in the past 40-odd years, on the prop of support for Israel. A new relation is called for, aptly captured in the slogan of the National Foundation for Jewish Culture: "independence and interdependence." Several more words about our relation to Israel, then, before turning to imagining the very different Jewish community in America.

It is clear, as little else is to me, that the "myth" of Israel, which has sustained American Jews for close to two generations, is no longer serviceable. The headlines we confront almost daily betray the sustaining images of David defeating Goliath, deserts made to bloom, and life-giving pioneers rising proudly from the ashes of the death camps. There is much to be proud of in Israel, of course, but no myth stands ready to replace those images, no leader to fill the shoes of Golda or Ben-Gurion—and it is not certain that the majority of American Jews will be able to relate to Israel without them. In the absence of myth, one has only reality, and American Jews are woefully ignorant of Israeli reality. Steven M. Cohen's data have shown that only a third of American Jews are aware that Menachem Begin and Shimon Peres belong to different political parties, or that the only conversions approved by Israel's official rabbinate are those performed by Orthodox rabbis. Even the American Jewish elite, far more knowledgeable about such matters, is largely illiterate in Hebrew and ignorant of contemporary Israeli culture, even in translation. The prospects for interdependence are bleak unless this abyss of ignorance can be overcome.

The political realities, furthermore, pose moral problems to American Jews for which we are unprepared. We need Israel to give us things it no longer can supply: evidence that we are a light unto the nations; evidence that given the change, Jews could apply Jewish tradition in a way that enhances human dignity and diminishes injustice; achievements that enable us to feel good about our tradition and ourselves, and a political path so correct in American eyes that it keeps away the specter of dual loyalties. We need these things from Israel, but that is not what the Jewish state is for. It cannot meet all those needs, and should not try. Israel exists to serve its own citizens. It rests, like every other state, on force. It faces mundane, uninspiring problems and fails, as all states do, to solve them. Even in the best of times, it commits terrible injustices. And these are not the best of times. It is not helpful to Israelis—who already rely upon us for money and for political clout with the government upon whom their survival depends—to receive unsolicited advice, particularly in public, which suggests that we could better handle their pressing problems.

I am not advocating silence on our part. We cannot be silent. It is not our style, first of all, and we are driven to speak by moral imperatives at the heart of what makes us Jews, and proud Jews. But we should recognize that we act, at least in part, from motives attached to *our* needs rather than Israel's. We should remember that we are not ultimately responsible for their destiny. We have sloughed off that responsibility by choosing to live here rather than there— thereby wounding Israelis, body and soul, in a way for which they cannot entirely forgive us. Were we in their shoes, moreover, I doubt that we would do better. In short, we as a community are in a bind that is both moral and tactical. How shall we speak responsibly when we lack ultimate responsibility for the consequences of our advice? And how shall we retain close ties to Israelis who grow more distant from us with each passing year, regardless of their politics, and are joined to us not only by a shared history but by the exchange of anger, guilt, envy, and resentment?

There are no easy answers to such questions, and this is not the place for them in any case. I counsel the obvious: a renewed commitment to Hebrew literacy, exchange programs that lead large numbers of Americans and Israelis to know each other and the two communities, trust on our part that they will not jettison commitments at the heart of Zionism and on their part that we will criticize them responsibly. The relevant point here is that we must learn to see ourselves as a unique Jewish community alongside others that are very different, that we cannot look to other communities, past or present, Israeli or Diaspora, for full-scale models of what Jewish life in this country might look like. Israel is one among several loci of our Jewish commitment, one among several sources of inspiration, even as it remains our paramount partner in confronting the 21st century's version of modernity. It is the path not taken, on which it behooves us to walk as much as is humanly possible from a near distance. Closer to hand, I believe, will be American-born models that I will now sample, and the continuing encounter with tradition, exemplified here by a partial reading of Pirke Avot.

Community

The primary lesson I draw from books such as Alasdair MacIntyre's *After Virtue* is that we should watch out for the notions of self and society presumed by the philosophy and social science that we read, the better to challenge those notions with our own. "Any contemporary attempt to envisage each human life as a whole, as a unity, whose character provides the virtues with an adequate telos must beware of modernity's atomization of our lives into role-sets, reflected in the refusal of much modern philosophy to address existential issues of the greatest moment."[1] In place of the "self detached," MacIntyre urges us to presume a self "embedded in the story of those communities from which I derive my identity. I am born with a past; and to try to cut myself off from that past, in the individualist mode, is to deform my present relationships."[2]

Michael Sandel makes a similar critique of liberal, "rights-based" political theory, dominated of late by the massive presence of John Rawls's *Theory of Justice*. He rejects the view of community as individuals venturing forth from the private sphere in pursuit of private interest to be achieved jointly with others doing the same. In Sandel's counter-conception, community would describe "a mode of self-understanding partly constitutive of the agent's identity." It is not a matter of mere "association" or "participation" or "cooperation," nor of what is "common" or "collective."[3] Community connotes

> allegiances [that] go beyond the obligations I voluntarily incur and the "natural duties" I owe to human beings as such. . . . To some I owe more than justice requires or even permits . . . in virtue of those more or less enduring attachments and commitments which taken together partly define the person I am.[4]

This is music to a Jew's ears; the fact that it emerges from a Jew's mouth may not be entirely coincidental. It is crucial, as we think about Jewish community, that we commit ourselves to community in the stricter rather than the looser sense. Here I shall invoke the stipulations of Robert Bellah and his co-authors in *Habits of the Heart*. "Whereas a community attempts to be an inclusive whole, celebrating the interdependence of public and private life and of the different callings of all," life-style enclaves (their term for communities more weakly conceived) are "fundamentally segmental and celebrate the narcissism of similarity." They "involve only a segment of each individual, for they concern only private life, especially leisure and consumption. And they are segmental socially, in that they include only those with a common lifestyle."[5]

We have good reason for not wanting to travel the road to communities of obligation too quickly. There is ample cause for Jewish suspicion of the conservative appeal to organic wholes. Such wholes have generally not wished to retain us as a distinct part. They have not, when they were wholes, tended to be tolerant of dissent or encouraging of diversity. Jews are overwhelmingly liberals for good reason in the modern period. But I think recent political theories such as those of Sandel and Walzer point down a road that Jews can walk with some confidence, precisely because as American Jews we can build what walls we build knowing those walls will not be impervious to the wider world outside them, that traffic at our gates will be heavy. With Walzer, we can envision "a pluralist society of diverse communities and cultures within the larger political community," that is to say, within a state that in turn rests "upon the cooperation and mutual involvement of all the groups."[6] With Sandel, we can seek to maintain the distance between someone else's headlong pursuit of ultimate perfection and our own, while remaining convinced that in maintaining this distance at all costs, liberalism "forgets the possibility that when politics goes well, we can know a good in common that we cannot know alone."[7] We need a true pluralism of significant difference, within and outside the Jewish community. That may or may not be possible in this country, but one thing is certain: pluralism from within is possible only insofar as it is possible without. The Israeli counter-example witnesses powerfully.

I do not present this lesson as a *chidush* (new insight). It is not news to us. The Jewish bet on America, the gamble that America really will be different, rests on the possibility that pluralism will be more than a shibboleth here. That is why Jews such as Horace Kallen and Kaplan, and now Walzer and Sandel, have been advocating it so relentlessly. What does seem new to me is the situation in which such calls arise. America may now be poised to experiment with true pluralism, a pluralism rendered necessary by the diversity of its population and made conceivable by its economic fecundity, in a way not possible 50 years ago. From where I sit, at a West Coast university, the minority presence is visible indeed. Diversity is the American future. We will have either real pluralism or cultural hegemony by the few; if the latter, it is doubtful we will have much serious Jewish community. The stakes for us could not be higher, and the moment just might be uniquely auspicious.

That is why I have surveyed recent political theory. American Jews have been wary of standing visibly apart, with good reason. Kaplan's proposals for *kehillot* fell largely on ears deafened to them by the cries of anti-Semites. Yet we need to build more communal structures, embracing more and more areas of life, if Judaism is to be rendered a serious aspect of the lives of most American Jews, if indeed it is to remain as serious as it is to as many. Steven Cohen and Charles Liebman, far apart in their estimates of "The Quality of American Jewish Life," agree that serious Judaism, however defined, is now restricted to a small elite of at best 20–25 percent of our population.[8] If we are to protect that elite and widen it, we will need to push back the constricting thrust of sec-ularization, reconquering more and more areas of life for Jewish expression and commitment.

How to do so is another matter. I have intentionally been vague—as are the political theorists I cited—about what the nature of these Jewish communities or structures might be. My caution stems from two sources. First, I have learned from Gershom Scholem that one cannot define in advance the boundaries of au-thentic Judaism. That does not mean that all is equally valid. There will be cre-ations both profound and trivial, inspiring and perverse. But what will come to count as authentic Judaism a century or two from now cannot at present be known, for it will be a function of what is tried, of what *we* try. This is no less true of the nature of Jewish community. Second, for reasons set forth earlier, there are no road maps to guide us, no ready-made precedents to apply. We will have to work such matters out by trial and error, as friendships and marriages are worked out in our day, building upon experience and moving from trust to trust. The near-total *hefker* (open-endedness, uncontrollability) of the present makes our responsibility to be creative, while remaining authentic Jews, all the greater. I offer only the barest of suggestions.

At a minimum, we can further reanimate our synagogues with *havurot* meant for life-cycle celebrations and Sabbath study, building outward from re-ligious commitments to political action, ecological concern, and so on. This al-ready happens in many shuls. At the next stage of the continuum, we can have adult and family camps, community-run schools that become foci of other com-munal activity, neighborhood cooperatives that begin with kosher or vegetarian food distribution and go on to wider spheres of social, political, and religious activity. Every effort that serves Jewish bodies is an opportunity to serve Jewish spirits as well. Day-care centers for working parents are an opportunity to build community, as are geriatric facilities. Professional loyalties that have alienated Jews from the Jewish community are a possible road back. We need Jewishly learned Jewish physicians to work on hospital policies regarding neonates and treatment of the terminally ill, and Jewishly learned Jewish scientists to work on national scientific policy objectives. We desperately need Jewish retreat centers for meditation and spiritual growth that are noncognitive in orientation. We need communal living arrangements of a variety of intensities.

Whatever we do, if it is to fall anywhere on the continuum of substantial Jewish community, must involve: (1) face-to-face interaction over a significant period of time; (2) joint activity arising out of central commitments; (3) ties of serious mutual obligation, and (4) a sustained dialogue with Jewish tradition. I will entrust the definition of "significant," "central," "serious," and "sus-tained" to those involved. I am fairly certain, however, that if we fail to widen and deepen the degree of Jewish community that we have at present, we may not be able to sustain the commitment of our elite, given the societal forces to which they, no less than the majority of American Jews, are subject. We need stronger

Jewish communities if we are to have Judaisms in America that will matter to significant numbers of Jews in coming decades.

Theology

There is another reason for my sense of urgency, and it takes us squarely into the realm of theology as I conceive it. God-talk is not the only or even the predominant mode of such theology, necessary as it is. I tend in any event to leave such talk to others who, thank God, can do it better than I. My own vision of theology is rather like Heschel's; the polarity of Halakhah and aggadah, or, in Jacob Neusner's elegant formulation, life lived and life reflected upon. I seem to have a profound existential need, of the sort which I think underlies Buber's *I and Thou,* for human community. I cannot imagine that life would be worth living in the absence of that community and the friendships it nourishes. Theology emerges only from the conservation it engenders. More than that, I feel commanded to work for such community, commanded by mitzvot so many in number and so pervasive that the tradition to my mind is defined by them. And so, I am doubly driven to worry about what the rabbis of old and the Hasidim worried about: first because what I need is imperiled by the lack of real community—I need Shabbat, for example, and cannot make it alone—and second because it seems imperative to me that the concept of mitzvah be widened in our day so that is comes to include the many areas of decision making that determine the character of our lives. That too cannot be done without communities. Our aggadah and our Halakhah are mutually dependent.

Pirke Avot, inasmuch as it makes a coherent statement about the ideal world, seems to me at one with the halakhic definition of that world provided in the Mishnah as a whole.[9]

The object is stability, structure, harmony; this means an all-encompassing ordering, a present tense that restores priests to their sanctuary and Israel to its holiness. I turn to this text, in a very different time, with very different objectives. I use the tradition not as a recipe but as a language. It gives me a set of snapshots—here a Mishnaic ideal, there a Hasidic reality—out of which I, a Jew like Ishmael and Nachman, attempt to draw a picture of what a response to the demands of Torah might look like in my time and place. Look with me then for a moment at the ideal world pictured by our sages in Pirke Avot, chapters four and six. Their model, not surprisingly, is a community of learning. The leitmotif of that model, the word which recurs repeatedly and more than any other defines the human relations that it structures, is *kavod.*

In 4:1 Ben Zoma tells us that the wise person is one who learns from everyone; the mighty, one who subdues his own *yetzer* (inclination),[10] the rich, one who is happy with what he has, and the honored or respected person (*mekhubad*), the one who honors or respects fellow creatures, as it is said: "For them that honor me I will honor, and they that despise me shall be lightly esteemed"

(I Sam. 2:30). All we will learn from the entire chapter is here in the opening epigram. Note first that wisdom comes from people and not from books; second, that the proof text for happiness in one's portion promises happiness in both this world and the next; third, that the reciprocity of human respect is learned from God's respecting (or making weighty) those who respect God and making light of those who do not. We might diagram the foundations of this community as a flow of *kavod* downward from God to us, horizontally back and forth among human beings, and upward again to God. What we do in this time is grounded in eternity; what we do in this place extends to infinity. Within the coordinates so defined, *kavod* is ours to give and to receive, happiness available to all who will accept it.

Mishnah two, in a similar mood, urges no distinction between light and heavy duties or transgressions, and teaches that the reward of mitzvah is mitzvah. The system is again in dynamic stasis. Mishnah three warns us to despise no one and deem nothing impossible, for each man has his hour and each thing its place. Mishnah four urges us to be "very very humble of spirit," considering our imminent death, and warns against profaning God's name in secret. Mishnah five advises us to learn in order to teach and in order to do, and warns us against using our learning for private gain. Finally, mishnah six,—we need go no further in the chapter because it is all of a piece—stipulates that the person who honors the Torah is himself honored by humanity, and vice versa.

Honor is of two sorts. There is the honor that depends upon status, and is inherently scarce. It puffs up ego, precludes humility, seeks a name for self rather than the name of God. Exodus 14–15 plays on usages of the root k-b-d in this sense. Pharaoh's heart is not only hardened but made heavy, swollen with self-importance; God, by making the chariots sink heavily in the mud, will be honored, raised in stature in the eyes of those who witness this event. Eyes are crucial to this kind of *kavod*. It has to be seen to exist; it exists in the seeing of it. It is external, the result of rank or achievement.

There is, however, an inner weightiness, a character so deeply engraved that it is not easily washed away, a rootedness of self secure against prevailing winds. No human being is totally immune to the loss of this honor, and the total institutions studied by Erving Goffman can strip us of it quite effectively. We need each other's confirmations of self. But the core is within, a function of who we are and what we stand for; our text would say: of before Whom we stand. When mishnah 12 urges us to honor our students as we would ourselves, our friends as we would our teachers, and our teachers as we would Heaven, it is this sort of honor it has in mind. Notice that the adage rests on a clear understanding of hierarchy, which it urges us to raise by one degree. The teaching can have only three parts: raising our inferiors to equals, our equals to betters, and our betters to God. That is the total system. The basis of the hierarchy is our mastery of God's Torah—the source of our true *kavod*.

Chapter six, added to the tractate at a later period, expands upon this lesson precisely. "The sages taught in the language of the Mishnah: Blessed be He [or:

he] who chose [chooses] them and their teaching.'' Once again the first mishnah, indeed the first words, encapsulate the chapter. ''Anyone who engages in
Torah for its own sake merits many things, and, still more, is deserving of the
whole world. He is called friend, beloved [*re'a ahuv*], lover of God, lover of
humanity, rejoicer of God, rejoicer of humanity; and it [Torah] clothes him with
humility and reverence, and fits him to be *tzadik, chasid,* upright and faithful . . . It magnifies and exalts him above all things.''

Note R. Meir's extravagant language, its emphasis upon the eros of those
who fill their days with Torah. This is a passionate statement of the reward
stored up for lovers of Torah, a reward conceived in overflowing terms of love
and joy. The theme continues in mishnah three, a still more direct retelling of the
teachings of chapter four. ''He who learns one chapter from his friend, one halakhah, one *pasuk* [verse], one expression, even one letter, must treat him with
kavod.'' A proof text is brought from the story of David and Achitofel, and again
the lesson is offered, from chapter to *pasuk* to letter, until it reaches this remarkable conclusion. ''There is no *kavod* but Torah, as it is said 'The wise shall inherit *kavod*' [Prov. 3:35], and 'The perfect (*temimim*) shall inherit good' [Prov.
28:10], and there is no good but Torah, as it is said 'I give you good teaching,
forsake not my Torah.' (Prov. 4:2)'' We have all learned something from everyone we know, and therefore owe them *kavod,* meaning that we owe them Torah.

What might that mean? In a community of scholars, the core meaning
would seem to be that I owe my fellows, those who share in my love of the
Torah, whatever insights into Torah I have gained in their company. To rabbis
bent (as we are) on the *chidush,* on impressing the teacher, on leaving our names
on disciplinary chains that stretch way back, this recognition of shared author-
ship is no small matter. But there is more. We owe each other Torah: the fullest
realization of the life of mitzvah of which we are capable, because it *is* life, it is
the source of our *kavod,* and only if we give it to each other do we have it from
God. This is no religion concerned with human solitariness, as Alfred North
Whitehead would have it. It is rather the credo of human beings drunk on the
love of their lives together. Such people can (mishnah four) be ''happy and well
off'' with bread and water, will value Torah more than priesthood and kingship
(mishnah five), will not covet *kavod* (in its inferior sense), and will certainly try
to have their deeds reach beyond their learning. Mishnah six teaches that Torah
is acquired in 48 ways, among them love, loving God, loving humanity; loving
rightness, reproof, the straight and narrow. Note that love had previously been
a reward for immersion in Torah. Now it is a prerequisite. The circle is endless.
Hence the urgent need (mishnah nine) to live in a place of Torah, so that one can
retrace the circle's path, and so complete it by returning *kavod* to God. The
chapter and the tractate as a whole end as follows: ''All that the Holy One
Blessed be He created in His world He created only to give Him *kavod.*'' God
gets it from us, as we get it from each other.

I get a lot of pleasure from this particular text, and a measure of insight, for
three reasons.

First, it is true to my experience. All I value most is tied up in Torah. I have been fortunate enough to live in a time when models of Torah study and Torah living have been developed which enable me to respond authentically to a text such as Pirke Avot. Anthropology, psychology, and history, which served to distance previous generations from texts such as this one, have brought our generation closer. I can vividly recall intense moments of study and insight in *chevrutah*. I could not think of living in a place without Torah. And thus it saddens me to think that many American Jews live precisely in such places, even if Torah is now as close to them as their local bookstore and the sukkah around the corner. Missionary zeal offends me, do-gooders out to increase their own self-esteem by saving souls are anathema to me, and yet for all that I think we now have a Jewish reality in this country of which the majority of American Jews are ignorant. They do not see it in their synagogues, in those rare moments when they happen to be in one, and they certainly do not see it on television or in the movies. Where then will they experience it? We owe them something. All the doubts concerning America that I raised in part one of this paper convince me that most American Jews will not wish to depart significantly from the cultural or societal mainstream. But we owe them a compelling presentation such as they still have not had of the product line—the contemporary American Judaisms—that had been developed over the past four decades.

The second thing that inspires me in this text is the open-endedness of its definition of Torah, the democracy proclaimed within its elitism, the total dedication to widening the bounds of Torah until they surpass the violated borders of Eretz Israel and extend throughout the entire exiled world. I do not find rigidity here, but rather energy. I find pluralism rather than imperialism. There will be structures—Judaism remains a commitment to the details—but the details themselves seem to evolve, the process seems unlimited within the framework established by the original revelation. This is what Heschel had in mind, I believe, when he urged us to accept the principle of *Torah min hashamayim* (Torah being divinely revealed) as definitional of Jewish faith, while being aware that Ishmael and Akiba, like Jews ever since, radically disagreed as to the precise meaning of *Torah min hashamayim*. Jews are dedicated to building just Jewish communities with God in their midst—lots of them, as history attests, with many and varied blueprints.

Finally—the hard part, and yet the part that matters most—Torah is *min hashamayim*. It is God's. Our dignity ultimately rests on the Source of all Being. Our Torah, even if we do not believe it to be God's actual word, is a way that conforms to how God would wish us to walk. The system I diagrammed earlier has its beginning in God, and its end. "Great is Torah, for it gives life in this world and the next" (6.7).

This is not hyperbole, even if, once more, it is not a specific account of things that remain, for Jews, beyond all human knowing. Even without the Holocaust, we would have known that the "death problem" is everywhere in our century, our world. We have Weber's ruminations based on Tolstoy's and Nietzsche's; we have Ernest Becker and Saul Bellow and Woody Allen; we have our own nightmares and repressions. Witnesses abound. There is no need for us to say more than Pirke Avot said in this regard, but we should affirm what needs affirming—that, as Psalm 73 avers, "You shall guide me with your counsel, and afterwards receive me to *kavod*." There is a pastoral dimension to Jewish faith that we have not performed as well as we need to because we have felt unable to promise all we hope for while retaining authenticity in our culture. This too is a task we need to work on, within the communities we must build—the only place where it can usefully occur.

This brings me, finally, to God. Most of the time, I find myself unable to believe what I would like to believe about God, but equally unwilling to settle for what others would have me believe. My pluralism extends to this domain too, of course. What works for you may not work for me, and vice versa. Heschel "speaks to me" about God. Kaplan does not. I wish to speak briefly about what I need, in the context of Pirke Avot, in the hope that it will fulfill Pirke Avot's requirement that I reciprocate the Torah that I have received.

I need a correspondence between the words that I say, the actions that I perform, and the Lord "Who spoke, and the world came into being." The correspondence need not be, cannot be, one to one. I do not need to know that God spoke the words of the Torah to Moses, but only that the words that grew up around those which Moses heard articulate a way in which God would have me walk. I do not need to know that God hears the words of prayer as you hear me, but I am dissatisfied with process theologies that suddenly turn personalist, in order that prayer may continue.

Leonard Fein, for example, moves me immensely in his book, *Where Are We?* but I cannot rest content with his notion that a leap of love is required rather than a leap of faith. "To make a leap of love means to love God, whether or not He (or She, or It) exists. It is in loving God rather than in only talking God, that we move from metaphor to meaning.["11](#) No. Too fast. Nor am I entirely satisfied with Arthur Green's far more sophisticated notion that in speaking to God in prayer I perform "an act of personification, lending a human face to that which has none without us."[12] It is not that I presume to get beyond metaphor. I cannot. But I must leap, *do* leap in moments of faith, to a correspondence between my metaphors and a reality that authorizes them even if it is not the author of them. That may not be all one can hope for, but it is a faith to which I would gladly say *dayyenu*. I hope that in the next decades I, we, will be able to reflect on God in ways in which modern Jewish thought as a whole has rarely done until now. The moment once again seems precious; the place, again, seems the intimate space of community rather than the pulpit or the classroom.

The agenda, then, is community of a new and stronger sort, learning that reaches more Jews with more messages, and reflection on several matters to which we have thus far given much too little attention. Concretely, we will have to work very hard simply to retain the allegiance of the quarter of our American Jewish population now bound in vital connection to their people and its traditions. Reasonably, we cannot hope to add more than another 10 percent to that number—fully half a million souls! I expect that in 25 years, with any luck, we will be pretty much where we are today: wrestling with the Holocaust, perplexed about Israel, concerned about assimilation and anti-Semitism, incorporating women into our midst and the insights of feminism into our theologies, rebuilding our communities, teaching our Torah. That may not be as ecstatic a vision as Rabbi Meir's. But it is far better than we had any reason to hope for only 25 short years ago.

A Response

Jacob J. Staub

Talking about "community" these days is something of a perilous enterprise. It is an overused term, the meaning of which seems to vary according to the hopes and dreams of the writer. "Community" is what so many of us seek from the Jewish civilization to which we are committed, but our hopes will not be fulfilled unless we first define the realistic possibilities more clearly, so that we can act to realize those possibilities.

I am thus delighted at the opportunity to respond to Arnold Eisen's essay. Over the last several years, I have found Eisen's work to be very helpful in explicating our problems with community formation. Those of us who have abandoned as unrealistic Mordecai Kaplan's proposals for an organic community and an international covenant among all Jews nevertheless face a concern as pressing now as it was 50 years ago. If Judaism is a civilization, how can we hope to sustain it when even the most committed North American Jews are so tangentially involved in Jewish communities, so preoccupied with competing concerns of life, so protective of their personal autonomy? We have already read much in this volume about the privatization of Jews' identification. Eisen's approach can help us to think through appropriate responses. This essay is therefore largely an endorsement and elaboration of his points.

I will touch briefly on four points: first, the breakdown of Jewish communities caused by political emancipation, and new possibilities for generating real communities in an age of voluntarism and autonomy; second, the effects of individual autonomy on the way we define and ought to define Jewish identity; third, needed responses to the growing chasm between factions of our people; and last, a few thoughts for developing a theology that reflects our basic communal aspirations.

The Challenge of Voluntarism

We have lived for over a century under conditions in which individual Jews can determine the nature and extent of their involvement in Jewish life. Among all the dislocations that we have faced in the modern era, this political revolution arguably has been the most disruptive to the fabric of Jewish life. Whereas prior to our political emancipation our ancestors lived in Jewish communities whose laws were the Law, whose culture and social services and educational systems were part of the air that Jews breathed, we now face a situation in which a Jew can determine whether and how to identify Jewishly.

That much is obvious. As we reflect on the issue of community, however, it becomes clear that for all our creative innovations, we have not yet dealt successfully with the implications of our community's breakdown. Heaven knows, we have tried. We have partially followed Kaplan's proposal and formed Jewish community centers, where Jews can spend their leisure time with other Jews. We have promoted identification with Israel as a way of inducing vicarious national pride. We have chosen to emphasize the dangers of anti-Semitism in ways that keep us together through mistrust of Gentiles. Some of us have asserted that Halakhah remains binding, ignoring the fact that we have lost the communal mechanisms to enforce it and the organic cultural context that once locked our forebears into our traditions. Some of us have applauded the individual autonomy that has freed us from halakhic coercion. We have welcomed a situation in which Jews decide on their own how seriously to integrate Jewish traditions and commitments into their lives.

Yet as Arnold Eisen has stated so clearly, none of us—except those Orthodox who choose to live separately—has yet managed to scale the hurdles of voluntarism. Problems arise when Judaism, even for the most committed of non-Orthodox Jews, amounts to a series of autonomous choices about integrating Torah into our lives. What are those problems? In our so-called communities, we lack the moral power, and often even the inclination, to stand firmly for the value of ritual practice, for the value of ethical living in the home, in the community, and in our professional lives, for the value of acting as Jews in the sphere of social and political action. And lacking the moral power to stand for those values, we are reduced to numbering ourselves through lowest common denominators. We count Jews through dues payments, through federation campaign contributions, through bar and bat mitzvah ceremonies, through the spouses we choose, through the votes we cast in presidential elections. We are reduced to sales techniques, to outreach that accepts Jews as they are, and that rejoices in the slightest indication of their interest. We are reduced to groping for new ways in which Jewish commitment can make a substantial difference in a person's life, can address the angst and isolation that come from the absence of community. We are encouraged, with good reason, by the fact that Jews, like all others, feel the lack of community, but we have not yet found the way to create Jewish groups that fill that void.

Our nostalgic yearnings notwithstanding, the traditional world of the Jewish community is long gone. There will be no speedy return to the world in which Jews lived effortlessly with other Jews, finding meaning in Jewish teachings and practices and thus developing creative Jewish responses to the neverending series of challenges they faced. We may indulge in the hope that in the decades ahead, many non-Orthodox Jews will see the light and will feel "commanded'' in some sense by Jewish imperatives of one sort or another. That hope is doomed to be frustrated, however, unless we can do much better in developing communities that address the subversive impact of the reality of individual autonomy upon our ability to have Judaism function centrally in the warp and woof of Jews' lives.

Recognizing this challenge, both the Reconstructionist and the *havurah* movements have sought to create *havurot* and participatory communities that provide a feeling of connectedness and give their members a decision-making authority that motivates study and increased practice. Some communities have gone even farther by creating support system networks that enable members to give and receive some of the support and nurture that Jews once expected from their communities.[13]

These efforts have succeeded in attracting countless numbers of Jews who are interested in maximizing their attachment to community, but the communities have not yet succeeded in hurdling the inviolable autonomy of their members, who remain only as long as the compromises required of them do not overstep their personal principles or life-style choices. The congregations and *havurot* are effective as service organizations, and there is reason to hope that, as long as they continue to serve, their members will remain involved with them. But, by and large, they have not succeeded in producing many Jews who admit that the collective voice of their co-members represents an imperative—a formulation of the divine will, so to speak—that ought to shape their personal, everyday decisions. Matters of professional or sexual ethics, of *menshlichkeit* or personal religious observance, are generally beyond the scope of such voluntary ''communities,'' and that limitation undermines the viability of the Jewish standards that emerge from such groups.

Thus when I attempt to imagine the future of Jewish communities, I grope for a new way to synthesize the absolute reality of our personal freedom with the need, both of individuals and of the Jewish people, to connect to a transcendent reality to which we can voluntarily give the authority to inform and enrich our lives. I imagine communities, voluntarily formed, whose members agree to be bound by the decisions of the collective in all areas of life—not because they accept literally that traditional versions of Halakhah are divinely commanded and therefore binding, but because they believe that the commandments of Torah can emerge in their full sanctity and power only when individuals cede some of their autonomy to a group of Jews who are seriously grappling with the imperatives of our traditions and the imperatives of contemporary life. I imagine Jews joining such collectives not only because they satisfy personal needs that are otherwise unmet, but also because they come to see that sparks of meaning and transcendence are most easily generated among people who have truly and completely cast in their lot with each other.

Even as I imagine joining such a collective, I grow palpably claustrophobic at the prospect of losing my privacy and liberty. Yet I continue to imagine it, because the alternative—paying my dues to various associations with which I feel lukewarm involvement—is clearly neither the path to true human interconnection nor to the flourishing of the Jewish people as a whole.

Clearly, most Jews will not choose to join such communities for the foreseeable future. Participatory *havurot* and support system networks will continue to enrich the lives of some of us, and those forms ought to be promoted. Others of us will be much more peripherally involved, and we would do well to include those on the periphery as far as they are willing. But were even a minuscule percentage of Jews voluntarily to join real communities, those "pockets of Jewish energy" might generate a vital and viable set of Jewish paths to sustain us through the next century. Their shared study of Torah, for example, would generate midrashim reflecting the gritty problems of people striving to resolve real contemporary conflicts. Their ethical standards, their *tefillot,* their ceremonies would bear the sacred authority of having functioned to bring Jews together, perhaps leading the way to a renewal of Judaism that is otherwise but a faint hope.

Defining Jewish Identity

As we imagine the formulation of discrete communities, however, we would also do well to contemplate the definition of Jewish commitment. It appears that the traditional criteria for Jewish identity—by birth or through *giyur* (conversion)—require some reexamination. People with Jewish parents can no longer be assumed to identify as Jews, and people without Jewish parents who have not undergone conversion can no longer be assumed not to identify as Jews.

The confusion has been well focused in the course of the debate about patrilineal descent. The Federation of Reconstructionist Congregations and Havurot in 1968 established a double standard for Jewish identity—birth alone for those with Jewish mothers, but birth plus affirmation of identity for those with Jewish fathers. The Reconstructionist Rabbinical Association (RRA) righted that inequity in 1979 by accepting birth alone to either a Jewish mother or a Jewish father. Then in 1983 the Central Conference of American Rabbis (CCAR) established a different equitable standard—requiring public and formal acts of identification for both matrilineally and partilineally descended Jews.

This is not the place for a discussion of the many issues raised by patrilineal descent. The struggle exhibited by these contradictions, however, points to a substantial problem that faces us all: we have lost a clear sense of communal demarcation between those who are in and those who are out.

Requiring timely public and formal acts of identification of people with Jewish parents, as the CCAR did, may raise unacceptably the threshold of who qualifies for a minyan. The truth, however, may be that birth is no longer sufficient. In the more traditional communal settings of previous centuries, Jewish parentage implied a level of commitment and involvement that is no longer applicable. It may thus be productive to think about a universal ritual that would affirm Jewish identity at birth.

Initiating new rituals is always a perilous enterprise, and it is often more prudent to transform an ancient one that is resonant with sacred associations. With that in mind, I think of *tevilah,* ritual immersion, as a promising possibility that was suggested to me by David Seidenberg. Though we may think of *tevilah* these days primarily in terms of conversion, its ancient associations are much richer than that—as symbolic rebirth out of the waters of the spiritual womb, as reenactment of the crossing of the Red Sea, as a periodic aid of renewing purification. In North America we would have to overcome the associations of baptism, but that can be done, as my family discovered when, following the example of Michael and Sharon Strassfeld, we chose a *brit mikveh* ceremony as a convenantal affirmation for our daughter. Clearly, we do not want to become a faith community only, but we need to reclaim the lost power of ritual to help define community limits.

But why is this so? Why not welcome, within reasonable bounds, anyone who wants to join us, on the basis of their intentions alone? Because accepting outreach too readily fails to establish the demands required of community members. Real communities have ritual by which they affirm their mythic and symbolic approaches to reality, and our current hesitation at using them may reflect our inability to take Judaism seriously as more than an attractive leisure-time activity.

The Challenge of Diversity

The current alarm over the imminent schism in the Jewish world may be exaggerated. One need not, however, doubt that there will be one Jewish people in the year 2000 to acknowledge that the Jewish people now consists of many discrete components whose resemblance and allegiance to one another is weakening. The so-called Jewish community might be better designated in the plural—as a coalition of Jewish communities.

Here, as much as anywhere, I rely on Kaplan, whose message of unity in diversity is as current as ever. It would be a terrible and tragic mistake for our various factions and streams to abandon our dearly held commitments and principles in an effort at conflict avoidance. The vitality of our future depends on the flowering of multiple, distinct approaches to Jewish living, and many of those will be absolutely incompatible with one another. Nevertheless, our collective fate may depend on serious efforts to reduce gratuitous acrimony. We will do best if we represent (or reflect) streams with strong convictions and commitments so that we can and will negotiate from strength.

For that possibility to emerge, we need to reshape our emphasis on Jewish peoplehood, currently defined by our broadest common denominator, to include a proud affirmation of our differences. A Jewish coalition that stresses unity alone will find itself threatened at every turn by serious, energetic, innovative Jews at the forefront of adapting to our unprecedented challenges. We need instead to promote allegiance to a unity of diverse streams whose loyalty to one another is not dependent on jointly held principles and who are willing to work cooperatively despite their differences.[14]

Adjusting Our Theology

Insofar as we believe that theology is an essential foundation of any communal enterprise, work is required to adjust our discourse about God to reflect the realities for which we strive. Our understanding of monotheism too often works against the divine ends of our sacred enterprise.

We are not one, and if admitting this causes us to feel as if we are betraying the unity of God, then we must redouble our efforts to remind ourselves that the one God is and has always been beyond the multiplicity of divine images and epithets, beyond the ever-changing diversity of the Jewish people, beyond our necessarily imperfect attempts to embody that which is beyond embodiment. To be monotheistic is not to be monolithic, and our quest to establish a oneness in creation may be among the more dangerous forms of our idolatry.

Moreover, the unity of God often presents us with an image of a transcendent, immutable, monarchical deity that retains the nominal allegiance of too many Jews, but that subverts, at every turn, many of our most earnest efforts at community formation. That image stands in opposition to the contemporary affirmation that growth and change are the staples of the physical, social, and psychological worlds; it undercuts efforts at sanctifying participatory decision making; and it implicitly calls into question the ultimate value and godliness of human innovation.

It will be no small feat to alter the framework of our theological discourse so that we can take ourselves seriously as communities that indeed do the work and reflect the image of God. We ought to question the notion that the divine must by definition be timeless, eternal, and unchanging, working to replace it with the teaching that God, as manifest in creation, is forever in process, forever unfolding in new ways. It will require the imaging of God's power as shared, of God's wisdom as ultimately cognizant of the goodness of diversity, of God's compassion as yearning for those who struggle through doubts, as much as or even more than for those whose beliefs are certain. It will require that such images of God be sustained and infused by living communities in their worship and in the mutual commitments of their members. For it is not true that new interpretations of old beliefs can never achieve authenticity as long as they are known to be the inventions of human beings; their power rather correlates with the degree to which they are lived by the communities that affirm them.

This version of our communal future is a long way from implementation. The creation of radiant centers of Jewish creativity and commitment, of comfort with diversity, of a Jewish people powerful enough to transform its members—

these are goals worthy of our best efforts. Their implementation will require sustained efforts that may prove to be beyond us, but we cannot allow ourselves to be limited by our current situation in our efforts to imagine a future that is worth pursuing.

Notes

Section I (*Pages 12–58*)

1. Catherine Keller, "Goddess, Ear, and Metaphor: On the Journey of Nelle Morton," *Journal of Feminist Studies in Religion*, Fall 1988, pp. 66–67.

2. Richard R. Niebuhr, *Experiential Religion* (New York: Harper & Row, 1972), p. 103.

3. Charles Silberman, *A Certain People: American Jews and Their Lives Today*, (New York: Summit Books, 1985).

4. On this aspect of American Jewish communal life see Jonathan Woocher, "The Civil Judaism of Communal Leaders," *American Jewish Year Book, 1981*, (Philadelphia: Jewish Publication Society), pp. 149–169. The seminal essay on American civil religion was written by Robert Bellah, "Civil Religion in America," *Daedalus*, Winter, 1967, pp. 1–21.

5. Deborah E. Lipstadt, "From Noblesse Oblige to Personal Redemption: The Changing Profile and Agenda of American Jewish Leaders," *Modern Judaism* October, 1984.

6. Steven M. Cohen, *American Modernity and Jewish Identity*, (New York and London: Tavistock, 1983).

7. Calvin Goldscheider and Alan Zuckerman, *The Transformation of the Jews*, (Chicago: University of Chicago Press, 1984), p. 9.

8. Steven M. Cohen, *American Assimilation or Jewish Revival* (Bloomington: Indiana University Press, 1988), p. 8.

9. Calvin Goldscheider, *Jewish Continuity and Change: Emerging Patterns in America* (Bloomington: Indiana University Press, 1986).

10. Donald Feldstein, *The American Jewish Community in the 21st Century: A Projection* (New York: American Jewish Congress, 1984), p. 34.

11. Calvin Goldscheider, *The American Jewish Community: Social Science Research and Policy Implications* (Atlanta: Scholars Press, 1986), pp. 9–10.

12. Steven M. Cohen and Leonard J. Fein, "From Integration to Survival: American Jewish Anxieties in Transition," *Annals*, July 1985, pp. 75–88. Charles Liebman, "American Jewry: Identity and Affiliation," *The Future of the Jewish Community in America*, David Sidorsky, ed. (Philadelphia: Jewish Publication Society, 1973), p. 130.

13. There is an inherent danger in defining the objectives of Jewish studies programs as a means to heighten Jewish identity on campus. While the programs serve that purpose for many students, the faculty is quite vigilant about maintaining academic integrity and differentiating between what occurs in the classroom and in a Hillel. This has prevented Jewish studies programs from going the way of the many ethnic studies programs that proliferated in the early 1970s.

14. Calvin Goldscheider, *Jewish Continuity.*

15. Stephen Isaacs, *Jews and American Politics* (New York: Doubleday, 1974).

16. Herbert Alexander, *Pro-Israel PACs: A Small Part of a Large Movement,* paper presented at International Conference on the Domestic Determinants of U.S. Policy in the Middle East, sponsored by the Jaffee Center for Strategic Studies of Tel Aviv University.

17. Simon Rawidowicz, "Israel: The Ever-Dying People," *Studies in Jewish Thought,* Nahum Glatzer, ed. (Philadelphia: Jewish Publication Society, 1974), pp. 210ff. It is noteworthy that on a popular level many of those who parted company with Silberman were most vexed by his contention that anti-Semitism was no longer a significant problem for American Jews. The inclination of American Jews to posit the existence of a higher degree of anti-Semitism in the American public than polls show exists is a fascinating phenomenon. Why does the most secure Jewish community in history tend to feel that its security is at best tenuous? Is it a response conditioned by a particular sensitivity to history, that is, the knowledge that the German Jewish community of the late 1920s also felt quite secure and impervious to attack? Or is it reflective of a deeper insecurity, a feeling of being not quite "at home"? Is it possible that the broader Jewish public is sensitive to sentiments that scholars who study the Jewish community are not? Are those on the firing line aware of something to which the residents of the ivory tower of the academy are oblivious?

18. There are many problems with the use of the term "assimilation." Daniel Bell has summed them up most succinctly by asking, "What is there [for American Jews] to assimilate to?" See Daniel Bell, "Where Are We?," *Moment,* May 1986, pp. 15–22. On this issue see also Nathan Glazer, "New Perspective in American Jewish Sociology," *The American Jewish Year Book, 1987* (Philadelphia: Jewish Publication Society), p. 17.

19. See *New York Review of Books,* November 21, 1985, pp. 18–22; *New Leader,* October 7, 1985, pp. 16–19; *Commentary,* November 1985, pp. 108–114.

20. Steven M. Cohen, "The Quality of American Jewish Life-Reasons for Optimism," *Jewish Sociology Papers* (New York: American Jewish Committee, 1987).

21. Arthur Hertzberg, "The Triumph of the Jews," *New York Review of Books,* November 21, 1985, p. 22.

22. Charles Liebman, "Reconstructionism in American Jewish Life," *American Jewish Year Book, 1970* (Philadelphia: Jewish Publication Society), p. 23.

23. Steven M. Cohen, *American Assimilation or Jewish Revival* (Bloomington: Indiana University Press, 1988), p. 14.

24. Leonard Fein, *Where Are We? The Inner Life of American Jews* (New York: Harper and Row, 1988), p. 171.

25. Liebman, "Reconstructionism," p. 23.

26. Hertzberg, p. 21.

27. Donald Feldstein, p. 34.

28. Jack Wertheimer, "Jewish Ethnicity: Searching for the New Limits," *Melton Journal,* Winter 1984, p. 19.

29. John Higham, *Ethnic Leadership in America* (Baltimore: Johns Hopkins University Press, 1978), p. 2.

30. Ira Silverman, *Sh'ma,* November 13, 1987, p. 1.

31. Samuel Heilman, "Jews in the Land of Promise," October 7, 1985, p. 18.

Section II (*Pages 59–116*)

1. Isa Aron, "Instruction and Enculturation of Jewish Education," unpublished manuscript, pp. 3–4.

2. Sheldon A. Dorph, "A New Direction for Jewish Education in America," in *Studies in Jewish Education and Judaica in Honor of Louis Newman*, Alexander M. Shapiro and Burton I. Cohen, eds. (New York: Ktav Publishing House, 1984), p. 108.

3. Barry Chazan, "The State of Jewish Education" (New York: JESNA, 1988), p. 8.

4. Susan Rosenblum Shevitz, "Communal Responses to the Teacher Shortage in the North American Supplementary School," in *Studies in Jewish Education*, Volume III, Janet Aviad, ed. (Jerusalem: The Magnes Press, Hebrew University, 1988), pp. 25–61.

5. Ronald Reynolds, "Goals and Effectiveness in Jewish Education: An Organizational Perspective," in *Studies in Jewish Education*, Volume III, Janet Aviad, ed. (Jerusalem: The Magnes Press, Hebrew University, 1988), pp. 91–115.

6. For more exact figures see Sylvia Barack Fishman, *Learning about learning: Insights on Contemporary Jewish Education from Jewish Population Studies*, Cohen Center for Modern Jewish Studies, Brandeis University, 1987.

7. Margaret Mead, *Culture and Commitment* (New York: Columbia University Press, 1978).

8. One excellent source on family therapy is Salvador Minuchin, *Families and Family Therapy* (Cambridge: Harvard University Press, 1974).

9. For the life cycle of the Jewish family, see Edwin H. Friedman, "Systems and Ceremonies: A Family View of Rites of Passage," *The Family Life Cycle*, E.A. Carter and M. McGoldrick (eds.) (New York: Gardner Press, 1980).

10. As I was asked to address this subject personally, from the perspective of a practicing artist, I focus on poetry, which is the art form I practice and know best. I suspect that at least some of what I have to say may be applied to the other arts as well.

11. Jewish-American singer/songwriters like Bob Dylan or Paul Simon might well imagine this, having themselves become legends in their own time. But performing artists (and especially pop performing artists) are in a different category from other artists in our culture. And although poetry was certainly once a performing art, today it exists for the most part on the printed page. Even those contemporary American poets who put on a great show—like Allen Ginsberg or Maya Angelou, to name two random examples—do not attain the kind of popular recognition garnered by performers of less talent.

12. From "I Am . . . " by Mani Leyb, translated by John Hollander, in Howe, Wisse, and Shmeruk, eds., *The Penguin Book of Modern Yiddish Verse* (New York, 1987), p. 28.

13. From a letter dated March 4, 1975, from Malka Heifetz Tussman to Marcia Falk, printed in *Am I Also You?* (translations from the Yiddish of Malka Heifetz Tussman by Marcia Falk, Berkeley, 1977), p. 10.

14. In a talk on women's prayer delivered at a conference, "Illuminating the Unwritten Scroll: Women's Spirituality and Jewish Tradition," University of Southern California, Los Angeles, November, 1984.

Section III (*Pages 117–146*)

1. As an aside, it is no accident that Jewish journalists seemingly the most critical of Israel, such as Ted Koppel of ABC, or Tom Friedman of the New York Times, personally fit this sociodemographic profile of Israel's Jewish critics.

2. For a further exposition of the ideas in this section, see Charles Liebman and Steven M. Cohen, *Constructions of Judaism: The Israeli and American Experiences* (New Haven: Yale University Press, 1990).

3. *Los Angeles Times*, "Los Angeles Times Poll Number 149: Israelis and Palestinians, March 25–31, April 4–7, 1988."

4. Michael Walzer, "Liberalism and the Jews: A Symposium," *Commentary*, January 1980, pp. 76–77.

5. Quoted in Charles Liebman, "Jewish Ultra-Nationalism in Israel: Converging Strands," *Survey of Jewish Affairs, 1985*, William Frankel, ed. (Rutherford, NJ: Fairleigh Dickinson University Press, 1985), pp. 28–50.

6. Quoted in Eliezer Schweid, *The Land of Israel* (Rutherford, NJ: Associated University Presses, 1985), pp. 171–72.

7. The Jewish tradition certainly contains elements that are consonant with these sentiments, as well as elements that are antagonistic to them. Some politically progressive religious Israelis argue—and I think correctly—that Meir Kahane's racist, antidemocratic and theocratic views constitute one intellectually reasonable, albeit morally detestable, interpretation of traditional Jewish sources.

Section IV (*Pages 147–244*)

*Acknowledgment from Martha Ackelsberg: Conversations with many people have contributed to the development of the ideas in my essay. I wish especially to acknowledge the help of Judith Plaskow and Denni Liebowitz and my ongoing discussions and struggles with the women of B'not Esh.

1. On the history and development of Jewish families see Steven M. Cohen and Paula Hyman, eds., *The Evolving Jewish Family* (New York: Holmes and Meier, 1986); also Charlotte Baum, Paula Hyman, and Sonya Michel, *The Jewish Woman in America* (New York: Dial Press, 1976).

2. On changes within Jewish families and communities, and for interpretations of their significance, see Steven M. Cohen, *American Modernity and Jewish Identity* (New York: Tavistock, 1983), especially ch. 6; and Andrew Cherlin and Carin Celebuski, "Are Jewish Families Different?" *Journal of Marriage and the Family* (November 1983), pp. 903–910. I am grateful to Steven Cohen for calling the latter article to my attention.

3. Martin Buber, "The Holy Way: A Word to the Jews and to the Nations," ch. VII of *On Judaism*, Nahum N. Glatzer, ed. (New York: Schocken, 1967), pp. 110, 112.

4. This term was introduced by Barbara Breitman and Barbara Johnson at a workshop they coordinated at a B'not Esh gathering in May 1986.

5. Note, for example, the title of a February 1986 symposium at the 92nd Street Y in New York: "Lifestyles and Sexual Norms: Personal Choices and Communal Imperatives." Susan Handelman's article, "Family, a Religiously Mandated Ideal," *Sh'ma,* March 20, 1987, suffers from some of these perspectives. See also Anne Roiphe's article, "The Jewish Family: A Feminist Perspective," *Tikkun,* Vol. 1, No. 2, 1986, pp. 70–76, and my letter in response to it, *Tikkun,* Vol. 2, No. 2, 1987, p. 4.

6. Marcia Cohn Spiegel, "Breaking the Silence," plenary address, New Jewish Agenda National Conference, July 1987; reprinted in *Genesis 2.* See also *Lilith,* No. 20, Summer 1988; Faith Solela, "Family Violence: Silence Isn't Golden Anymore," *Response,* Spring 1985, pp. 101–106.

7. I develop other aspects of this argument in "Sisters or Comrades? The Politics of Friends and Families," *Families, Politics, and Public Policies,* I. Diamond, ed. (New York: Longman, 1983), pp. 339–56; in "Families and the Jewish Community: A Feminist Perspective," *Response,* Spring 1985, pp. 5–19; and in "Redefining Family: Models for a Jewish Future," in *Twice Blessed,* Christie Balka and Andy Rose, eds. (Boston: Beacon Press, 1989).

8. Much of the discussion that follows is taken from my "Redefining Family: Models for the Jewish Future."

9. The "Family Partnership Act" in San Francisco, for example, would extend a variety of benefits to unmarried heterosexual couples (whether elderly or young) as well as to gay or lesbian partners.

10. See, for example, Arthur Waskow, "Down-to-Earth Judaism: Sexuality," pp. 46–49, 88–91, and Bradley Sharvit Artson, "Judaism and Homosexuality," pp. 52–54, 92–93, both in *Tikkun,* March/April 1988; David Teutsch, "Rethinking Jewish Sexual Ethics," pp. 6–11, and Sharon Cohen, "Homosexuality and a Jewish Sex Ethic," pp. 12–16, both in *Reconstructionist,* July–August 1989; Judith Plaskow, *Standing Again at Sinai: Judaism from a Feminist Perspective* (San Francisco: Harper and Row, 1990), ch. 5.

11. I have explored some aspects of this question in "Rabbis Are People Too: Politics, Spirituality, and the Jewish Community," *Reconstructionist,* September 1986, pp. 19–24, 32.

12. Discussions with Denni Liebowitz and the women of B'not Esh has greatly enriched my thinking about these issues.

13. See Solomon Freehof, *Reform Responsa* (Cincinnati: Hebrew Union College Press, 1960), pp. 3–23; Steven Passamaneck, *A Motion for Discovery* (Los Angeles: Hebrew Union College, 1977). See also the Reform movement's Centenary Perspective and its official commentary in Eugene B. Borowitz, *Reform Judaism Today* (New York: Behrman House, 1978), vol. I, pp. xxii–xxiii; vol. III, pp. 15–55; and the official Reform guide for ritual behavior, *Gates of Mitzvah,* Simeon J. Maslin, ed. (New York: Central Conference of American Rabbis, 1979), esp. pp. 2–5.

14. See, for example, J. O. Urmson, "Saints and Heroes," *Essays in Moral Philosophy,* Abraham I. Meldon, ed. (Seattle: University of Washington Press, 1958), pp. 209ff; Stanley Hauerwas, *A Community of Character* (Notre Dame: University of Notre Dame, 1981).

15. See Rachel Biale, *Women and Jewish Law* (New York: Schocken, 1984), pp. 93–96.

16.   See Erich Fromm, *The Art of Loving* (New York: Harper and Row, 1956).

17.   That work honors the worker: B. *Nedarim* 49. That idleness leads to lewdness and mental instability: M. *Ketubbot* 5:5; that it leads to thievery: T. *Kiddushin* 1:11.

18.   See Norman Lamm, *Faith and Doubt* (New York: Ktav, 1971), p. 192. He cites B. *Berakhot* 35b and *Eruvin* 13b.

19.   Calvin Goldscheider and Alan S. Zuckerman, *The Transformation of the Jews* (Chicago: University of Chicago Press, 1984), p. 240.

20.   Elihu Bergman, "The American Jewish Population Erosion," *Midstream*, October 1977.

21.   U. O. Schmelz and Sergio Dellapergola, *Basic Trends in American Jewish Demography* (New York: American Jewish Committee, 1988).

22.   Marshall Sklare, "Forms and Expressions of Jewish Identification," cited in Will Herberg, *Protestant-Catholic-Jew* (New York: Doubleday, 1955), p. 204.

23.   Steven M. Cohen, *Ties and Tensions: The 1986 Survey of American Jewish Attitudes Toward Israel and Israelis,* (New York: American Jewish Committee, 1987).

24.   Thomas Luckmann, *The Invisible Religion* (New York: Macmillan, 1967).

25.   Steven M. Cohen, "Jewish Attitudes to Issues of Jewish Unity and Diversity," unpublished report to the American Jewish Committee, November 1987.

26.   Mark L. Winer, Sanford Seltzer, and Steven J. Schwager, *Leaders of Reform Judaism: A Study of Jewish Identity* (New York: Union of American Hebrew Congregations, 1987), p. 55.

27.   Cited in Herberg, *Protestant-Catholic-Jew*, p. 49.

28.   Gary A. Tobin and Alvin Chenkin, "Recent Jewish Community Population Studies: A Roundup," *American Jewish Yearbook* (New York: American Jewish Committee, 1985).

29.   Howard W. Polsky, "A Study of Orthodoxy in Milwaukee," *The Jews*, Marshall Sklare, ed. (New York: The Free Press, 1958), pp. 325–335.

30.   Sidney Goldstein and Calvin Goldscheider, *Jewish Americans: Three Generations in a Jewish Community* (Englewood, NJ: Prentice-Hall, 1968).

31.   Marshall Sklare, *Jewish Identity on the Suburban Frontier* (New York: Basic Books, 1967), p. 4.

32.   Gerald B. Bubis, "Religious Diversity and Jewish Identity—Fostering Cooperation Between Agencies and Congregations," *Journal of Jewish Communal Service*, Fall 1988, pp. 9–13.

33.   For suggestions on the format of this essay, I owe special thanks to Joshua Sher and Phyllis Berman.

34.   Edwin H. Friedman, *Generation to Generation: Family Process in Church and Synagogue,* (New York: Guilford Press, 1985), esp. pp. 14ff.

35.   Friedman, p. 23.

36.   Friedman, pp. 162–163.

37.   Nahum M. Sarna, *Exploring Exodus: The Heritage of Biblical Israel* (New York: Schocken, 1987), p. 218.

38. I express my thanks to Janet Walkup, Gloria Leitner, Lawrence Kushner, and Arthur Waskow for the help and criticism they offered while I was preparing this essay.

39. Peter Marin, "Introduction" in Anders Holmquist, *The Free People* (New York: Outerbridge & Dinstfrey, 1969), unpaginated.

40. Johannes Pederson, *Israel: Its Life and Institutions* (London: Oxford University Press, 1964), Vols 1–11, p. 263.

41. Heszel Klepfisz, *Culture of Compassion: The Spirit of Polish Jewry from Hasidism to the Holocaust* (New York: KTAV, 1983), p. 47.

Section V (*Pages 245–268*)

1. Alasdair MacIntyre, "The Virtues, the Unity of a Human Life, and the Concept of a Tradition," *Liberalism and its Critics*, Michael Sandel, ed. (New York: New York University Press, 1984), pp. 125, 143.

2. See Alasdair MacIntyre, *After Virtue* (South Bend: Notre Dame, 1981), pp. 203–209.

3. Michael J. Sandel, *Liberalism and the Limits of Justice* (Cambridge, England: Cambridge, 1982), pp. 148–151.

4. Sandel, p. 179.

5. Robert Bellah et al., *Habits of the Heart* (New York: Harper & Row, 1986), p. 72.

6. Michael Walzer, *Spheres of Justice* (New York: Basic Books, 1983), pp. 39, 223. I would trust to the balance of state and communities even more than Walzer. Where he fears that widespread private education in schools dedicated to advancing particular ways of life would deprive adolescents of precious possibilities, making for "less diversity, less tension, less opportunity for personal change" than the current system of public schools, I would argue that Jews can safely invest in private education precisely because the wider culture is so utterly pervasive.

7. Sandel, *Liberalism*, p. 183.

8. Steven M. Cohen and Charles Liebman, "The Quality of American Jewish Life: Two Views" (New York: American Jewish Committee, 1987), pp. 6, 27, 50–52.

9. I follow Neusner here, because his generalizations about the corpus were borne out completely in my own work on Avodah Zarah, and also seem confirmed most conveniently by the Mishnah's sections. Jacob Neusner, *Method and Meaning in Ancient Judaism* (Missoula: Scholars Press, 1979), pp. 1–11. For my own work see *Galut: Modern Jewish Reflection on Homelessness and Homecoming* (Bloomington: Indiana, 1986), ch. 3; and "Building Communities in Our Own Day," *Reconstructionist*, June 1988, pp. 9–12.

10. I have left the pronouns as they are in the original: exclusively male.

11. Leonard Fein, *Where Are We?* (New York: Harper & Row, 1988), p. 28.

12. Arthur Green, "Judaism and Spirituality: A Jewish Mysticism for our Age" (Boston: Brandeis University, 1986), p. 15.

13. Harriet Feiner, "The Synagogue as a Support System," *Reconstructionist*, January–February 1985, pp. 25–30.

14.   See, for example, Tsvi Blanchard, "Common Ground: Plowing the Rich Soil of Cooperation Among Jews," *Reconstructionist,* April–May 1989. An Orthodox rabbi, Blanchard is successfully pioneering Guidelines for Respectful Conversion that enable Jews to cooperate despite the enormity of their differences.

Authors' Biographies

MARTHA A. ACKELSBERG

Dr. Martha Ackelsberg is Professor of Government at Smith College, where she has taught since 1972. She received her B.A. from Radcliffe College and her M.A. and Ph.D. from Princeton University. Her teaching at Smith includes courses on urban politics, political theory, and feminist theory. A founding member of Ezrat Nashim (the first Jewish feminist group) and of B'not Esh (a Jewish feminist spirituality collective), she has spoken and published widely, in both scholarly and Jewish communal journals, on urban politics, women's political activism, feminist theory, Spanish anarchism, and changing roles for women.

Her book, *Free Women of Spain: Anarchism and the Struggle for the Emancipation of Women* (Indiana University Press, 1991), explores the social and political vision of the Spanish anarchist women's organization, Mujeres Libres, active in Spain at the time of the Spanish Civil War.

STEVEN M. COHEN

Dr. Steven M. Cohen is Professor of Sociology at Queens College. He writes and lectures widely on changing patterns of American Jewish identity, the Jewish family, intermarriage, the politics of American Jews, and their relationship with Israel. His recent books include *American Modernity & Jewish Identity* and *American Assimilation or Jewish Revival?* He also co-edited *Perspectives in Jewish Population Studies* as well as *The Jewish Family: Myths and Reality,* and has conducted several public opinion surveys of American Jewry. His articles have appeared in *Moment* magazine, the *American Jewish Yearbook,* and several scholarly journals. He has been a visiting professor at Brandeis University, Hebrew University, and Yale University, and is now a visiting professor at the Jewish Theological Seminary.

Dr. Cohen lives in New Haven with his wife, Susan Wall, the principal of New Haven's Solomon Schechter School, and their two children. He is on the boards of the Jewish Telegraphic Agency, the National Foundation for Jewish Culture, and the New Haven Jewish Federation. He also chairs the federation's Communal Planning Committee.

ELLIOT N. DORFF

Elliot Dorff was ordained by the Jewish Theological Seminary of America in 1970 and earned his Ph.D. in philosophy from Columbia University in 1971. Since then he has directed the rabbinical and master's programs at the University of Judaism, where he currently is Provost and Professor of Philosophy. He is a member of the Conservative movement's Committee on Jewish Law and Standards and Commission on the Philosophy of the Conservative Movement. In Los Angeles he serves as a member of the board of directors of Jewish Family Service and chairs its Jewish Hospice Commission. He is also a member of the ethics committees at the Jewish Homes for the Aging and UCLA Medical Center.

Rabbi Dorff's publications include some 40 articles on Jewish thought, law, and ethics together with four books: *Jewish Law and Modern Ideology; Conservative Judaism: Our Ancestors to Our Descendants; A Living Tree: The Roots and Growth of Jewish Law;* and *Mitzvah Means Commandment.*

He is married and has four children.

ARNOLD EISEN

Dr. Arnold Eisen is Associate Professor of Religious Studies and Aaron Roland Fellow at Stanford University. He is the author of *Galut: Modern Jewish Reflections on Homelessness and Homecoming* and *The Chosen People in America,* both published by Indiana University Press, as well as numerous articles, including "Saving the Remnants of Jewish Faith in a Faithless Time." Dr. Eisen holds degrees from Hebrew University (Ph.D.), Oxford (B.Phil.), and the University of Pennsylvania (B.A.) and has held teaching positions at Columbia and Tel Aviv Universities.

MARCIA FALK

Dr. Marcia Falk, Affiliated Scholar at Stanford University's Institute for Research on Women and Gender, is a poet, scholar, and translator of national reputation. She received her B.A. in Philosophy from Brandeis University and her Ph.D. in English and Comparative Literature from Stanford. She has been both a Fulbright scholar and a postdoctoral fellow in Bible and Hebrew literature at Hebrew University in Jerusalem.

Dr. Falk's book publications include *The Song of Songs: A New Translation and Interpretation* (Harper San Francisco, 1990); *With Teeth in the Earth: Selected Poems of Malka Heifetz Tussman* (translations from the Yiddish, with introduction, Wayne State University Press, 1992); and two books of poems, *This Year in Jerusalem* (State Street Press, 1986) and *It Is July in Virginia* (Rara Avis Press, 1985). She has also completed a volume of translations of the Hebrew poet Zelda, entitled *The Spectacular Difference.*

Marcia Falk's current work is in composing Hebrew liturgy, and she has published her new prayers, along with theological essays, in several journals, including *Reconstructionist*. Her *Amidah* prayer appears in the new Reconstructionist Friday evening prayerbook.

LEE FRIEDLANDER

Rabbi Lee Friedlander is co-rabbi, with his wife Joy Levitt, of the Reconstructionist Synagogue of the North Shore in Roslyn Heights, New York. Rabbi Friedlander received his rabbinic ordination in 1975 from the Reconstructionist Rabbinical College. He is a past chairperson of the Jewish Reconstructionist Foundation and past president of the Reconstructionist Rabbinical Association. Rabbi Friedlander has published articles in *Reconstructionist* and is editing part of the forthcoming Rabbi's Manual for the Reconstructionist Rabbinical Association.

EVERETT GENDLER

Rabbi Everett Gendler, a native of Iowa, studied at the University of Chicago, the Jewish Theological Seminary (ordained as rabbi, 1957), and Columbia University. He has served congregations in Mexico, Brazil, Cuba, and Princeton, New Jersey, and for some years has been serving as rabbi to Temple Emanuel, Lowell, Massachusetts, and as Jewish Chaplain and Instructor of Philosophy and Religious Studies at Phillips Academy, Andover, Massachusetts.

A member of the Rabbinical Assembly, the Central Conference of American Rabbis, and a corresponding affiliate of the Reconstructionist Rabbinical Association, Rabbi Gendler has served on the R.A. Committee for Racial Justice and on the C.C.A.R. Commission for Worship. He has also been a member of the executive committees of the Fellowship of Reconciliation, the Jewish Peace Fellowship, and the War Resisters League, and has been active in a number of conservationist groups.

Rabbi Gendler has contributed to numerous journals, among them *Response, Reconstructionist, Reform Judaism, Conservative Judaism, The Christian Century, Hadassah Magazine*, and *Natural History*, and to such volumes as *Contemporary Jewish Religious Thought, Ecology: Crisis and New Vision, Protest: Pacifism and Politics*, and *The Jewish Catalogs*.

ARTHUR GREEN

Dr. Arthur Green is President of the Reconstructionist Rabbinical College. He is a scholar in the field of Jewish mysticism and Hasidism and seeks to relate his work in those areas to a contemporary Jewish theological agenda. He is the author of *Tormented Master: A Life of Rabbi Nahman of Bratslav,* translator of two volumes of Hasidic sources, and editor of *Jewish Spirituality.*

Dr. Green was ordained by the Jewish Theological Seminary and received his Ph.D. from Brandeis University. He served as an associate professor of religious studies at the University of Pennsylvania from 1973 to 1984, when he became the dean of the Reconstructionist Rabbinical College. He was the founder of Havurat Shalom Community in Somerville, Massachusetts, in 1968.

KATHY GREEN

Kathy Green currently teaches at the Reconstructionist Rabbinical College. She received a master's degree in psycho-educational processes (Temple University) and a second master's in child development (Beaver College). Her work concentrates on Jewish educational programs and curriculum development in Jewish elementary schools.

Kathy Green is the co-author of the *Jewish Family Book* and numerous articles that have appeared in the *Melton Journal* and *Religion & Intellectual Life* and other books and journals.

She, her husband Arthur, and their daughter live in the Germantown section of Philadelphia, where they are active members of a growing Jewish community.

OMUS HIRSHBEIN

Omus Hirshbein was born in New York City and grew up in Los Angeles. His father, Peretz Hirshbein, was the noted Yiddish dramatist, novelist, and poet; his mother, Esther Shumiatcher Hirshbein, was also a well-known poet and lecturer. He was educated at Los Angeles City College, the Aspen Music School, and the Juilliard School. From 1949–64 he made recital and orchestral appearances throughout the United States and Canada.

Mr. Hirshbein served as Administrator of New York's Hunter College Concert Bureau from 1964 to 1973. In 1974 he became the Education Director of New York's 92nd Street YM/YWHA, and was instrumental in reactivating that institution's long-neglected Arts and Humanities program. He became the Y's Performing Arts Director in 1979 and its Director of Arts and Humanities in 1988.

Mr. Hirshbein serves on the board of the Bloomingdale House of Music. Since 1982 he has served on the New York State Council on the Arts as Chairman of its Presenting Organizations Panel and as a member of its Music Panel. He has also served the National Endowment for the Arts as an Inter-Arts Program panelist, and as chairman of the Multi-Music and Challenge panels. In

1981 he was the recipient of the City of New York Mayor's Award of Honor for Arts and Culture.

Mr. Hirshbein lives in Manhattan with his wife Jessica and two sons.

RICHARD J. ISRAEL

Rabbi Richard J. Israel is a research associate at the Cohen Center for Modern Jewish Studies at Brandeis University.

Until recently the director of central services and Judaica of the Jewish Community Center of Greater Boston, Rabbi Israel was the director of the Hillel Council of Greater Boston (the Hillel regional office) from 1971 to 1985, and before that was the director of the Yale University Hillel Foundation for 13 years.

Rabbi Israel served as rabbi of the Jewish Religious Union of Bombay, India, and was the associate director of the Hillel Council of UCLA. He is a past president of the National Association of Hillel Directors and of the Yale Religious Ministry, and has been a lecturer in the Department of Urban Studies, Southern Connecticut State College.

He publishes regularly in a wide range of Jewish periodicals and has more than 100 articles in print. He is the author of a book entitled *Jewish Identity Games,* published by the B'nai B'rith Hillel Foundations, and has written articles for each of the volumes of the widely read *Jewish Catalog.*

Rabbi Israel is married to Sherry Israel (née Feinberg), who teaches in the Hornstein program in Jewish Communal Service at Brandeis University. They have four children and two grandchildren and live in Newton Centre, Massachusetts.

BURT JACOBSON

Rabbi Burt Jacobson graduated from the Jewish Theological Seminary of America in 1966, and was a Fellow in the Melton Research Center for Jewish Education from 1966 to 1970. He was a co-founder of Havurat Shalom in Somerville, MA, as well as a contributor to *The First Jewish Catalog.*

The author of *Teaching and Traditional Liturgy* (Melton Research Center), Rabbi Jacobson is the founder and rabbi of Kehilla Community Synagogue in Berkeley, CA. He has also authored a variety of contemporary liturgies for the Sabbath and Holidays and is the co-editor of *Or Hadash: New Paths for Shabbat Morning* (Pnai Or). His most recent book is *Crossing the River: Bar/Bat Mitzvah and the Journey toward Jewish Adulthood.*

PHILIP N. KLUTZNICK

A prominent Chicago attorney and businessman, Philip Klutznick has devoted much of his life to public service in both domestic and international spheres. He has served in various federal government posts under seven presidents, beginning with the Eisenhower administration.

Mr. Klutznick was a member of several U.S. delegations to the United Nations. Since 1976 he has served as vice chairman of the Committee for Economic Development (CED) Board.

In the business world, Mr. Klutznick is primarily associated with real estate development. He founded and headed the Urban Investment and Development Company in Chicago. In Israel he helped plan the construction of the industrial center and deep-water port of Ashdod.

Mr. Klutznick has devoted himself to many causes in the field of humanitarian and civic affairs, serving as a member of President Ford's Advisory Committee on Indo-Chinese refugees and of the National Council of Boy Scouts of America.

Long prominent in the Jewish community, Mr. Klutznick was president of the World Jewish Congress, chairman of the Institute of Jewish Policy Planning, and international president of B'nai B'rith. He is currently President Emeritus of the World Jewish Congress and Honorary International President of B'nai B'rith.

His many committee associations include service as president of the Memorial Foundation for Jewish Culture, member of the board and chairman of the United States Committee of Friends of Beth Hatefutsoth (the Diaspora Museum in Israel), and member of the advisory committee of the Kennedy School at Harvard University.

Mr. Klutznick began his national Jewish career as the international president of B'nai B'rith Youth in 1925. He continues to serve the national and international Jewish communities as a major communal spokesman.

Mr. Klutznick is married to the former Ethel Riekes, and they have five children and fourteen grandchildren.

LAWRENCE KUSHNER

Lawrence Kushner was born in Detroit in 1943. He graduated Phi Beta Kappa in philosophy from the University of Cincinnati in 1965 and was ordained as rabbi by the Hebrew Union College in 1969. Upon ordination, Kushner served as rabbinic fellow-in-residence in Congregation Solel of Highland Park, Illinois.

Rabbi Kushner assumed his present pulpit at Congregation Beth El of Sudbury, Massachusetts, in 1971. Its 350 families have attained national prominence for their innovation and creativity. They have translated, edited, and published their own prayerbook, *V'taher Libenu,* the first nonsexist liturgy. He originated the concept of synagogue *havurot,* and has designed and led over 50 adult and family *kallah* weekends for personal religious growth.

He serves as Rabbinic Chairman of Reform Judaism's Commission on Religious Living and as a member of the board of the Union of American Hebrew Congregations. In 1986 he was appointed to the faculty of the rabbinic school of the Hebrew Union College–Jewish Institute of Religion in New York City, where he teaches a weekly class every other semester. He has written and lectured widely on the themes of personal and institutional spiritual renewal.

He is the author of *God Was in This Place* and *I, I Did Not Know* (Jewish Lights Publishing, 1991); *The Book of Letters: A Mystical Alef-Bait* (Jewish Lights Publishing, 1990); *Honey From the Rock: Visions of Jewish Spiritual Renewal* (Jewish Lights Publishing, 1990); *The River of Light: Spirituality, Judaism, Consciousness* (Jewish Lights Publishing, 1990); *The Book of Miracles: A Young Person's Guide to Jewish Spirituality* (Union of American Hebrew Congregations, 1987); *The Invisible Chariot: An Introduction to Kabbalah for Young Adults,* with Deborah Kerdeman (Alternatives in Religious Education, 1986).

He and his wife, Karen, have three children.

HILLEL LEVINE

Rabbi Hillel Levine received his rabbinic ordination from the Jewish Theological Seminary, and his Ph.D. in sociology and Jewish history from Harvard University. From 1973 to 1980 he taught sociology and Jewish history at Yale University, where he founded the program in Judaic studies. From 1980 to 1982 he was deputy director for museum planning of the United States Holocaust Memorial Council in Washington. He is currently Professor of Sociology and Religion at Boston University, and Director of its Center for Judaic Studies. He directs the Washington Internship on Community and Polity, to train advocates for the Jewish community and for not-for-profit organizations. In the spring 1989 he taught Jewish history at the Chinese Academy of Social Sciences and several universities in the People's Republic of China. Rabbi Levine is the author of several studies in sociology and Jewish history, including *Economic Origins of Antisemitism: Poland and Its Jews in the Early Modern Period* (Yale University Press, 1991) and a study of bankers, bureaucrats, blacks, and Jews and changing neighborhoods.

DEBORAH E. LIPSTADT

Dr. Deborah E. Lipstadt is an adjunct professor of religion and Jewish studies at Occidental College and Director of Research at the Skirball Institute on

American Values, an arm of the American Jewish Committee. She is currently writing a book on Holocaust denial. Dr. Lipstadt is a consultant to the United States Holocaust Memorial Museum, where she is designing the Museum's Interactive Learning Program on American Response to the Holocaust. In addition, she is directing a research project on the impact of the American experience on the values of ethnic and religious groups in Los Angeles.

She is the former director of the Brandeis Bardin Institute. Prior to going to Brandeis she was a professor of modern Jewish studies at the University of California, Los Angeles. She received her B.A. from the City College of New York and her M.A. and Ph.D. from Brandeis University and studied for two years at the Hebrew University in Jerusalem.

Dr. Lipstadt is the author of *Beyond Belief: The American Press and the Coming of the Holocaust* (Free Press/Macmillan). The book is an examination of how the American press covered the news of the persecution of European Jewry between the years 1933 and 1945.

EGON MAYER

Egon Mayer is Professor of Sociology at Brooklyn College and former president of the Association for the Sociological Study of Jewry. His area of specialization is the study of religious and ethnic values in social behavior and community organization.

Dr. Mayer received his B.A. from Brooklyn College in 1967; his M.A. from the New School for Social Research in 1970; and his Ph.D. from Rutgers University in 1975.

Dr. Mayer is the author of numerous articles and research reports, and serves as consultant to several national and local Jewish organizations. He has directed major studies on Jewish intermarriage, which were published under the titles *Intermarriage and the Jewish Future* (1979) and *Children of Intermarriage* (1983). His widely acclaimed book on intermarriage, *Love and Tradition: Marriage Between Jews and Christians*, was published in 1985 and released in paperback in 1987. Dr. Mayer is also the author of a book on the Orthodox and Hasidic communities of Boro Park, entitled *From Suburb to Shtetl* (1979). Dr. Mayer has written and lectured extensively throughout the Jewish community on various aspects of Jewish social life, the family, the changing nature of Jewish identity, and the challenges of communal organization.

RELA GEFFEN MONSON

Dr. Rela Geffen Monson is a graduate of the Joint Program of Columbia University and the Teachers Institute of the Jewish Theological Seminary of

America. She received a master's degree in sociology from Columbia and a Ph.D. from the University of Florida. Currently she is Professor of Sociology and Dean of Academic Affairs at Gratz College in Philadelphia. She is a fellow of the Center for Jewish Community Studies and serves on the advisory committee of the National Jewish Family Center of the American Jewish Committee. She is President of the Association for the Social Scientific Study of Jewry.

Dr. Monson's major research interests are in the fields of sociology of religion and sociology of the family. Her publications include *Jewish Women on the Way Up, Bringing Women In: A Survey of the Evolving Role of Women in Jewish Organizational Life*, and *Jewish Campus Life.*

Dr. Monson serves on the Philadelphia board of the American Jewish Committee, the publication committee of the Jewish Publication Society, and the board of Akiba Hebrew Academy. Professionally, she serves on the board of directors of the Association for Jewish Studies.

DEBORAH DASH MOORE

Dr. Deborah Dash Moore is Professor of Religion at Vassar College. A historian of American Jews, she devotes her scholarship to the study of their 20th-century urban and social history. Her book, *At Home in America*, examines the experience of second-generation Jews in New York City during the interwar decades. She has also explored the themes of ethnic leadership, religious innovation, and Jewish community in articles and a book on the B'nai B'rith. Currently she is editor of the *YIVO Annual* and of a collection of essays drawn from past volumes of the Annual, *East European Jews in Two Worlds*. She is also writing a book on American Jews during the postwar period, specifically looking at the migration of northeastern and midwestern Jews into Miami and Los Angeles.

MICHAEL PALEY

Rabbi Michael Paley received his B.A. from Brandeis University and M.A. from Temple University. He studied at the Reconstructionist Rabbinical College and Yeshivat Hamiutas in Jerusalem. He received private ordination.

Rabbi Paley was formerly associate chaplain and the director of Hillel at Dartmouth College, where he founded the Conference on Judaism in Rural New England and the Edgar M. Bronfman Youth Fellowship in Israel.

Currently, Rabbi Paley is the Director of Earl Hall and St. Paul's Chapel at Columbia University.

JUDITH PLASKOW

Dr. Judith Plaskow (Ph.D., Yale University, 1975) has been learning, teaching, speaking, and writing about feminist theology for 20 years. She is Associate Professor of Religious Studies at Manhattan College and has also taught at New York University and Wichita State University.

She is author of *Sex, Sin, and Grace: Women's Experience and the Theologies of Reinhold Niebuhr and Paul Tillich,* and with Carol P. Christ is co-editor of *Womanspirit Rising: A Feminist Reader in Religion* and the soon-to-be-published *Weaving the Visions: New Patterns in Feminist Spirituality.* She and Elisabeth Schussler Fiorenza co-founded and co-edit the *Journal of Feminist Studies in Religion,* an academic journal now in its fifth year.

Dr. Plaskow recently completed a Jewish feminist theology, *Standing Again at Sinai: Rethinking Judaism From a Feminist Perspective* (Harper and Row).

MARTIN J. RAFFEL

Martin J. Raffel, who has a law degree from the Hebrew University School of Law and a B.A. in political science from Franklin and Marshall College, is Assistant Executive Vice Chair at the National Jewish Community Relations Advisory Council and Director of the Israel Task Force. He is the primary resource at the NJCRAC for Israel-related issues, and on the basis of consultations with national and community member agencies he provides guidance to the community relations field in responding to developments affecting the security and status of Israel and U.S. foreign policy in the Middle East.

Before assuming his present position at the NJCRAC in 1987, Mr. Raffel served as vice president at the Reconstructionist Rabbinical College, executive director of the Pennsylvania Region of the American Jewish Congress, and assistant director of the Philadelphia chapter of the American Jewish Congress.

JOSEPH REIMER

Dr. Joseph Reimer is a member of the faculty of the Hornstein Program at Brandeis University, where he teaches courses in Jewish education, Jewish life cycle, and family life. A psychologist by training, Dr. Reimer received his doctorate from the Harvard Graduate School of Education, where he studied with Lawrence Kohlberg. His doctoral work and several subsequent publications concerned the topic of the moral development of kibbutz adolescents. He has also written about innovative programs in moral education and more recently on professionalizing the field of Jewish education and Jewish family education. His recent monograph, *The Synagogue as a Context for Jewish Education,* was distributed by the Commission on Jewish Education in North America, of which he served as a staff member.

RICHARD A. SIEGEL

Richard A. Siegel is currently Executive Director of the National Foundation for Jewish Culture. While at the National Foundation, he has also served as executive producer for numerous festivals and conferences, including the "First Jewish Theatre Festival," "Jews and Judaism in Dance," "Art and Identity in the American Jewish Community," and "Independence and Interdependence: Israel-North America Cultural Exchange." As executive producer for "One People, Many Voices"—a three-part radio series on Jewish music in America produced by National Public Radio—he won the Corporation for Public Broadcasting Award for the Arts and Humanities. He is co-editor of *The Jewish Catalog* (Jewish Publication Society, 1973) and *The Jewish Almanac* (Bantam, 1981).

JACOB J. STAUB

Dr. Jacob J. Staub is Dean of the Faculty and Director of the Department of Medieval Civilization at the Reconstructionist Rabbinical College.

Dr. Staub is the author of *The Creation of the World to Gersonides* (Brown Judaic Studies, Scholars Press), the co-author of *Exploring Judaism: A Reconstructionist Approach* (Reconstructionist Press), and the co-editor of *Creative Jewish Education: A Reconstructionist Perspective* (RRC Press/Rossel Books). From 1983 to 1989 he served as editor of *Reconstructionist* magazine. He holds a Ph.D. in Jewish philosophy from Temple University and rabbinic ordination from the Reconstructionist Rabbinical College. Dr. Staub serves as Chairman of the Academy for Jewish Philosophy and has been a recipient of a Mellon Foundation Fellowship (1982–83) in Jewish Philosophy. Prior to his return to the RRC in 1983, he was an assistant professor of religion at Lafayette College.

DAVID A. TEUTSCH

Rabbi David Teutsch is a professor and Executive Vice President at the Reconstructionist Rabbinical College in Wyncote, Pennsylvania. He is the editor-in-chief of *Kol Haneshamah,* the new Reconstructionist siddur series.

For four years the executive director of the Federation of Reconstructionist Congregations and Havurot, Rabbi Teutsch joined the staff of the Reconstructionist movement in 1980. A founder of the National Havurah Committee, Rabbi

Teutsch has served as program director of CLAL (then called the National Jewish Resource Center).

He wrote his doctoral dissertation on organizational ethics, receiving his Ph.D. from the Social Systems Sciences Program at the Wharton School of the University of Pennsylvania in 1991.

An honors graduate of Harvard University, he was ordained in 1977 at Hebrew Union College in New York. He has served as a congregational rabbi and founded a day school.

Rabbi Teutsch lives in Philadelphia with his wife Betsy, an artist and calligrapher. They have two children.

ESTHER TICKTIN

Esther Ticktin was born in Vienna and came to the U.S. in 1940 with her family. She studied at Brooklyn College and Herzliah Hebrew Academy, and received her B.A. in 1947. With her husband, Max, she spent 1947–1948 in Jerusalem, returning to the U.S. to continue her studies. She received her Ph.D. in psychology in 1978.

Dr. Ticktin was a member of the community that created the Upstairs Minyan, one of the first completely egalitarian *havurot*. She continued her association with havurot in Fabrangen when the family moved to Washington, D.C., in 1972. Through this association she became involved with the Jewish feminist movement and B'not Esh, a woman's group that explores the feminist roots of Jewish spirituality.

Dr. Ticktin has a private practice in psychoanalytic psychotherapy, and continues her involvement in Fabrangen.

ARTHUR WASKOW

Arthur Waskow is the director of the Shalom Center, and a Fellow of the Institute for Jewish Renewal. From 1982 to 1989, he was a member of the faculty of the Reconstructionist Rabbinical College.

Waskow founded and co-edits the journal *New Menorah*, and is the author of *The Freedom Seder* (1969), *Godwrestling* (Schocken, 1978), *Seasons of Our Joy* (Bantam, 1982), and *These Holy Sparks: The Rebirth of the Jewish People* (Harper and Row, 1983). He is also co-author of *The Shalom Seders* (Adama, 1984) and *Before There Was a Before* (Adama, 1984). He has recently completed *Becoming Brothers*, and is now writing *Ancient Torah, Future Earth: The Spiral Shape of Human Hope*.

Born in Baltimore in 1933, Waskow earned a B.A. from Johns Hopkins University and a Ph.D. in United States history from the University of Wisconsin. He worked as a legislative assistant for a U.S. congressman, and wrote *The Limits of Defense* (Doubleday, 1962) and three other books on nuclear strategy, deterrence, and disarmament. He was a founding fellow of the Institute for Policy Studies. He wrote two books on the roles of violence and nonviolence in the process of American social change: *From Race Riot to Sit-in* (Doubleday, 1965) and *Running Riot* (Herder and Herder, 1970).

Waskow was a member of the board of the National Havurah Committee from 1978 to 1980 and from 1983 to 1987, and is a member of the board of the P'nai Or Religious Fellowship and the editorial boards of *Reconstructionist* and *Tikkun* magazines.

JONATHAN WOOCHER

Dr. Jonathan Woocher (Ph.D., Temple University) is Executive Vice President of the Jewish Education Service of North America (JESNA), the continental planning, coordinating, and service agency for the field of Jewish education. Prior to assuming this position, Dr. Woocher was associate professor in the Benjamin S. Hornstein Program in Jewish Communal Service at Brandeis University.

Dr. Woocher is the author of *Sacred Survival: The Civil Religion of American Jews*. His articles on Jewish communal and religious life have appeared in a number of journals. Dr. Woocher is also a co-editor of *Perspectives in Jewish Population Research*. He serves as a fellow of the Center for Jewish Community Studies in Jerusalem.

Dr. Woocher has been deeply involved in Jewish communal activities as a program developer, consultant, scholar-in-residence, and lecturer for both national and local organizations.

DAVID A. WORTMAN

Rabbi David A. Wortman has served as executive director of the Jewish Community Relations Council of Greater Philadelphia since August 1988. He was formerly executive director of the Board of Rabbis of Greater Philadelphia and the Jewish Chaplaincy Service for six years.

Rabbi Wortman holds M.A. and M. Phil. degrees from Yale University and a MAHL degree from Hebrew Union College, from which he was ordained in 1973. He also studied at the University of Wisconsin and at Hebrew University in Jerusalem. A visiting lecturer at the Lutheran Theological Seminary of Philadelphia, he has taught at St. Joseph's University, Yale University, and Yale Divinity School.

Rabbi Wortman serves as chairman of the United Jewish Appeal Rabbinic Cabinet Soviet Jewry Committee. He was the chief writer and editor of the "Exodus Haggadah." He provides editorial commentary to "Connections," a television news program of the interfaith religious community, and is a member of the steering committee of the Delaware Valley Media Ministry. A frequent lecturer, he represented the United States at the US-USSR Emerging Leaders Summit, which was held in Philadelphia in December 1988.